SOCIAL REFORM IN THE UNITED STATES NAVY, 1798–1862

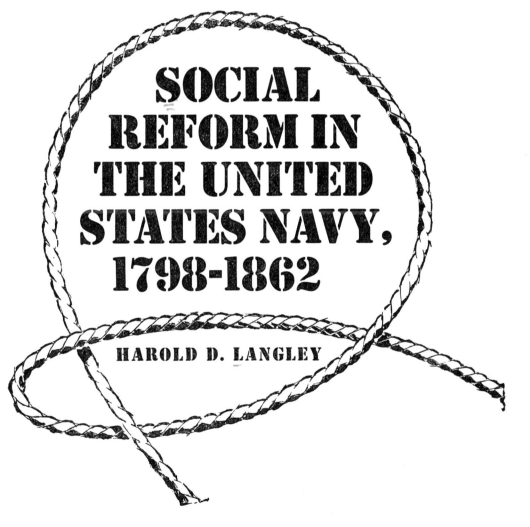

SOCIAL REFORM IN THE UNITED STATES NAVY, 1798-1862

HAROLD D. LANGLEY

UNIVERSITY OF ILLINOIS PRESS, URBANA · CHICAGO · LONDON, 1967

257336

TO MY MOTHER

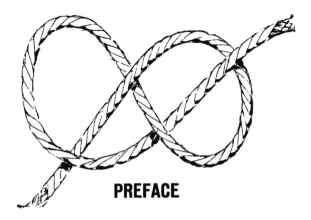

PREFACE

The growing participation of the rank and file of American society in the excitement and work of politics during the first half of the
nineteenth century, and the increase of interest and activity in
the welfare of all parts of the population, have been characterized
by American historians as the rise of the common man. While historians have noted that this interest in improving the lot of mankind embraced agitation on behalf of the Negro slave, workers,
women, children, the poor, the insane, and the imprisoned, among
others, its impact on the military organizations of the country has
not been examined or appreciated. The purpose of this study is to
examine the impact of this nineteenth-century reform fever on the
United States Navy, and specifically on the common sailor.

The United States Navy offers a particularly fruitful field for
such an investigation. To begin with, it was frankly patterned on
the British Navy. This fact had a bearing on the attitude of those
Americans who relished the notion that they had thrown off all
vestiges of their colonial past, and were building a proud new
nation with its own traditions. Also, the monarchical organization
and class outlook of the Navy were quite out of step with the
democratic spirit of the country. Every warship was like a little
kingdom that was ruled with a firm hand by a captain, assisted by
junior officers who were analogous to nobles. At the bottom of this
social structure were the seamen, who were characterized as serfs,
peasants, or unruly rabble, but seldom as freemen. The captain
was the absolute ruler of this domain and life on board ship was
usually lived far away from the sight and supervision of the au-

thorities at home. Thus there arose among Americans a difference of opinion as to how the needs of discipline and order in the military life could best be harmonized with the democratic attitudes of the country and its people.

There was also a heritage of at least some public concern about the hazards associated with the sailor's life. Resentment over the practice of impressment antedated the American Revolution and continued down through the War of 1812. Worry about the fate of American sailors held captive by the Barbary pirates was one of the factors that led to the establishment of a Navy. Public interest in the lot of the common sailor did not end with the War of 1812, but it took new forms. The three decades that preceded the Civil War were notable for the number of reform movements that swept the land. Agitation to improve the lives of the naval and merchant seamen was a part of that era of reform. And while other reform movements tended to become less active as the antislavery agitation grew, those for the sailor were helped by this climate of opinion. The life of the sailor was compared with that of the slave, and in at least some areas the slave came out better in the comparison.

Throughout most of the period under discussion, the Navy needed men, and particularly American-born men, to fill its ranks. This need provides a focal point for an examination of the recruiting process, and of the concern of civil and military leaders over the number of foreigners in the Navy and their reliability in the event of a war. Some reformers were struck by the possibility of solving two or more problems at the same time. If poor and idle American boys in the cities could be induced to join the Navy, they would learn a trade, reduce the problem of juvenile delinquency, and solve the Navy's manpower needs. The practice would gradually eliminate the number of foreigners in the fleet, and improve its quality and reliability.

To illustrate the influence of nineteenth-century reformers in improving the conditions of service of the sailor in the United States Navy, I have investigated four main themes: (1) The origins, membership, and activities of societies dedicated to working among sailors, and particularly the American Seamen's Friend Society; (2) the manpower situation in the Navy, including some attention to the history of recruiting; (3) the agitation against corporal punishment, which may also be considered as a chapter in the history of American penal practices; (4) the movement to abolish the sailor's ration of whisky or grog, which is a part of the story of the temperance crusade. These developments are set against a brief history of the Navy and its problems during this period.

I have used the term "humanitarian" in the sense of a person who is devoted to promoting the welfare of humanity, especially through the elimination of pain and suffering. In this study, the term refers to those who worked to improve the living conditions of the naval seaman.

There are those who will argue that taking away the sailor's grog was not a humanitarian action. The answer to this is that in the minds of the reformers, drunkenness was the cause of a good deal of the degredation, suffering, and privation that the sailor endured. While the grog ration in itself did not cause drunkenness, it stimulated an appetite for more alcohol, and to quench this thirst the sailor went to great pains. Both the effort to get liquor and the effects of over-indulgence frequently brought the sailor to ruin. The attack on the grog ration was an effort to get at the cause of other troubles. The reformers also attempted to control the sailor's living conditions ashore. Whether on sea or land, the sailor was urged to renounce liquor voluntarily.

The full implementation of most of the reforms discussed in this study depended upon the political processes of the Congress. I have tried to trace the patterns of action in this area as much as existing records will permit, and to indicate the political and/or sectional affiliations of the contenders. My use of party designations for individuals active in the period before 1840 — a period during which our party machinery was evolving — is intended to be suggestive in terms of possible attitudes of members of state factions.

Many people have helped to make this book possible. For their gracious assistance, I am obligated to the staffs of the Library of Congress, the University of Pennsylvania Library, the District of Columbia Public Library, the Scranton Public Library, the Mullen Library of the Catholic University of America, the Duke University Library, the University of North Carolina Library, the United States Naval Academy Library, the Navy Department Library, the library of the Marine Corps Historical Section, the Massachusetts Historical Society, the Andover-Harvard Theological

Library, the Historical Foundation of the Presbyterian and Reformed Churches, the Princeton University Library, Colonial Williamsburg, the Chicago Historical Society, the Eleutherian Mills Historical Library, the New Hampshire Historical Society, the New Jersey Historical Society, the Historical Society of Pennsylvania, and the Department of Archives and History, Raleigh, North Carolina. To the present and past staffs of the Manuscript Division of the Library of Congress, and especially to C. Percy Powell, Elizabeth McPherson, John De Porry, and W. S. Langone, I want to express my appreciation for their help over a period of several years. Similar assistance has long been given to me by Miss Camille Hannon of the National Archives Library, and by the present and past staffs of the Navy Branch and Central Search Room of that institution.

Throughout the long period of research, writing, and revision, Dr. Roy F. Nichols, the Vice Provost of the University of Pennsylvania, has been a constant source of inspiration and encouragement. I am also grateful to the late Arthur C. Bining, and to Wallace E. Davies and Thomas C. Cochran, of the University of Pennsylvania, for reading portions of this study and giving me helpful criticisms.

I owe a special debt of gratitude to Merle Curti of the University of Wisconsin, who, in spite of his own busy schedule, read a version of this manuscript and gave me valuable suggestions.

For their assistance and encouragement at various stages in the research, writing, and revision of this work, I am grateful to Irving Brant, Byron Fairchild, Fred Meigs, Rear Admiral John D. Hayes, U.S.N. (Ret.), D. Michael O'Quinlivan, Schafer Williams, John Finan, Russell F. Weigley, Mrs. Daniel Goggin, James R. Masterson, and Donald Jackson, Editor of the University of Illinois Press. Various drafts of this manuscript or parts of it were typed by Mrs. Douglas Houston, Mrs. Margaret Martin, Mrs. Carl Hevener, Mrs. Emita Nelson, Miss Elizabeth Baird, and the final version was typed by my wife, Patricia. To these good ladies I must say that my words of thanks are but a poor index of my appreciation.

Finally I need only point out that I alone am responsible for any errors of fact or interpretation in this book.

Washington, D. C.   H. D. L.
June 1966

CONTENTS

"The strangest thing in the world, perhaps, when we consider the common nature of men, is our strangeness to one another: the ignorance in which we live of one another. Hence comes much of our hardness, severity, cruelty, to our fellows. . . . Growing knowledge, the press, the school, civilization, Christianity, are melting away those barriers, and bringing men into contact and sympathy. These are the foundations of that larger brotherhood which is stretching out its hand to hitherto neglected classes — the laborer, the sailor, the slave himself. Men cannot hate, when they come to know one another. When I look into my brother's heart, and see his need, his pain and sorrow, his darkness and error — image refection of my own — no matter what his garb is, I must feel for him."

The Sailor's Magazine, [London], 1849

PART
ONE

THE NAVY AND THE NATION

"It is Time We should establish an American Character — Let that Character be a Love of Country and a Jealousy of it's honor — This Idea comprehends every Thing that ought to be impressed upon the Minds of all our Citizens, but more especially of those Citizens who are also Seamen & Soldiers. — "

Secretary of the Navy Benjamin Stoddert, 1798

THE FORMATIVE YEARS, 1798-1815

When the American Revolution ended and the independence of the United States was acknowledged, the government operating under the Articles of Confederation turned to the task of putting the new nation in order. The Army was disbanded except for a handful of troops who were retained to guard powder supplies. The Continental Navy went out of existence when the last of its ships was sold in 1785. Such complete demobilization did not meet with the approval of all Americans. Many prominent men believed that it was folly to expect a nation to endure without armed forces. They were right. Indian depredations on the frontier soon led to the enlargement of the Army for the protection of the settlements. On the ocean frontier American ships sought markets in the far corners of the world, since independence had ended the privileged trading position of America with Britain and her colonies. Independence also meant the withdrawal of the Royal Navy's protective shield, and Americans involved in shipping and trade now began to work for the creation of a United States naval force to protect our expanding commerce.

Elsewhere in the United States prominent men were concerned about the ability of the government to meet the various needs of the nation. Their concern led to correspondence, to talk about revising the Articles of Confederation, and eventually to the meetings in Philadelphia that produced the Constitution of the United States. Among the delegates to the Constitutional Convention were some pro-navy men, and it was they who were responsible for incorporating in the Constitution the clause that Congress would have the power to "provide and maintain a navy." During the debates that preceded the ratification of the Constitution by the various states, it was men of this persuasion who argued that a navy was necessary for defense, for strengthening our diplomacy, and for stimulating and unifying the national economy. Once the Constitution was adopted and the new government was launched, pro-navy men began to plan for a standing navy.[1]

Such plans did not go unopposed. Representatives from the back country of the Middle and South Atlantic states fought against the creation of such a force. One of the most famous members of this opposition group was Senator William Maclay of Pennsylvania. When members of the Federalist faction urged that a fleet be built to protect ourselves from the pirates of Algiers who had captured American ships and imprisoned their crews, Maclay noted in his diary that "the Indian war is forced forward to justify our having a standing army, and eleven unfortunate men, now in slavery in Algiers, is the pretext for fitting out a fleet to go to war with them." [2] He had no sympathy for the line of argument that it was better to spend half a million dollars for a fleet than to pay a ransom to the pirates.

Increased depredations by the Algerian pirates finally induced Congress to approve a naval armament act in March 1794 that authorized the building of six frigates. The vote on this measure was so close that to placate the opposition an amendment was added providing that in the event of a peace with Algiers no further progress would be made with the naval program. In 1795 a treaty was negotiated with Algiers which bought protection for our commerce at a cost of $800,000 in ransom money and a yearly gift of $24,000. But the return of the peace did not end plans for a navy. After another verbal battle in Congress, the President was author-

---

[1] Harold and Margaret Sprout, *The Rise of American Naval Power, 1776–1918* (Princeton, N.J., 1946), pp. 15–27. For a detailed study of the origins of the Navy see Marshall Smelser, *The Congress Founds the Navy, 1787–1798* (Notre Dame, Ind., 1959).

[2] Edgar Stanton Maclay, ed., *Journal of William Maclay, United States Senator from Pennsylvania, 1789–1791* (New York, 1890), p. 383.

ized to complete three of the six frigates.[3] These ships, the *Constitution*, the *United States*, and the *Constellation*, were destined to play an important role in the building of naval discipline, tradition, and *esprit de corps*.

In spite of the peace arrangements with Algiers, the Federalist faction believed that the new frigates might still be necessary, for we had no treaties with Tunis and Tripoli. This need was emphasized by President Washington in his message to Congress in December 1796. He declared that our commerce would always be insecure and our citizens in peril unless we could protect our trade in the Mediterranean. He urged that the United States "set about the gradual creation of a Navy."[4]

The new threat to our commerce did not come from the pirates of the Mediterranean but from France, when war between that country and England broke out in 1793. France considered that the United States was still bound by the Alliance of 1778, but Washington issued a proclamation of neutrality. This neutral state tended to operate to the advantage of Britain as the dominant sea power. Washington's action was bitterly criticized by the farmer-artisan class, which was now being organized politically by Madison and Jefferson. This group denounced attempts to build a regular naval establishment as a plot to bring the country into war to aid Britain. In selling goods to both sides, American merchants reaped profits and ill will. Soon our ships were being seized by both France and Great Britain. Tensions with Great Britain were eased by the negotiation of the Jay Treaty of 1795, but this treaty further antagonized France, and diplomatic relations were broken off. Decrees issued in 1796 and 1797 ordered French cruisers and privateers to attack American shipping; between July 1796 and June 21, 1797, 316 ships flying American colors were seized by the French.[5] Slowly Congress and the people became aroused to this threat. Those who had been champions of the alliance with France now found themselves hard put to justify her actions. In March

---

[3] Sprout, pp. 28–30; John A. Carroll and Mary Wells Ashworth, *George Washington: First in Peace* (New York, 1957), pp. 346–347; Allan F. Westcott, ed., *American Sea Power Since 1775* (rev. ed.; Philadelphia, 1952), pp. 29–30; Smelser, pp. 87–101.

[4] Charles W. Goldsborough, *The United States Naval Chronicle*, I (Washington, D.C., 1824), 62; Smelser, pp. 87–88.

[5] Westcott, p. 33; Smelser, pp. 102–115.

1798 John Adams became President of the United States. He had long been an advocate of a navy, and now, with the backing of Federalist majorities in both houses of Congress, he began to see his hopes fulfilled. Bills were passed to complete the building of frigates and authorizing the President to augment the navy by other means. On April 30, 1798, Congress established the Navy Department, with Benjamin Stoddert as its first Secretary.[6]

The selection of Stoddert was an extremely fortunate choice. A man of vision and energy, he saw eye to eye with the President and the leading naval officers on the need for an efficient, well-disciplined naval force. During his term of office the Navy grew from a force of 3 ships in 1797 to 50 vessels by the end of 1799. As the Navy expanded, he impressed upon its officers the necessity of keeping a well-disciplined crew and of instilling in them a respect for the honor of the flag. Early in July 1798 Congress authorized retaliations on French ships anywhere on the seas. A state of war existed in fact if not in law, and Stoddert needed officers who were equal to the occasion. A favorite commander of the Secretary and of President Adams, and one who came to be highly regarded in British maritime circles, was Captain Thomas Truxtun.[7]

Truxtun was a product of the hard school of the merchant service, where, without marines to support them, the officers had to rely on their physical powers to maintain discipline. His 32 years of previous service included the command of various ships of the Continental Navy which were very successful in their actions against the British. Truxtun saw the need for establishing firm discipline in the young Navy and for attracting and holding the best officer material. In those days the captains chose most of their lieutenants and warrant officers, and the futures of these officers usually depended on the whim of the captain. Truxtun made his discipline severe so that only those who possessed great stamina and devotion to duty would remain in the Navy. He was determined to keep the inefficient and the lazy out of the officer ranks as

---

[6] Sprout, pp. 38–39; Smelser, pp. 118–159; Dudley W. Knox, *A History of the United States Navy* (rev. ed.; New York, 1948), pp. 45–46.

[7] Charles O. Paullin, "Early Naval Administration Under the Constitution," *United States Naval Institute Proceedings* [hereafter cited as *U.S.N.I.P.*], XXXII (1906), 1015–30; Sprout, pp. 39–41, 51–52; Smelser, pp. 160–207; Eugene S. Ferguson, *Truxtun of the Constellation* (Baltimore, 1956), pp. 147–148, 150–151, 169, 171–174.

far as possible. The strict discipline with which he held his officers was passed on to the seamen. Yet Truxtun was quick to point out to his midshipmen that "rigid discipline and good order are very different from tyranny." In Truxtun's view the character of a gentleman and that of an officer should never be separated. He was the most outstanding leader during the Quasi-War with France and his victories served to attract young and ambitious men to his command. More than any other officer he left his stamp of discipline and devotion to duty on the early Navy. Young officers such as Edward Preble, William Bainbridge, Stephen Decatur, Isaac Chauncey, Charles Stewart, James Barron, John Rodgers, and Oliver H. Perry served their apprenticeships during the Quasi-War and imbibed the strict discipline of the early Navy. These men and this code of discipline dominated the service for many years to come.[8]

In the closing months of the Adams administration and at the end of the undeclared war with France, the opposition of the Jeffersonian faction made itself felt in Congress. Stoddert's plans to create a naval reserve and to establish three ranks of admiral failed. Congress reduced the number of officers in the Navy to 9 captains, 36 lieutenants, and 150 midshipmen, all of whom were to draw pay only while on active duty. It also authorized the selling of all but 13 naval vessels, and 7 of these could be taken out of active service. Construction work in the various naval yards was halted.

One of the most influential members of Jefferson's cabinet was Albert Gallatin, the Secretary of the Treasury. Gallatin thought that the Navy was a luxury the country could ill afford, particularly at a time when the government was in debt. Secretary of the Navy Robert Smith urged the creation of a strong naval force to protect our commerce. Jefferson, determined to have a peaceful administration and a harmonious cabinet, took what might be regarded as a neutral position in regard to naval policy. Smith was told that the Navy would not be further reduced, but at the same time Gallatin's

---

[8] Captain Thomas Truxtun to Lieutenant Simon Gross, Aug. 30, 1797, *Naval Documents Related to the Quasi-War Between the United States and France* [hereafter cited as *Quasi-War*] (7 vols.; Washington, D.C., 1935–38), I, 14; Paullin, p. 1022; Ferguson, pp. 148, 220, 259–260; David D. Porter, *Memoir of Commodore David Porter of the United States Navy* (Albany, N.Y., 1875), p. 24; Gardner W. Allen, *Our Naval War with France* (Boston, 1909), p. 137.

financial plans were supported. The result was that Smith's recommendations for supplies were usually cut in half. When Smith
carried through his plans, Gallatin fretted about where the money
would come from.[9]

Smith's position was not an enviable one. In view of this state of
affairs, the outbreak of a war with Tripoli helped the naval establishment to survive. The Secretary had a penetrating mind and a
good knowledge of men, as well as some experience in nautical
affairs. Charles W. Goldsborough, Chief Clerk of the Navy Department, considered Smith as fortunate a choice for Secretary as Stoddert had been. But the Tripolitanian war pointed up the fact that
poor organization and incompetence prevailed at the Navy Department. Some of this was no doubt due to the lack of harmony between Smith and Gallatin. In the last analysis, Smith deserves credit
for waging a successful naval war off the coast of Africa on an
appropriation that was designed to cover the maintenance costs of
three frigates operating in home waters.[10]

Smith's orders were inclined to be vague and allowed his officers
a great deal of leeway in carrying out his instructions. The gallant
exploits of Commodore Preble's force off Tripoli showed that an
efficient naval force could blockade an enemy and command
respect. This service in the Mediterranean was an important follow-
up to the beginnings of naval discipline under Truxtun. Service
under Preble drove home the earlier lessons and taught some new
ones. Naval officers of this period were individualistic if nothing
else, but it is possible to observe some common traits of character
among those who served with Preble. By and large they were decisive, resolute, and resourceful; they possessed an offensive spirit,
and had a tremendous feeling of *esprit de corps*.[11] These traits were
of great value to the new Navy, particularly when its future role
was in doubt. But these same characteristics could also work to the
disadvantage of a Secretary who was inept, unimaginative, and
who lacked the capacity to inspire and to fight for the service he

---

[9] Sprout, pp. 52–55; Charles C. Tansill, "Robert Smith," in Samuel F.
Bemis, ed., *The American Secretaries of State and Their Diplomacy*, III (New
York, 1927), 151, 155; George E. Davies, "Robert Smith and the Navy,"
Maryland Historical Magazine, XIV (1919), 308.

[10] Tansill, p. 155; Davies, p. 308.

[11] Knox, p. 64; Fletcher Pratt, *Preble's Boys: Commodore Preble and the
Birth of American Sea Power* (New York, 1950), pp. 28–29, 399–404.

headed. The officers believed in their branch of service, and if leadership did not come from the Secretary it was bound to come from a dedicated group of officers.

One precedent in the war with Tripoli had a very bad effect on our naval department. Preble used some small gunboats to operate in the shallow waters where larger ships could not penetrate. Their utility in these operations convinced Jefferson that they were the ideal solution to our problem of naval defense. It was his policy to urge the construction of these small craft as a substitute for more expensive frigates. All but six or eight of these gunboats would be laid up along the coast, ready to drive a hostile enemy from our shores if necessary. They would be manned by a naval militia at the various ports. By storing these gunboats in sheds on land the government would be saved great sums for maintenance and manpower. Jefferson admitted that these boats were useless for protecting our commerce; his aim was to protect our coasts. It was his firm conviction that large vessels tended to bring on attacks rather than to ward them off.[12]

In the face of this situation the career naval officers had little choice but to acquiesce. With their chosen profession virtually cut out from under them they were left to fare for themselves. Many resigned from the service. Some went on furlough and sought temporary employment in the merchant service. Later the Embargo destroyed this form of employment. A small but devoted group weathered the gunboat era.

After protecting American commerce and seamen from the Algerians, the Tripolitanians, and the French, the naval officers now watched the deterioration of the fleet at the very time when American commerce and American seamen were being harassed anew by the English and the French. In its effort to destroy the power of Napoleon Bonaparte and his allies on the continent of Europe, Great Britain attempted to enforce an extensive blockade. Americans who traded with the various ports of Europe found themselves caught between the blockades proclaimed by both England and France. Their ships were liable to seizure by both powers. Once

---

[12] Sprout, pp. 58–60; Henry Adams, *A History of the United States of America* (9 vols.; New York, 1909), IV, 24; Alfred T. Mahan, *Sea Power in Its Relations to the War of 1812* (2 vols.; London, 1905), I, 187, 260.

again the neutral trade was a hazardous but profitable venture for American shippers who were willing to gamble.

But the stakes of the game were not just ships and cargoes. Hard pressed to man her navy, Great Britain resorted to seizing sailors from American ships. The grounds for such seizures were that the sailors taken were Englishmen who had either deserted from, or declined to serve in, His Majesty's service. The right of naturalization was not acknowledged, however, so to protect themselves from such impressments American sailors secured "protections," documents certifying that they were American citizens. But the value of such documents was compromised by the practice of sailor landlords or shippers of selling such protections to aliens or to any man who felt he needed one. Learning of such practices, British officers paid no attention to these papers. As a result many native-born and naturalized Americans were seized and forced to serve under the British flag. Once a man had been impressed it took long diplomatic negotiations to secure his release. Even so, there was no sure way for the government to know of every case of illegal impressment, and sometimes it was very difficult to prove nationality. Meanwhile the impressed man was prevented from returning home for many years and exposed to the danger of death in combat. Despite the enormous injustices involved, many shippers and politicians, and perhaps sailors as well, felt that impressment was just another risk of seaborne trade.[13]

The situation became worse. In 1805 a British warship lying off New York impressed men from three American ships, leaving one with less than half of her crew. The following year three British warships operating off Sandy Hook harassed American commerce and killed a seaman with a cannon shot. The United States government demanded that the British officer responsible be punished, and Great Britain court-martialed him. Public sentiment was becoming more and more aroused by such outrages.

Jefferson believed that Great Britain, heavily in debt and suffering military setbacks, could not resist the demands of other powers.

---

[13] James F. Zimmerman, *Impressment of American Seamen* (New York, 1925), pp. 1–134; Mahan, I, 114–133; Bradford Perkins, *Prologue to War: England and the United States, 1805–1812* (Berkeley, Calif., 1961), pp. 84–96; Roger H. Brown, *The Republic in Peril: 1812* (New York, 1964), pp. 12, 16–18, 21–23; Irving Brant, *James Madison: Secretary of State, 1800–1809* (Indianapolis, Ind., 1953), pp. 171–175, 254–258.

But the British Minister to the United States believed that the American government was weak and its people divided and hostile to taxation, so that if the British squadron on the North American station were increased, all hostile actions against Great Britain would cease.[14]

For the Navy and the nation 1807 was a dark year. In January the President officially informed Congress of the conspiracy of Aaron Burr, who had served as Vice-President during Jefferson's first term. The plot appeared to threaten Spain's possessions along our southwestern borders, and may have involved a secession of a portion of the Union. Burr was arrested, tried, and acquitted, but doubts about the aims of the conspiracy, and the extent of the involvement of influential persons, remained.[15]

June brought the disgraceful *Chesapeake* affair. When the United States frigate *Chesapeake* sailed from Norfolk, Virginia, she had among her crew deserters from two British warships. This was known to British diplomatic and naval officers. On his own authority the British naval commander at Halifax, Nova Scotia, ordered his captains to search for the deserters if they met the American frigate. H.M.S. *Leopard* met the *Chesapeake* on June 22, 1807, about ten miles off the coast of Virginia. The American frigate was fired upon and forced to surrender. The *Leopard's* officers boarded the *Chesapeake* and removed four men, three of whom were Americans. The four had deserted from the British service, but the three Americans were escaping from an earlier impressment. The men were taken to Halifax where the three Americans were put in prison and the Englishman was hanged. But this was not all. The British gunfire had killed 3 and wounded 18 of the *Chesapeake's* crew. When that frigate returned to Norfolk with news of the outrage the American public was greatly aroused and the nation was on the verge of war. Eventually the matter was settled by diplomacy.[16]

Meanwhile in July Jefferson ordered British warships out of American waters, but some defiantly remained. Secretary of State Madison later told the British special envoy, George Rose, that if the United States had had the force to do so she would have com-

---

[14] Zimmerman, p. 104; Brant, pp. 257, 367–370; Perkins, pp. 82–83.
[15] Brant, pp. 340–359.
[16] Adams, IV, 1–39; Zimmerman, pp. 135–155; Mahan, I, 155–171, 255.

pelled obedience to the President's order. The inadequacy of the gunboat policy was now being realized.[17]

Many naval officers regarded the *Chesapeake* affair as a disgrace to that service. Captain James Barron, the *Chesapeake's* commander, was charged with failing to prepare his ship for action and with surrendering prematurely. The veteran officers of the French and Tripolitanian wars considered it unthinkable that a naval officer should ever be charged with such failings. Barron was court-martialed and suspended for five years without pay. While he was found guilty only of failing to prepare his ship for action, there was a feeling in naval circles that he lacked the aggressive spirit that they had come to expect as a *sine qua non* of an American naval officer. Indeed, the decision of the court did not foster the idea of caution. To Jefferson the *Chesapeake* incident proved his conviction that frigates invited trouble.[18]

The impressment problem remained unsolved, and the passing months saw new attempts by both Britain and France to restrict trade with Europe. British Orders in Council were answered by Napoleon's Berlin and Milan decrees. Those who wondered how America would cope with the new restrictions soon got a surprising answer. December of 1807 brought the Embargo.

Congress, responding to Jefferson's urging, passed a law forbidding all American and foreign shipping to leave our harbors except when engaged in coastal trade. The President hoped that the need of the British and French for our exports would force them to come to us and to agree to respect our commerce. Unfortunately things did not work out that way. Neither France nor England yielded, but the enforcement of the law brought economic disaster to New England. Illegal trade flourished with Canada and occasionally ships allegedly loaded for American ports brought their cargoes to Europe. The tightening of the enforcement machinery, including the posting of bonds for the delivery of cargo, discouraged such activities.[19]

---

[17] Brant, pp. 381, 384, 406.

[18] Sprout, pp. 61–62; Mahan, I, 256–257; Adams, IV, 20–24; Pratt, pp. 52–53, 112; Charles Lee Lewis, *The Romantic Decatur* (Philadelphia, 1937), pp. 94–96.

[19] Brant, pp. 395–403, 448–451, 463; Perkins, pp. 150–183; Mahan, I, 182–215; Reginald Horsman, *The Causes of the War of 1812* (Philadelphia, 1962), pp. 110–112, 124–125.

Naval officers were disheartened by the progression of events. Remembering that on previous occasions a display of force was effective for safeguarding our commerce, they could not appreciate the Embargo. Under Jefferson the nation's response to affronts was not to fight, pay protection, or turn the other cheek, but to stay home and lock the doors.

At the end of Jefferson's second term Congress replaced the Embargo with the Non-Intercourse Act, which allowed Americans to trade with all nations except France and England.

By 1809 Paul Hamilton, Secretary of the Navy under President Madison, had come to appreciate the folly of the gunboat program and asked for "fast sailing frigates and smaller cruisers."[20] But Congress was in no mood to increase the Navy, and in 1810 even debated reducing it further. Two years later, when the War of 1812 began, the Navy consisted of "sixteen seagoing vessels, twelve of which were probably equal to any vessels afloat in the same class." In the opinion of the officers, the practice of laying up frigates in port had hastened their decay.[21]

Meanwhile the United States continued to press its claims in regard to the *Chesapeake*. The diplomatic negotiations were hampered by the fact that the United States linked the *Chesapeake* incident with the whole long-standing impressment issue. The British were willing to disavow the former but not the principle behind the latter.

The passage of time gave the Navy an opportunity to settle the *Chesapeake* matter in its own way. While protecting American shipping off our coasts the United States frigate *President* hailed the British sloop-of-war *Little Belt* in May 1811. The *Little Belt* replied with a cannon shot and the *President* answered in kind. Each ship brought guns to bear on the other. After about 15

---

[20] Sprout, p. 63; Perkins, pp. 165, 226–232; Mahan, I, 186–188, 213–214; Horsman, pp. 142–143, 218–220.

[21] Adams, VI, 362–363; Charles O. Paullin, "Naval Administration Under Secretaries of the Navy Smith, Hamilton and Jones, 1801–1814," *U.S.N.I.P.*, XXXII (1906), 1299–1300, 1318; Theodore Roosevelt, *The Naval War of 1812* (4th ed.; New York, 1889), pp. 72–73. The figures on the Navy's strength at the outbreak of war are from Adams. Irving Brant says the strength was 17 vessels. Of this number 8 were frigates, but 3 of these had deteriorated badly. The rest of the total was made up of the 20-gun ship *John Adams* and 8 small brigs and sloops. See Brant, *James Madison: The Commander in Chief, 1812–1836* (Indianapolis, Ind., 1961), p. 39.

minutes of fighting the *Little Belt* was badly damaged and had 9 men killed and 23 wounded. The larger, more powerful *President* sustained no casualties and no serious damage: the *Chesapeake* was avenged! On the diplomatic front, however, the *Chesapeake* incident was not settled until November 1811.[22]

On June 1, 1812, President Madison presented to Congress documents which showed a series of actions by Great Britain that were "hostile to the United States as an independent neutral nation." Among these was the impressment of thousands of American citizens into the British Navy and forcing them to serve "under the severities of their discipline," as well as subjecting them to exile and to the risk of their lives. Madison also spoke of the blockade of American ports, the harassment of our commerce in our own territorial waters, and the plundering of our shipping in every sea. He charged that American commerce was being sacrificed not because it interfered with Britain's belligerent rights, but because she wished to destroy a threat to her own monopoly of commerce and navigation. The President also pointed out the activities of British traders among Indian tribes on the frontier and the subsequent hostility of such tribes toward Americans. He declared that Britain was already at war with the United States and he asked Congress for a resort to force to defend our national rights. Congress responded by voting for war, but the vote, 79–49 in the House and 19–13 in the Senate, showed an ominous lack of support for the measure. The maritime states of New England, as well as New York, New Jersey, and Delaware, voted against war.[23]

The first of the naval victories was the triumph of Captain Isaac Hull's *Constitution* over the *Guerriere*. The same Boston newspaper that joyfully proclaimed this victory also carried the news of the surrender of Detroit by General William Hull, the captain's brother. Within 24 hours, Captains John Rodgers and Stephen

---

[22] Mahan, I, 257–259; Zimmerman, pp. 135–155; Irving Brant, *James Madison: The Presidency, 1809–1812* (Indianapolis, Ind., 1956), pp. 94–95, 106–107, 123–124, 196–198, 316–327, 349, 364–365, 408.

[23] The text of the war message may be found in James D. Richardson, *A Compilation of the Messages and Papers of the Presidents, 1789–1897* (10 vols.; New York, 1897) II, 484–490. For a discussion of the causes of the war see Mahan, I, 41, 134–140, 276–282; Brown, pp. 112–130; Horsman, pp. 260–267; Perkins, pp. 403–417, 421–437; Brant, *James Madison: The Presidency,* pp. 470–483; Brant, *James Madison: Commander in Chief,* pp. 13–22.

Decatur sailed into Boston harbor with the news that they had accomplished nothing in their own two-month cruises. Thus Hull's victory came at the precise moment when the public spirit needed uplifting. The populace was thrilled.[24] Hull's exploit was commemorated with poems, songs, cheers, and toasts. Other victorious ship duels in succeeding months made national heroes of naval officers and built an enormous amount of prestige for their arm of service.

But spectacular victories at sea did not hide the faults of the Secretary of the Navy. Hamilton's administration was criticized by the press, and he himself, despite the efforts of President Madison and others to help him, was becoming an inebriate. Finally, on December 20, 1812, he resigned. He was succeeded by William Jones, a Pennsylvania merchant who had seen both land and sea service during the Revolution.[25]

Secretary Jones addressed himself to the problems of his office with an intelligent zeal. Within a short time he asked for ships, for a reorganization of the department, for the establishment of a purchasing agency, and for additional personnel in the department and in the fleet. He also outlined the new strategy of building light, fast ships for protecting our coasts and for commerce raiding. He directed the build-up of our forces on the lakes that was to result in Perry's victory on Lake Erie and McDonough's triumph on Lake Champlain. Broad policy matters were worked out with the President and with Representative William Lowndes and Senator John Gaillard of the naval committees. His forceful leadership was an important factor in putting the department on a more efficient basis.[26]

Jones was firmly convinced that the practice of giving and accepting ship duels with the Royal Navy was unwise. The Navy that had begun to prove itself was about to be restrained somewhat. To lend additional authority to his order to stop these duels it was issued in the name of President Madison. Jones also issued detailed

---

[24] Adams, VI, 376–377.

[25] Brant, *James Madison: Commander in Chief*, pp. 25, 125–126, 128, 164; Leonard D. White, *The Jeffersonians: A Study in Administrative History, 1801–1829* (New York, 1951), p. 271.

[26] Kenneth L. Brown, "Mr. Madison's Secretary of the Navy," *U.S.N.I.P.*, LXXIII (1947), 969–970.

orders to his commanders for planned cruises in specific areas. These planned cruises did result in some splendid victories, but the Navy officers felt that the results would have been more spectacular if they had been allowed to cruise and fight at will.[27]

In 1814 Jones submitted a plan for the reorganization of the Navy Department which included the appointment of a three-man board of officers who would advise the Secretary. He also recommended the creation of a naval academy for the proper training of midshipmen to be future leaders. Although the Secretary did not get his naval academy, his plan did lead to the establishment of the Board of Naval Commissioners in February 1815.[28]

Such were the formative years of the United States Navy. Conceived in an atmosphere of hostility and born amid a war, within 17 years it grew from the small but spirited child loved mainly by the Federalists to the strong young adult that was the pride of the whole nation. The Navy had fought and won its right to existence. Its fighting officers had won glory, position, and prestige as a result of their efforts. They felt a sense of pride over what they had accomplished with limited resources. Looking back over their early history they saw that the major problems and setbacks they had faced were due to the failures of civilian leadership. There was a tendency to believe that the Navy and national honor had been preserved in spite of the politicians. This attitude and the aura of glory that surrounded its leading officers were to have an important influence on the Navy in the years to come.

The future of the Navy depended upon the public's support of its goals. In urging the creation of the Navy the Federalists had argued that such a force was necessary for the defense of national honor, the protection of our commerce, and the safeguarding of our seamen. When the Democratic-Republicans applied this same line of reasoning as a justification for a war against Great Britain, the Federalists and others with maritime interests were furious. If the imprisoned sailor in Algiers was the least of the concerns of the Congress during Washington's administration, under Madison the Congress acquiesced in making the impressed sailor in the British

---

[27] *Ibid.,* p. 972.
[28] *Ibid.,* p. 975.

service a major cause of a war. Both the Federalists and the Democratic-Republicans were responsible for linking together in the public mind the concepts of national honor, economic interest, and individual freedom, and for making the Navy a major defender of all three. Soon this type of identification would create new problems when the needs of the Navy, the varied interests of the nation, and the spread of democracy all competed for public support.

THE YEARS OF DECLINE AND REFORM, 1815-62

News of the end of the War of 1812 reached the United States in February 1815. Amid the celebrations New England shippers promptly sent vessels to sea to recapture markets and to make up for the losses suffered from the British blockade. The movement to the American West, slowed by the war, soon reached large proportions. The whole country reflected an optimistic, expansive mood. It was a time for doing things. Gone were the days of our precarious independence and the humiliations resulting from weakness. The country had just emerged with honor from a war with Great Britain — the country that had contributed so much to the defeat of Napoleon. The conduct of the American Army at Chippewa, Lundy's Lane, Baltimore, and New Orleans instilled a feeling of pride and patriotism. The same was true of the victories of our naval vessels.

But the joys of peace and the sense of pride in the country's achievements did not make some men forget that New England had not supported the war in a wholehearted way. The anti-war feeling which produced the Hartford Convention and threats of secession from the Union might erupt again. Something must be done to overcome sectional jealousies. This problem was on the mind of Justice Joseph Story of the Supreme Court when he wrote to a friend in February 1815. Story thought that the national authority should be extended "over the whole extent of power given by the Constitution." As a part of this program he suggested, among other things, the establishment of a national bank; "great military and naval schools; an adequate regular army"; and the laying of the broad foundations for a permanent Navy. "By such enlarged and liberal institutions, the Government of the United States will be endeared to the people, and the factions of the great States will be rendered harmless. Let us prevent the possibility of a division, by creating great national interests which shall bind us in an indissoluble chain." [1]

Story's dream of making the Army, the Navy, the Bank of the United States, and other federal institutions serve as substitutes for sectionalism was not to be realized. But throughout the period of this study there was hope among the friends of the Navy that a sense of national pride would lead to public support for a strong Navy.

In the Navy there was reason to believe that a bright new day was dawning. Its victories in the War of 1812 had won it wide popular acclaim. Even at New Orleans, the last land battle of the war which everyone remembered better than any others, the naval force and guns of Master Commandant Daniel Patterson contributed significantly to Andrew Jackson's victory. Stirred by public support, Congress might now be induced to put the Navy on a proper footing. Congress responded in 1816 by passing a law for the gradual increase of the Navy through the expenditure of $1,000,000 a year for six years to build nine 74-gun ships-of-the-line, twelve 44-gun frigates, and three steam-propelled "batteries" for harbor defense. The latter item was still in the experimental stage.[2] Friends of the Navy had reason to be optimistic.

The Navy's role as the protector of our commerce was underscored anew. No sooner was the War of 1812 over than the Navy began offensive actions against Algiers for interference with our trade. By the fall of 1815 this task was completed. Not long after this pirates operating in the West Indies posed a new threat to our commerce. Between 1822 and 1829 the Navy eliminated this menace. The importance of naval power was highlighted again in 1823 when President James Monroe announced to the world the Ameri-

---

[1] Story to Nathaniel Williams, Feb. 22, 1815, cited in William W. Story, *The Life and Letters of Joseph Story* (2 vols.; Boston, 1851), I, 254.
[2] *U.S. Statutes at Large*, III, Chaps. 138, 321; Sprout, pp. 86–92.

can policy in relation to the Western Hemisphere that bears his name. The Monroe Doctrine ultimately depended on the support of the British fleet to make it effective, but in any period when the doctrine might be tested, the American Navy could be counted on to contribute its strength to the cause of hemispheric defense. Small squadrons were maintained in the Mediterranean, the South Atlantic, the Pacific, and the West Indies, where they "showed the flag" and advertised our ability to protect our commerce. A Home Squadron was organized in 1841 to patrol our own coasts, and two years later the African Squadron was created to fight the slave trade.[3]

YEARS OF DECLINE

Despite these responsibilities the friends of the Navy soon found that their hopes for better days were premature. By 1821 there was a reaction against building up a large force, and the appropriations for the Navy Department were steadily reduced. This reversal of policy was due in part to the effects of the business depression known as the Panic of 1819, to the increased demands for the expenditure of federal funds on projects that would benefit various sections of the country, and to anti-Navy sentiment in Congress. In addition there was the distraction occasioned by Missouri's request for admission to the Union in 1819 which touched off a sharp debate on slavery and pointed up the rising sectional rivalries. The Missouri Compromise arrangement, governing the limitations of slavery in the territories, established the formula for the admission of free and slave territory in the West for the next 30 years. The need for institutions which could nourish the concept of union was demonstrated, but there was no disposition in the Congress to encourage the use of the Navy for such a purpose.

The lack of any strong desire on the part of the Congress to make up for the years of neglect or to plan for the future caused the Navy to decline slowly from its wartime level. With each passing year the gap between needs and their fulfillment widened. Various Secretaries of the Navy tried to do the best they could with the materials at hand. Often this meant concentrating on one or two goals and letting other things drift. During the last part of Monroe's presi-

---

[3] Sprout, pp. 94–95; Knox, pp. 136–138.

dency and throughout the administration of John Quincy Adams, Secretary of the Navy Samuel L. Southard (1823–29) agitated for a variety of reforms. He was particularly interested in curbing a growing attitude of insubordination among the officers. This goal was also pursued by John Branch (1829–31), Levi Woodbury (1831–34), Mahlon Dickerson (1834–38), and James K. Paulding (1838–41) during the administrations of Presidents Andrew Jackson and Martin Van Buren. In an era characterized by a great deal of talk about the plight of "the common man" such curbing of abuses of rank and authority by naval officers seemed to be a most appropriate activity for Jacksonian Secretaries.[4]

The Jacksonians had no desire to create a larger or more powerful naval force. To protect our commerce, reliance was placed on frigates and other small ships that were less expensive to maintain. Secretary Paulding was subjected to heavy pressure from younger officers to build steam frigates for the Navy. The Secretary, however, like many of the older officers, did not believe that steam had fully demonstrated its utility for ocean operations. He considered the "steam fever" to be one of the passing manias of the time, and he wrote that he would "never consent to let our old ships perish, and to transform the Navy into a fleet of sea monsters."[5] Yet in the end he compromised between pro- and anti-steam factions, and Congress authorized the building of three steam warships.[6] It was the beginning of a technological revolution.

Technology was not the only thing that demanded attention. The officer corps needed a reorganization from bottom to top. At the bottom were the midshipmen, whose commissions were usually dispensed by members of Congress without regard to the needs of the service. The Secretary of the Navy had no effective way of screening out the undesirable young men and no systematic way of training them. Since the time of Captain John Paul Jones various friends of the Navy, including several Secretaries, had urged that a naval

---

[4] Charles O. Paullin, "Naval Administration Under the Navy Commissioners, 1815–1842," *U.S.N.I.P.*, XXXIII (1907), 601–641; William I. Paulding, *Literary Life of James K. Paulding* (New York, 1867), pp. 270–275; Ralph M. Aderman, ed., *The Letters of James Kirke Paulding* (Madison, Wis., 1962), p. 258.

[5] Paulding, pp. 277–278.

[6] Sprout, pp. 110–115.

academy be established for the proper training of officers. The idea
was resisted by many in Congress on the grounds that it would tend
to build up an aristocracy of officers, which they believed West
Point was already doing. It also seemed to smack too much of aping
Great Britain. Besides, many congressmen and some naval officers
believed that experience on the high seas was the best teacher.
Midshipmen were taught various subjects on board ship by the
chaplain or schoolmaster at such times when the captain was willing to dispense with their services, but it was a haphazard arrangement at best.[7]

Faced with a lack of sympathy for this problem on the part of
Congress, the Navy resorted to other expedients. Special schools
were established at Boston, Norfolk, and later at Philadelphia.
Attendance was voluntary and small groups of young officers were
granted leaves to attend these schools. It was better than nothing,
but it was no substitute for a regular naval academy where all
young officers could be given a uniform and systematic education
to prepare them for the responsibilities of command.[8]

Midshipmen who completed their course of studies on land or
on ship were given a synthetic promotion and the title of passed
midshipman until such time as they could attain the regular rank
of lieutenant. Promotion to any rank entailed a long wait. Lieutenant Maury estimated that a midshipman appointed in 1839
could expect to reach the rank of lieutenant by 1870, and many a
young midshipman decided on another career in the interval.[9]

The situation was almost as discouraging for persons holding the
rank of lieutenant, commander, or captain. Congress, fearful of
establishing a naval aristocracy, refused to authorize any rank
higher than that of captain. For most of the period before the Civil
War the captaincies were held by officers who had won the rank

---

[7] Henry L. Burr, *Education in the Early Navy* (Philadelphia, 1939), pp.
42–54, 111–115, 122–127, 143–145, 189–191, 197–199, 207–209; James Russell Soley, *Historical Sketch of the United States Naval Academy* (Washington, D.C., 1876), pp. 7–61.

[8] Burr, pp. 147–165.

[9] Harry Bluff [Matthew F. Maury], "Scraps from the Lucky Bag,"
Southern Literary Messenger, VI (1840), 319. In the British Navy of the
nineteenth century there were many instances of slow promotion, but among
the most extreme were the case of a 65-year-old midshipman, and the case
of an officer who was a midshipman for 34 years before being promoted. See
Michael Lewis, *The Navy of Britain* (London, 1949), p. 274.

during or soon after the War of 1812. There was no system of retirement, and the lieutenants had to look to the angel of death to provide vacancies in the top ranks.

At the top of the rank structure were the captains, who were given the complimentary title of commodore when they commanded squadrons. In the course of a cruise they often found themselves at a disadvantage when dealing with commanders of foreign squadrons, who, for the most part, held higher ranks. The commodores looked forward to the day when Congress would create the rank of admiral, but this did not come about until the Civil War, when all but one of the old War of 1812 captains was dead.

The naval forces on active duty were never large enough to provide commands for all the captains who desired them, so there were long periods of time between cruises. At such times, and when advancing years made them unfit for sea duty, the captains found themselves ashore and awaiting orders. The luckier ones were assigned to comfortable berths as commandants of naval yards.[10]

The bleak outlook for promotions made it advisable for officers to cultivate political friendships. By the 1840's it was a well-known maxim in the Navy that a cruise in Washington was worth two around Cape Horn. Such lobbying by officers tended to undercut the authority of the Secretary and it had pernicious effects upon discipline. This situation was complicated by the fact that the various Secretaries were politicians with no background in naval or maritime affairs. For most, it was a steppingstone to other posts. It was only natural that some officers would adopt the attitude that they knew better than the Secretary what was best for the Navy.

---

[10] Paullin, "Naval Administration . . . 1815–1842," p. 628; Leonard D. White, *The Jacksonians: A Study in Administrative History, 1829–1861* (New York, 1954), pp. 233–237. Matthew F. Maury served 30 years as a lieutenant before being promoted to a commander. The situation was not much better in the Army. In 1836 the Adjutant General calculated that it would take 58 years for a brevet second lieutenant to become a colonel. See Francis P. Prucha, *Broadax and Bayonet* (Madison, Wis., 1953), p. 54. In the British Navy, where the ranks of admiral existed, the situation was also very bad. It was estimated that if Lord Nelson had not been killed in battle in 1805, he would not have become Admiral of the Fleet until 1844, when he would have been 86 years old! See Michael Lewis, p. 273.

Several Secretaries found that maintaining the subordination of officers was one of their most persistent problems.[11]

Jealousy, factionalism, and an exaggerated sense of honor led to numerous minor quarrels among officers, and often to duels. Between 1798 and 1848, 33 naval officers were killed in duels. The death of the popular hero, Captain Stephen Decatur, in 1820 as a result of a duel with Captain James Barron caused such adverse public reaction that it led to a decline in such encounters between senior officers. Spirited young midshipmen kept up the practice for some time, however.[12]

Naval justice also left something to be desired. Junior officers often had cause to complain about the tyranny of their superiors. There is evidence that commanders were not always concerned about the letter of the law in naval regulations except where it concerned their own prerogatives. The aura of hero worship that surrounded the old veterans tended to protect them from the charges of their subordinates. Heroes were humored. It was common knowledge in the Navy that senior officers were virtually immune to any serious punishment. Anyone with a complaint usually had to wait until the end of a three-year cruise before filing it with the Navy Department, and investigations took time. Senior officers could usually rest assured that pressing a matter was too much trouble for most of their subordinates to worry about; an officer who preferred charges risked his career and his service reputation. The strong sentiments of the junior officers on this subject were expressed by Lieutenant Matthew F. Maury when he wrote that the "laws of the navy are kept in two vials — one of which is closely sealed, and seldom permitted to be opened — the other, large mouthed and convenient, ready at all times with its wrath to be emptied upon the younger, and therefore the weaker and more frail members of the corps." [13]

A midshipman named William Leggett, who left the Navy in 1825 following a court-martial for insubordinate behavior, went on to another kind of fame. As a civilian he published a collection of

---

[11] A Few Officers of Both the Line and Staff, *Suggestions upon Naval Reform* (n.p., 1850), p. 15.

[12] Charles O. Paullin, "Duelling in the Old Navy," *U.S.N.I.P.*, XXXV (1909), 1156–57.

[13] Harry Bluff [Matthew F. Maury], "Of Reorganizing the Navy," *Southern Literary Messenger*, VII (1841), 13.

poems entitled "Leisure Hours at Sea," established a short-lived literary publication, and, in 1829, became one of the editors of the New York newspaper *The Evening Post*. Under the senior editorship of William Cullen Bryant the *Post* became an important voice of the Jacksonian group in New York. Leggett, who took over the editorship when Bryant went to Europe in 1834, became the leading theorist of the Locofoco faction of the Democrats. He fought against the monopolies of the banks, and argued for the simple way of life associated with an agrarian economy. Regarding the influence of the Navy on Leggett's subsequent career, a contemporary biographer had this to say: "The vexations to which he was subjected during the period he was in the naval service, undoubtedly had great influence on his future character. There are some minds which despotism crushes and breaks; stronger natures find in it a discipline from which they gain new hardihood and energy. . . . The hatred which Mr. Leggett has shown to tyranny, in all its forms, was rendered the more intense by his having tasted its bitterness." [14]

Given the general situation in regard to the organization, leadership, discipline, and opportunities for professional advancement, it is not surprising that many young officers resigned their commissions in despair and chose other occupations.

There is little doubt that the Navy lost many fine officers through resignations, and that many of those who stayed in were of poorer quality. Nevertheless, among those who stayed there was a hard core of dedicated young men who were determined to improve the service and their own futures. It was men of this stripe who responded to the leadership of Matthew C. Perry and organized the United States Naval Lyceum at the New York Navy Yard in 1833. The Lyceum, which was dedicated to the spreading of knowledge among Navy officers, soon boasted a museum with Perry as its curator. Three years after its founding the Lyceum published the *Naval Magazine*, which was an outgrowth of their museum activities and the "first periodical in the United States conducted by naval officers." The magazine was edited by the Reverend Charles S. Stewart, a chaplain in the Navy. Similar efforts by like-minded

---

[14] "William Leggett," *United States Magazine and Democratic Review*, VI (1839), 20.

officers later resulted in the publication of the *United States Naval Magazine* and the *Army and Navy Chronicle*. In 1836 an American Historical Society of Military and Naval Events was organized.[15]

Ambitious men applied themselves as best they could. Lieutenant John A. Dahlgren pioneered in the improvement of naval ordnance. Young officers on survey duty charted our coasts. Others studied advances in steam navigation and in naval architecture. Some medical men improved themselves by studying abroad. Samuel Holbrook, a ship's carpenter, tells of meeting one of his former officers in the work crew of a merchant ship. The young officer asked not to be given away. He explained that after receiving the furlough he requested he had signed on board a merchant vessel in order that he might learn practical seamanship.[16]

The period also saw the publication of a number of works by individual officers of the Navy. Lieutenant Matthew F. Maury's *New Theoretical and Practical Treatise on Navigation*, published at his own expense, appeared in 1835 and soon brought the author wide acclaim. Between 1815 and 1830 Naval Surgeon William P. C. Barton published several volumes on botany and medicine. Naval Surgeon William S. W. Ruschenberger's account of his travels, *Three Years in the Pacific*, appeared in 1834. Lieutenant Alexander Slidell Mackenzie turned his talents to literature and history with published accounts of his travels in Spain and England, and biographies of John Paul Jones and Oliver H. Perry, as well as a collection of essays on naval subjects.[17]

It was but a short transition for much of this writing on naval topics to become a type of reform literature. An early example of this was an article on the Navy which appeared in *The North American Review* in 1830. Using the last annual report of the Secre-

---

[15] Paullin, "Naval Administration . . . 1815–1842," p. 637. Some of the members of the Lyceum who appear elsewhere in this study are Samuel F. Du Pont, Alexander Slidell Mackenzie, John C. Long, John W. Mooers, William L. Hudson, Guert Gansevoort, John Gamble, Lawrence Kearney, Silas H. Stringham, John D. Sloat, Doctors W. S. W. Ruschenberger and Usher Parsons, and Chaplain Thomas Lambert. James Fenimore Cooper was an honorary member.

[16] Samuel F. Holbrook, *Threescore Years: An Autobiography* (Boston, 1857), pp. 314–315.

[17] Paullin, "Naval Administration . . . 1815–1842," p. 638; Robert W. Neeser, *Statistical and Chronological History of the United States Navy, 1775–1907* (2 vols.; New York, 1909), I, 112, 114, 120–121.

tary of the Navy as a starting point for the presentation of his opinions, the author, a naval officer, discussed the history of navies before pointing out specific defects in his own. He also praised a recent book by a naval chaplain which described life in the U.S. Navy.[18]

Near the end of Paulding's term of office a series of articles appeared in *The Southern Literary Messenger* exposing the waste, mismanagement, inefficiency, and generally moribund state of the Navy. The articles, entitled "Scraps from the Lucky Bag," appeared under the name Harry Bluff, later identified as Lieutenant Matthew F. Maury of the Navy. Some idea of the power of these articles may be gained from the following excerpt: "Never before has the spirit of discontent, among all grades in the navy, walked forth in the broad light of day, with half such restive but determined steps. The period is fast approaching, when something must be done to stay the evils of the deranged system. Officers, and the friends of the Navy, have forborne, until forbearance has ceased to be a virtue. They feel that to remain longer silent with the Navy in its present condition, would be but to betray the interests confided to them by their fellow-citizens." [19]

The articles were an instant sensation and were reprinted for members of Congress.[20] Without a doubt they played an important part in the reorganization of the Navy which was soon to take place.

YEARS OF REFORM, 1840–62

When the Whigs came to power in 1841, with the inauguration of President William Henry Harrison, the post of Secretary of the Navy was given to George E. Badger of North Carolina. In May Badger reported that it seemed to be a general opinion both in and out of the Navy that a "thorough reorganization" was necessary. He

---

[18] "Report of the Secretary of the Navy to the President of the United States, December 1, 1829," *The North American Review*, XXX (1830), 360–389. Leonard D. White credits Lieutenant Alexander Slidell Mackenzie with the authorship of this article, but he does not give a source. See White's *The Jacksonians*, p. 214n.

[19] Harry Bluff, "Scraps from the Lucky Bag," p. 793. For background on this series of articles see Frances Leigh Williams, *Matthew Fontaine Maury, Scientist of the Sea* (New Brunswick, N.J., 1963), pp. 128–143.

[20] Paullin, "Naval Administration . . . 1815–1842," p. 640. Vice-President John Tyler was a charter subscriber to the *Southern Literary Messenger*.

hoped to present "a comprehensive and well digested system of reform" before the next regular meeting of Congress.[21] Badger never carried out his plan, for in September 1841 he resigned with his fellow cabinet members when John Tyler, who succeeded to the presidency after the death of Harrison, was read out of the Whig party.

Badger's successor was Abel Parker Upshur of Virginia, whose term of office (1841–43) brought new order, efficiency, and *esprit* to the Navy. In his first annual report Upshur served notice that he was a man of action. "I have had but a short experience in this department," he wrote, "but a short experience is enough to display its defects, even to the most superficial observation. It is, in truth, not organized at all." [22]

With the support of Congress, the new Secretary proceeded to set things right. The Board of Navy Commissioners, established in 1815 to assist the Secretary on matters relating to the building, arming, equipping, and employing of ships of war, had long out-lived its usefulness, but Congress had ignored suggestions for changes. In August 1842 Congress passed a law abolishing the board and replacing it with five specialized bureaus. They were charged with the responsibilities for Navy Yards and Docks; Ordnance and Hydrography; Construction, Equipment and Repairs; Medicine and Surgery; and Provisions and Clothing. The first two bureaus were to be headed by captains, the third by a skilled constructor; and the fourth by a naval surgeon. The fifth could be headed by either an officer or a civilian. The first incumbent of the Bureau of Provisions and Clothing was a civilian, Charles W. Goldsborough, who had long been associated with the Navy Department as chief clerk, and later as secretary of the board. He was followed by Gideon Welles, who, during his service between 1846 and 1849, acquired experience and made friendships that were to prove valuable when he later became Secretary.

The heads of these bureaus were appointed by the President with the approval of the Senate, but it was the Secretary of the Navy who determined their duties and to whom they were responsible. Since no attempt was made to form the bureaus into a board, and

[21] *Senate Documents*, 27th Cong., 1st Sess. (Serial 390), Doc. 1, p. 63.
[22] *Ibid.*, 2d Sess. (Serial 395), I, Doc. 1, p. 378.

since the Secretary was the only unifying force, the arrangement strengthened his position considerably.[23]

Secretary Upshur was also a strong advocate of naval improvements and expansion. Taking advantage of a diplomatic crisis with Great Britain over our boundaries, Upshur was able to get congressional approval for the construction of the first ironclad warship in the world. He was also convinced by Captain Robert F. Stockton that a steam vessel should be constructed with its screw propellor and its vital machinery below the water line, where it would be safe from enemy fire. This was a great step forward in naval technology. The vessel was named the *Princeton* in honor of Stockton's home town. The building of the ship was superintended by John Ericsson, a Swedish engineer whom Stockton brought to the attention of the Navy Department. Ericsson was responsible for arming the ship with two 12-inch reinforced wrought iron guns of his own design.[24]

Upshur's interest in the Navy extended beyond these important beginnings. He wanted to make it half as strong as the strongest maritime power in the world. The Whigs were generally inclined to be more favorable to the Navy than the Democrats, but this proposal was too much even for the pro-Navy men in Congress. An old friend of the Navy like John Quincy Adams thought that the program was too extravagant. The Democrats in the Senate, led by Thomas Hart Benton and Levi Woodbury, also opposed this ambitious plan. In the end a compromise program was enacted which fell far short of Upshur's ideas. Nevertheless, the zeal of the reformers was so great that the Navy prospered under Tyler's administration, and especially during Upshur's service as Secretary. Symbolic of the new interest in naval matters and of the growing influence of young reform-minded officers was the fact that President Tyler seriously considered offering the job of Secretary of the Navy to Lieutenant Matthew F. Maury, and actually did offer it to Captain Robert F. Stockton, who refused the post.[25]

Upshur left the Navy Department in 1843 to become Secretary of

[23] Charles O. Paullin, "Naval Administration, 1842–1861," *U.S.N.I.P.*, XXXIII (1907), 1440.

[24] Sprout, pp. 125–126; James P. Baxter, *The Introduction of the Ironclad Warship* (Cambridge, Mass., 1933), 13–14, 48–50.

[25] Paullin, "Naval Administration . . . 1815–1842," pp. 600, 627; Sprout, pp. 121–124; Charles Lee Lewis, *Matthew Fontaine Maury: The Pathfinder*

State. For the next ten years the administration of the Navy fell to a series of short-term Secretaries with the result that naval reform was sporadic. Upshur was replaced by David Henshaw, an ex-druggist, railroad promoter, and Massachusetts politician, who served from July 1843 to January 15, 1844. On the latter date the Senate refused to confirm his appointment — the only time during this period that it refused to agree to a presidential choice for the Navy Department. President Tyler then chose Thomas W. Gilmer of Virginia, who was confirmed. Gilmer was in office only ten days when he was killed by the explosion of an experimental cannon on board the *Princeton*. He was replaced by another Virginian, John Y. Mason, who served from March 1844 to the spring of 1845. In March 1845 George Bancroft of Massachusetts was appointed Secretary. Bancroft left this post in September 1846 and was succeeded by John Y. Mason. Mason's second term as Secretary lasted until 1849. Between 1849 and 1861 the Navy Department was administered by William Ballard Preston of Virginia (1849–50), William A. Graham of North Carolina (1850–52), John P. Kennedy of Maryland (1852–53), James C. Dobbin of North Carolina (1853–57), and Isaac Toucey of Connecticut (1853–57).

These men represented a period of predominately southern influence in the Navy Department, for even Toucey, the northerner, was sympathetic to the South. Two other southerners served in influential positions during this period: Stephen A. Mallory of Florida, who was Chairman of the Senate Committee on Naval Affairs, and Thomas S. Bocock of Virginia, who served as Chairman of the House Committee on Naval Affairs.[26] Their sympathies, background, and orientation were significant in a period that saw an increase in popular agitation for various humanitarian causes, including antislaveryism, which affected the Navy as well as the rest of the country.

With the coming of Gideon Welles to the Navy Department in 1861 a new era in naval administration began. Southern influence gave way to northern. Welles came to his post with three years of

---

of the Seas (Annapolis, Md., 1927), p. 40; Williams, p. 136. For Upshur's plans and contributions as Secretary of the Navy see Claude H. Hall, *Abel Parker Upshur: Conservative Virginian, 1790–1844* (Madison, Wis., 1963), pp. 120–193.

[26] Paullin, "Naval Administration, 1842–1861," pp. 1435–36.

experience as Chief of the Bureau of Provisions and Clothing. As
such he had had a chance to learn something of the service that he
now headed, and he was "an uncanny judge of men." He soon became known as a man who firmly believed in naval discipline and
in the impartial application of naval regulations regardless of rank
or influence. On more than one occasion he called naval courts to
task for handing down verdicts that were contrary to the evidence
that had been presented. He approached his job with a conscien-
tious zeal that made him drive himself and his subordinates very
hard. Under his leadership in the midst of war the Navy Department was transformed, and the service itself reached an all-time
high in efficiency.[27]

During the two decades preceeding the Civil War the reputation
of the Navy was enhanced by its role in various scientific, military,
and diplomatic enterprises. The exploring expedition under Lieutenant Charles Wilkes set sail in 1838 after years of bickering and
delay about its arrangements and command. Nearly four years later
it returned in triumph, having explored and surveyed islands in the
Pacific Ocean, a part of Antarctica, and the northwest coast of
North America from Puget Sound to parts of California. Other scientific expeditions set forth between 1850 and 1860 for such places
as the Arctic, the River Jordan and the Dead Sea, the isthmuses of
Darien and Chiriqui in Central America, the western and northern
Pacific Ocean, the western coast of Africa, and the La Plata River
and its tributaries in South America.[28]

The Navy played a brief but important role in the Mexican War
(1846–48), including blockade duty, giving support to the Army,
and in the seizure of California. Naval forces were also used in
actions against the Creek and Seminole Indians (1836–42), and in
the enforcement of American rights and interests in Nicaragua
(1853), China (1854–56), and Paraguay (1859).

---

[27] Charles O. Paullin, "A Half Century of Naval Administration in America,
1861–1911," *U.S.N.I.P.*, XXXVIII (1912), 1309–14; Howard K. Beale,
"Gideon Welles," *Dictionary of American Biography*, in Allen Johnson and
Dumas Malone, eds., XIX (1936), 629.

[28] Knox, pp. 154–166, 169–189. For background on the Wilkes expedition
see W. Patrick Strauss, "Preparing the Wilkes Expedition: A Study in Disorganization," *Pacific Historical Review*, XXVIII (1959), 221–232, and
Udolpho T. Bradley, "The Contentious Commodore: Thomas Ap Catesby
Jones of the Old Navy, 1788–1859," unpublished Ph.D. dissertation, Department of History, Cornell University, 1933, pp. 114–128.

Ships of the Navy carried a great many American diplomats to their posts, and naval officers played an important role in opening American trade with the Far East, especially with China and Japan. In the latter connection it should be noted that Commodore Matthew C. Perry, the founder of the Naval Lyceum, led the expedition which opened Japan in 1854.[29]

Despite these increased responsibilities there was no attempt on the part of Congress to evaluate soberly the role of the Navy in the life of the nation. The rapid settlement of California as a result of the discovery of gold in 1848, the increase in American trade with the Far East, the expansion of our industry and commerce — all seemed to point up the need for a larger and more efficient naval force. Yet little was done. The experiments in naval ordnance continued. Naval yards increased, and Congress subsidized the building of merchant vessels on the doubtful theory that they could be used as Navy ships in a time of emergency. Once again the Navy slipped into a period of decline, so that by 1853 the United States did not have a single vessel equal to any first-class warship of the Powers of Europe.[30]

Secretary Dobbin attempted to change this. In December 1853 he presented Congress with a naval policy and a reform program. He wanted a Navy that was large enough to protect our seas and our coasts. Many of the ships that we had were not worth repairing. The first step toward correcting the situation would be the construction of six new screw-driven steam frigates, as well as instituting reforms in regard to personnel. Congress approved the program by a vote that revealed a change in the old anti-Navy attitude of many Democrats and members from northern and western Pennsylvania, the South Atlantic and Gulf states, and Kentucky and Tennessee.[31]

It was a good start, and in 1854 Dobbin tried unsuccessfully to add another seven screw-propelled sloops-of-war. A diplomatic crisis with Great Britain over Central American problems provided yet another opportunity to urge preparedness for the possibility of war. Finally, in the last hours of the Pierce administration, Con-

---

[29] Knox, pp. 157–158, 169–179, 183–189; Sprout, pp. 135–147.
[30] Sprout, pp. 138–140.
[31] *Ibid.*, pp. 141, 143–144.

gress authorized the building of five shallow-draft steam sloops-of-war.[32]

During the administration of James Buchanan the emphasis was placed on a small Navy which relied on shallow-draft vessels to defend our coastline. The southern strength in Congress saw to it that the seven shallow-draft sloops-of-war authorized in 1857 would be able to operate out of southern harbors. This capability later worked to the disadvantage of the South during the Civil War. Toucey asked for more ships of this type in 1858, but it was not until February 1861 that Congress appropriated money to build seven more of them. By this time seven southern states had seceded from the Union and the members from the South still in Congress made an unsuccessful effort to keep these ships from being built.[33]

Meanwhile, the work of reforming the officer corps was slowly being pushed forward. The long-awaited Naval Academy became a reality during the administration of President James K. Polk while George Bancroft was serving as Secretary of the Navy. An arrangement was made whereby the Army's post at Fort Severn, Maryland, was transferred to the Navy. Bancroft then ordered several schoolmasters and chaplains and all the midshipmen to report there. Captain Franklin Buchanan, a strict disciplinarian and a temperance man, was placed in charge of the school. By the time Congress reassembled, the Naval Academy was in operation. The outbreak of the Mexican War, and the possibility of a war with Great Britain over Oregon, induced Congress to vote the necessary funds for the continuance of the academy.[34] Soon Captain Buchanan's discipline was weeding out the unfit, and gradually the caliber of the younger officers improved.

Congress also agreed that the number of midshipmen appointed yearly from each state or territory should be in proportion to the number of its representatives and delegates in Congress. This was the procedure followed in making appointments to West Point, and by 1853 it was formally applied to the Navy.[35]

---

[32] *Ibid.*, p. 145.

[33] *Ibid.*, pp. 146–149.

[34] *Ibid.*, p. 133n; Russel B. Nye, *George Bancroft, Brahmin Rebel* (New York, 1944), pp. 144–145; Soley, pp. 7–90.

[35] William Addleman Ganoe, *The History of the United States Army* (New York, 1924), p. 192; W. D. Puleston, *Annapolis: Gangway to the Quarterdeck* (New York, 1942), pp. 68–69.

The outlook for promotions also improved slightly. Many of the great names of the Navy were now gone. By 1851 only Captains Stephen Cassin and Charles Stewart remained of the group of distinguished officers from the War of 1812. Younger officers, such as those who had supported the Naval Lyceum, moved up to higher ranks. But Congress was still opposed to creating admirals, and the Navy had to wait until 1862 before that rank became a reality.

Promotion ladders were still being clogged by incompetent, inactive, and/or physically unfit officers who were of little use to the Navy. To do something about this problem Secretary Dobbin was instrumental in getting congressional approval in 1855 for a law to promote the efficiency of the Navy. Under its terms the President appointed a 15-man board of officers who were to study the duty capacities of their fellow officers and make recommendations. The board reported that 201 officers were incapacitated for duty. Of these, 49 were recommended for dismissal, 81 were to be retired on furlough pay, and 71 retired on leave of absence pay. The report caused a sensation. The older officers, having had no experience with retirement provisions, looked upon it as a slur on their characters. In drawing its conclusions the board made enemies in and out of the Navy. Many newspapers also took up the cause of the "degraded officers." At length the political pressure became so great that in 1857 Congress gave every dismissed officer the right to review his case before a board of inquiry. Such hearings resulted in the reversal of 62 decisions of the board during Secretary Toucey's regime. Thus the efficiency act of 1855 was not as successful as Dobbin and others had hoped.[36]

But in spite of the reappointments the board did not really fail. Between 1856 and 1859 many of the younger officers were promoted. Captains on active duty increased from 68 to 81, commanders from 97 to 116, lieutenants from 326 to 338. The older officers were restored to duty, but the younger ones retained their new ranks. According to Admiral Alfred T. Mahan, the service of these young officers in higher ranks in the years preceding the Civil War did for the Navy what the Mexican War service did for the Army. The officers who gained wider experience in command during this period were to see service during the Civil War. When

---

[36] Paullin, "Naval Administration, 1842–1861," pp. 1468–72.

the war began the wisdom of most of the board's actions was borne out in the cases of the older officers who could not serve.[37]

The troubles resulting from the board's actions point up the great influence of the old naval officers of this period. They had won many another contest with the Secretary of the Navy and the Congress, but this was their last stand. The board's actions left deep wounds on many. Matthew F. Maury, who had done important work for science and for a better Navy, was placed on the reserved list on leave of absence pay. Maury and other friends of naval reform were outraged that an officer who had won international fame for his work in science should be classified by his fellow officers as inefficient. What was even more unjust, no minutes were kept of the board's deliberations and no list of accusations was presented to Maury or any other officer. The board's action in Maury's case was supposedly due to the fact that a foot injury made him unfit for sea duty, but there are indications that some of his fellow officers were jealous of the fame he had attained while on shore duty. Maury and others fought the decisions of the board, and in 1858 he was restored to the active list and promoted to a commander, but the whole procedure had produced a great deal of bitterness in the Navy. The coming of the Civil War helped to blot out the memory of this attempt at naval reform.[38]

Another source of friction in the officer ranks was position in terms of protocol that the staff, or non-fighting, officers had in relation to the line, or fighting, officers. This problem involved the status of such specialists as medical officers, pursers, and engineering officers. Piecemeal attempts to resolve this problem were made by Secretaries in 1846 and 1847, but the subject was still disputed for many years. Congress finally settled the whole matter by law in 1859.[39]

The quests for status, discipline, and reform were also influenced by the activities of naval chaplains. From the beginnings of the Navy down to 1846 they had the responsibility (along with some schoolmasters) for educating the midshipmen on board, as well as attending to the spiritual needs of the officers and men. They saw

---

[37] *Ibid.*, pp. 1472–73; Alfred T. Mahan, *From Sail to Steam: Recollections of Naval Life* (New York, 1907), p. 23.

[38] Williams, pp. 272–308.

[39] Paullin, "Naval Administration, 1842–1861," pp. 1466–68.

the naval service from both sides: they could appreciate the bur-
dens of command without losing sight of the situation of those who
carried out orders. The chaplain was treated as an officer, but he
did not command. He was there to be kind, helpful, and understanding, and to act as a friend. This role as friend and adviser put
the chaplain in a position that could not be filled by any commissioned officer. If he was well liked his influence among the men
could be very great. According to George Jones, a good naval chaplain should be well educated, pious, prudent, modest, unobtrusive,
and self-reliant. He must possess dignity of character and be without a trace of meanness. He must also be firm and independent
where necessary, with an expanded and generous view of things,
gentlemanly in his manners, and free from seasickness.[40] Many of
the qualities that made for good chaplains made for zealous reformers.

Chaplains were assigned to frigates when on sea duty. Smaller
ships went without their services unless such ships were a part of a
squadron. During the administrations of Jefferson and Madison,
when the emphasis was on a small Navy, there were few chaplains
in the service. In 1810, for example, only three were on duty. Between 1811 and 1820 there were between three and twelve on the
rolls at various times. An average of nine chaplains were on the rolls
during the years 1821 to 1840, and some of these were on extended
furloughs. There was also a great turnover in chaplains, indicating
a dissatisfaction with their compensation and other matters.[41]

This state of affairs became increasingly critical at a time when
the fleet was slowly being expanded and when the nation was ex-
periencing a religious revival. All the large frigates as well as the
shore establishments rated chaplains. The Mediterranean, Pacific,
and other squadrons also wished to have at least one chaplain
attached to them, as did the exploring expeditions. The demand
was far greater than the supply, but it was not until 1841 that the
Navy Department appointed eleven additional chaplains.[42] But the

---

[40] Clifford M. Drury, chief comp., *The History of the Chaplain Corps,
United States Navy*, I (Washington, D.C., 1949), 86–87; A 'Civilian' [George
Jones], *Sketches of Naval Life* . . . (2 vols.; New Haven, Conn., 1829), II,
238–239.
[41] Drury, I, 22, 33, 61, 249–250.
[42] *Ibid.*, pp. 33, 63.

fact that there were not enough chaplains increased the influence of some of the more dynamic ones on active duty.

Chaplains had already begun to express their views in a way that would reach the public. The popularity of travel books encouraged them to write of their adventures in the Navy. The fact that such books were written by chaplains undoubtedly won for them a wider audience than many another salty tale. Women formed an important segment of this wider audience and their influence in the cause of reform was important. In the process of reading about far-off places civilian readers were introduced to an unromantic view of shipboard life which pointed up the problems in the Navy and the plight of the man in the ranks. A national interest in the hazards of the sailor's life, so evident in the earlier history of the country when the villains were foreign powers, had been replaced by other problems which competed for public attention. Now it was the task of the chaplains and a handful of seamen to inform and arouse the country to the indignities that were suffered by the crews of American ships at the hands of American officers. One of the earliest of these travel books was that published by Chaplain George Jones in 1829 under the title *Sketches of Naval Life*. Written in the form of letters, this book contained wonderful descriptions of places visited as well as vivid accounts of the harsher aspects of naval life. Another work, *A Visit to the South Seas in the U.S. Ship Vincennes . . .* by Chaplain Charles S. Stewart, was published in 1831. Chaplain Walter Colton wrote seven books of travel and adventure during his career. The publication of one of his letters in the Philadelphia *Independent North American* and the New York *Journal of Commerce* spread the news of the gold strike in California.[43]

While those who wrote books did much toward educating the public, chaplains with friends in high places played an important part in influencing politicians. Chaplain Charles S. Stewart was a close friend of Secretary of the Navy Samuel L. Southard and of Captain, later Senator, Robert F. Stockton.

William Ryland served as a chaplain in both the House of Representatives and the Senate of the United States. In the course of his congressional duties he met Senator Andrew Jackson and they be-

---

[43] *Ibid.*, pp. 33–38, 81–85; Neeser, I, 120.

came fast friends. When Jackson became President one of his first acts was to appoint Ryland as a naval chaplain and have him permanently attached to the Washington Navy Yard, where he was very popular.

President Jackson's attention was also drawn to Walter Colton, a graduate of Andover Theological Seminary and an ordained Congregational minister, who was serving as editor of the *American Spectator* and *Washington City Chronicle* in Washington, D.C. He accepted Jackson's offer of an appointment as a naval chaplain and served 22 years in that position. Of particular interest to this study were Colton's efforts to abolish flogging and the spirit ration in the Navy.[44]

Thomas Lambert was a friend and former law clerk of Levi Woodbury, who became Jackson's second Secretary of the Navy. Woodbury got Lambert an appointment as a naval chaplain in 1834 and the latter served in that capacity for 20 years. It is significant for this study that Lambert was the brother-in-law of Representative and Senator John P. Hale of New Hampshire, who figured prominently in the agitation against flogging.

After 1841 naval chaplains made important gains. Their duties were more clearly defined and regulations regarding divine services were more strictly observed. The number of chaplains in service was increased to 24 and more care was taken in appointing properly qualified clergymen to these positions. The establishment of the Naval Academy in 1845 relieved them of the duties of teaching midshipmen and left them more time to attend to the needs of the enlisted men.[45]

Long before the questions relating to naval administration, to ships, armaments, and officers were solved, serious problems developed in connection with the enlisted men. It became increasingly difficult to attract and hold Americans in the Navy. As a result the ranks included many foreigners. This reliance on non-Americans was both a blow to the pride of a young nation and a source of concern to all officers and many citizens. How reliable would such men be in the event of war? What could be done to make the Navy at-

---

[44] Drury, I, 45–46, 81–85; William W. Edel, "The Golden Age of Navy Chaplaincy, 1830–55," *U.S.N.I.P.*, L (1924), 880–883.

[45] Drury, I, 62–92. The role played by Chaplain George Jones in advocating the establishment of the Naval Academy is described in *ibid.*, pp. 72–73.

tractive to American-born young men? These were questions for which various Secretaries sought answers in order to make recommendations to Congress. In seeking solutions to this problem the Secretary was confronted with answers that reflected the spirit of the times. This was the era of "the common man." The growth of popular education, the extension of suffrage, the development of political parties and of the country itself, gave the average male citizen a great sense of participation in the events and decisions of his time. He had pride in his country's achievements and a generally optimistic outlook for the future. He disliked restraints on his independence and individuality. In view of all of this, why should he trade his situation and his prospects for the restricted, poorly paid, arduous, and often dangerous aspects of a military life? Friends of the Navy had no ready answers for these questions. They could only reply that Americans were needed to man the fleet, and that service to one's country was an honorable calling. In saying this they knew that it was not enough. So those who wished to see the United States Navy manned by Americans were forced to look closely at the enlisted man's life and to see what could be done to make it more attractive to our citizens. This quest brought them in contact with the chaplains and to an examination of their views on what needed to be done.

By this time the cause of religion among seamen had widespread support among civilians. Between the end of the War of 1812 and the Civil War, a spirit of reform captured the nation. Sparked and reinforced by the growth of organized religion, thousands of American men and women attempted to alleviate the various evils of society. Convinced that they were indeed their brother's keepers and positive that they could change the world, they organized societies dedicated to particular reforms. They raised funds, distributed literature, prayed, exhorted, and lobbied to bring about changes in society. From the point of view of the Navy, the most influential of these groups was the American Seamen's Friend Society.

The United States Navy began in adversity, fought its way to respectability by 1815, then gradually declined, and was slowly brought up to efficient status during the Civil War. It was consciously modeled on that of Great Britain, and that fact, plus its early emphasis on the training of officers and on improving the size, armament, and efficiency of the Navy, tended to create in the minds of some the image of a service which functioned on principles that were contrary to the democratic ideas of the country. On top of that, a navy was expensive. Between wars what could the Navy do to justify its drain on the national treasury? The men who shared such views tried to prevent the establishment of the Navy. Failing in this, they formed an anti-Navy bloc in Congress which helped to postpone any realistic appraisal of the role of the Navy in national defense and put all who were connected with the service on the defensive. Yet the critical attitude of some of this group helped to advertise the abuses in the service. The friends of the Navy fought to make it efficient and worthy of the nation. In so doing they also attempted to correct situations which strengthened the arguments of the opposition. But even among the friends of the Navy there was a difference of opinion over what should be done first, in what fashion, and how soon. Thus the actions of both the friends and the foes of the Navy ultimately helped to improve its personnel policies and to make the service as a whole more efficient.

Throughout this period the Secretaries had their problems in keeping the officer corps properly subordinated and in trying to train new leaders. They had their hands full with many troublesome details of administration and were inclined to put off many matters relating to the situation of the enlisted men. Suggestions for the abolition of flogging and of grog were regarded by many of the senior officers as dangerous innovations that could hurt the service. The Secretary generally had enough of a problem in keeping the officers subordinate, so why take the chance of creating disciplinary problems among the sailors, especially when so many experienced leaders seemed to be against it? The manner in which those changes came about will be presented in subsequent chapters. In the next chapter we examine the activities of various civilian groups who were interested in the welfare of the sailor, groups whose members believed that our naval service could and should reflect our national belief in the dignity of man without destroying discipline. Of special importance were the reform goals and naval membership of the American Seamen's Friend Society.

PART
TWO

RELIGION AND THE REFORMERS

"O ye moralists! talk not of the temptations of a city, the cor-
rupting tendency of brothels, the demoralizing influence of
theatres and public exhibitions, for city life with all its evil
accompaniments, is a career of godliness in comparison with
that which is endured on board a man-of-war."

Seaman Jacob Hazen, circa 1839

UPLIFTING THE SAILOR

Beginning in the late seventeenth century and extending for most of the eighteenth, Western civilization was transformed by the intellectual revolution known as the Enlightenment. It was a time when all authority and the existence of any absolute standard of truth were questioned. The leaders of this movement placed their confidence in human reason backed by the findings of science — the new standard of truth. They were optimistic and utilitarian, and they believed that society could be transformed by the rule of reason. In keeping with this hope, everything was to be studied, dissected, criticized, explained, and reformed according to natural law, natural ethics, and natural religion. As a result of their activities, politics and morals became secularized, free commercial intercourse was encouraged, education was broadened, and a sympathetic and humanitarian outlook on all of mankind was stimulated. The latter spirit led to protests against cruel and inhuman laws, the use of torture, and the excessive reliance on capital punishment. The Enlightened men argued that the punishment should match the seriousness of the crime, but it should also have as its goal the reformation of the criminal. If laws were clearly written and administered with justice and evenness, crime would become less common. The reformers also taught that the problems of the criminal, the debtor, the poor, and of all mankind must be

approached with reason and with an appreciation for the dignity
of man. This concern for the downtrodden eventually led to early
protests against Negro slavery.[1]

In attempting to free mankind from the evils of society the
leaders of the Enlightenment attacked organized religion. Christianity found itself under attack by the rationalists, by the worldly
wise, by the state, and by factions within itself. Large numbers of
the public were indifferent to formal worship. They put stock in
how a person acted rather than what he believed. Others who had
not lost their need for religion were bored by cold, legalistic dis-
putes over doctrines and interpretations. Organized religion was
losing its hold on all levels of society.

Protestantism made a special effort to win back the people
through revivals. These simple, spirited, infectious gatherings
attracted people who were entertained and moved by eloquent
oratory. Revival meetings brought spiritual matters down to an
individual level in language everyone understood. Preachers spoke
of the torments of Hell that awaited unrepentant sinners. Their
imagery prompted individual spiritual inventories. They stimulated public manifestations of belief and repentance in return for
peace of mind. Revivals gave people a great emotional release.

Along with reviving religion Protestantism emphasized that
every man was his brother's keeper. Faith must be manifested by
good works for other men. All men must one day render an account
of their stewardship on earth to God. Heaven was not on earth, as
some of the men of the Enlightenment said, nor was this the best of
all possible worlds. But Heaven might be won and past wrongs
atoned for, if each man would firmly embrace religion and help his
fellow man to do so. In helping to save his less fortunate neighbor
every man was helping to save himself. Such an approach to life
gave even the humblest of men a cause that was both selfish yet
shared by all of mankind.

England was at this time in the throes of an agricultural and
industrial revolution which brought thousands of people to the
cities, where they lived in poverty, apathy, and degradation.
Through the efforts of John Wesley and his associates many of

---

[1] Preserved Smith, *The Enlightenment, 1687–1776*, Vol. II of *A History
of Modern Culture* (2 vols.; New York, 1962), *passim*.

these people were brought back to religion. Faith gave them hope that their futures would be better, yet it resigned them to the workings of Providence. In this way a potentially dangerous element in urban life was neutralized.

A new appreciation for religion came about in the 1740's in the British colonies in North America as a result of the Great Awakening. Conservative elements in Protestantism objected to the emotional approach of the great revival preachers. Divisions appeared, but denominations such as the Methodists, Congregationalists, Presbyterians, and Baptists gained many converts as a result of revivals. Various local and regional revivals and camp meetings took place after the American Revolution and on into the early part of the nineteenth century.[2]

The stabilizing influence of religion on all classes of society was brought home to British and American leaders during the European wars that grew out of the French Revolution and the rise of Napoleon. The execution of the King of France, the Reign of Terror, and the whole apparatus of the revolutionary rule served as vivid object lessons of what happened to a society that rejected God and pushed rationalistic teachings too far. For the British, at least, interdenominational cooperation for the cause of religion was a spiritual and patriotic cause. It remained so after the revolutionary governments gave way to Napoleon, for now that leader was bent on spreading French rule throughout Europe.

To instill and to hold religion in the lives of the people, British Evangelicals preached, conducted Sunday schools, and distributed tracts. The latter were particularly useful in a day when books and other reading matter were out of the reach of the poor. Tract distribution led to the dispensation of Bibles and to the formation of the British and Foreign Bible Society.[3]

While the Evangelicals aimed at bringing the word of God to all men, a small group now became increasingly interested in that segment of society which they felt was usually out of the reach of organized religion and of all religious influence — the sailors of the naval and merchant service. The first systematic effort in modern

---

[2] *Ibid.*, pp. 393–406; Harvey Wish, *Society and Thought in Early America* (New York, 1950), pp. 143–183, 243–254.

[3] Charles I. Foster, *An Errand of Mercy: The Evangelical United Front, 1790–1873* (Chapel Hill, N.C., 1960), pp. 3–118.

times to promote the moral welfare of seamen seems to have been that undertaken by the Bible Society formed in London in 1790. Its founder, John Thornton, was a philanthropist and his group confined themselves to the distribution of Bibles. In 1804, after the founding of the British and Foreign Bible Society, Thornton's group redesignated themselves the Naval Bible Society. There was, however, no regular movement to distribute Bibles until after 1814. Such work as was done was largely the result of individual initiative.[4] Prominent among the individual workers for religion in the British Navy were James Gambier, Richard Marks, and George C. Smith.

Concerned about the lack of religion in the Navy, James Gambier had a chance to do something about it in 1793 when he assumed command of the 74-gun ship *Defence*, assigned to duty in the English Channel. His vessel soon acquired a reputation as a praying ship, though at the battle off Ushant in 1794 he proved that it was a fighting ship as well, for it was the first ship to break the French line. Gambier retained his interest in religion in the Navy throughout his subsequent career afloat and ashore. In 1812 he was instrumental in having the pay of chaplains increased — a move that improved their status and which, it was hoped, would induce more clergymen to become naval chaplains. Along with raising the chaplains' pay, the cause of religion was supported by giving the Book of Common Prayer and the New Testament to every mess on a ship. In later years, when the British and Foreign Seamen's Friend Society was established, Lord Gambier became its first president. Two of his relatives who were Royal Navy officers also held offices in societies devoted to improving the lot of the sailor.[5]

Richard Marks was a lieutenant in the British Navy and a veteran of the battle of Trafalgar when he became interested in religion in 1809. With a few like-minded men he held prayer meetings and Bible readings on board his ship. Leaving the Navy in 1810, he entered Cambridge University and subsequently the clergy of the

---

[4] *The Sailor's Magazine and Naval Journal* (hereafter cited as *The Sailor's Magazine*), III (1830–31), 234–235; *The Mariners' Magazine*, I (1825), 265.

[5] John K. Laughton, "James Gambier," in Sir Leslie Stephen and Sir Sidney Lee, eds., *Dictionary of National Biography* (London, 1960), VII, 833–835; *The Sailor's Magazine*, I (1828–29), 283, 339; *The Mariner's Magazine*, I, 265.

Church of England. In 1819 he published *Retrospect*, an auto-biographical account which brought him to the attention of an English gentleman who desired to be his patron. An ecclesiastical living was acquired for Marks which left him comfortably settled for the rest of his life. Meanwhile, his book on his earlier years in the Navy was reprinted several times in England and the United States, and he continued to use his talents for preaching and writing in the sailor's cause, which was then being pressed by George C. Smith.[6]

A major figure in the cause of reforming seamen through religion, George C. Smith spent his boyhood as apprentice first to a London bookseller and then to the master of an American ship. While serving as a cabin boy he was impressed into the British Navy. Here his talents enabled him to rise from the ranks to become a midshipman and later a master's mate. In the latter capacity he served under Horatio Nelson's command at the battle of Copen-hagen. At some point in his career he became interested in religion, and in 1803 he left the Navy to study for the ministry. After his ordination in 1807 he became a preacher to the fishermen and sailors at Plymouth and vicinity, and later the pastor of a Baptist chapel at Penzance. Between 1812 and 1816 he built six chapels in the neighboring villages and educated the men to staff them.[7]

But Smith's major interests were the religious education of sailors and soldiers and the establishment of philanthropic societies for their benefit. He was encouraged along this line by the news of a religious revival in the British Navy beginning about 1808. The cause of this revival is not known, but it may have been due in part to the activities of individuals reached by the Naval Bible Society. The long years of warfare against the French tended, like most wars, to stimulate the fighting man's interest in religion. Poor pay and an indefinite status kept many a clergyman from joining the Navy, and the shortage of chaplains was keenly felt during the war years. Sometimes a religious-minded officer like Gambier would read prayers on board ship, or designate someone else to do so.

---

[6] Undated letter of the Reverend George C. Smith to Joseph Eastburn, cited in Ashbel Green, *Memoirs of the Rev. Joseph Eastburn, Stated Preacher in the Mariner's Church, Philadelphia* (Philadelphia, 1828), pp. 142–143.

[7] George G. Bradley, "George Charles Smith," *Dictionary of National Biography*, XVIII, 450–451.

This helped, but it was not much of a substitute for regular services. As we have already noted in the case of Marks, individual initiative helped to fill some of the religious vacuum. Smith attempted to do something about this problem in 1810 by writing to prominent clergymen and urging them to support the establishment of a society for the evangelizing of seamen. He met with little encouragement. On his own he served as a volunteer chaplain to the British Army in Spain for a few months in 1814. The next year saw the final defeat of Napoleon and the return of peace. But war or no war, Smith was still concerned about the welfare of seamen. He traveled about England preaching in the open air to sailors and other groups of people. This type of approach did not please many people, but it led to the formation of the Home Mission Society in 1819. Meanwhile, in June 1817 Smith came to London, where he became acquainted with the work being done among seamen as the result of the efforts of a shoemaker named Zebulon Rogers.[8]

Rogers' work among sailors grew out of his meeting with Captain Simpson of the collier brig *Friendship* after they had both attended a Methodist service in London, and the two became close friends. While Rogers was visiting with Simpson on board the *Friendship* on June 22, 1814, he asked the captain if he thought the crew would come to the cabin and pray with him. Upon the captain's suggestion Rogers asked the crew himself, and after a moment or two of surprise, the crew filed into the captain's cabin, where both Rogers and Simpson read prayers. This assembly, the first prayer meeting held for sailors on the Thames River, led to subsequent meetings on board the *Friendship* when she was in port, to Rogers' being invited to other ships, and to invitations to other men on other ships to attend such services. The response was encouraging. Soon these gatherings began to be known as "Bethel Meetings." They took their name from the passage in the Old Testament where Jacob gave the name "Bethel" to the place in a field where he met with God. Despite the hostile reactions of some sailors and watermen, Rogers and his friends got permission to hold services on 13 ships that came to the port of London. To identify for all interested parties the ship on which a meeting would be held, it became customary to hoist a lantern on the top-gallant mast. The lantern soon

---

[8] *Ibid.; The Sailor's Magazine*, L (1878), 205.

gave way to a special flag designed by Rogers and made by his wife. This flag consisted of a blue field with the word "Bethel" emblazoned on it in white letters. Improvements upon this design were subsequently made by adding a red star in a corner (to signify the rising in the east), and later by the addition of a dove bearing an olive branch in its beak. The first Bethel flag was hoisted over the ship *Zephyr* late in March 1817. Such flags were the forerunners of the chaplain's pennant of later years.[9]

The steady growth of interest in religion led Rogers to enlist the help of a London timber merchant named Jennings, who was also a local Wesleyan Methodist preacher. In addition to the meetings afloat, Jennings began to hold meetings for seamen in his garden. Such was the situation when the Reverend George C. Smith arrived in London, attended a prayer meeting conducted by Rogers, and decided to devote himself to promoting this work.[10]

While preaching on shipboard and on shore Smith worked to establish a floating chapel. Negotiations to acquire a suitable ship and to raise the necessary funds prompted the friends of seamen to establish the Port of London Society in 1818. That same year the floating chapel — an old frigate whose interior was altered to provide a large room for meetings — was used by Smith and Rogers for services. Smith also induced ministers of various denominations to preach on board the ship.[11]

Smith now embarked on an organizing spree. An association of various religious denominations dedicated to spreading the Bethel idea was established under the name of the Bethel Union Society. In 1819 the British and Foreign Seamen's Friend Society was organized. Smith traveled around the country, establishing floating chapels and Bethel lofts in various ports. These activities resulted in the formation of seamen's societies in other parts of England as well as in Scotland and Ireland. Feeling that the cause also needed a periodical, in 1820 Smith began to edit and publish a monthly known as *The Sailor's Magazine*. The London group now began to look for a permanent chapel on shore, and a separate society was formed to acquire and maintain such a structure. The Mariner's Church at Wellclose Square on the London docks was opened for services by Smith in 1825. Between 1822 and 1830 he was responsi-

[9] *Ibid.*, III, 236; XII (1839–40), 60.
[10] *Ibid.*, I, 227–228.   [11] *Ibid.*, 229–230; VIII (1835–36), 10.

ble for the formation of several organizations devoted to the seamen, their families, and their orphans, including the erection of
the Sailor's Home in 1828, believed to be the first institution of its
kind in the world. Smith also raised funds for these enterprises by
undertaking preaching tours of Great Britain. Assisting him were
twelve orphan boys, half of whom were dressed as sailors and half
as soldiers, who sang patriotic songs and hymns at the meetings.[12]

Meanwhile chance gave Smith and his colleagues an opportunity
to encourage the Bethel cause in the United States. In 1820 John
Allen, a Presbyterian minister from Tennessee, made a trip to Great
Britain to see about a legacy. While in London he became interested in the work being done among sailors by Smith and his associates. Allen accepted invitations from them to preach at the
floating chapel and elsewhere on the Thames. When he left for
America in 1821 the executive committee of the British and Foreign
Seamen's Friend Society gave him a Bethel flag and asked that he
deliver it to those working for the cause of seamen in New York.
En route to the United States he raised this flag over the ship whenever he conducted religious services — the first time that a Bethel
flag had been flown over an American ship.[13]

In the United States an early effort to improve the lot of the sailor
had been undertaken by the Reverend Joseph Tuckerman, who had
seen and heard much of the brutal aspects of the sailor's life and of
the degrading effects of the grog shop and the brothel. His sympathies were aroused, and he decided to attack the evils. In May
1812 he founded the Boston Society for the Religious and Moral
Improvement of Seamen. Its 70 members were dedicated to the
distribution of moral and religious tracts among seamen and to
the establishment of regular divine services on merchant vessels.
The executive committee consisted of Gamaliel Bradford, Tristram
Barnard, William Ellery Channing, Richard Sullivan, Charles
Lowell, and Tuckerman. But in spite of its distinguished leadership the society grew slowly and soon declined. In 1817 it published
its eleventh and last tract. William Ellery Channing believed that
the society failed because it did not answer its purpose: neither
Tuckerman nor his co-workers were close enough to the sailor to
understand him, and the sailor had no interest in the society nor in

---

[12] *Ibid.*, I, 230–231.
[13] *Ibid.*, VII (1834–35), 348; VIII, 10–12, 32.

its cold and impersonal tracts. Furthermore, the community as a whole was indifferent to the cause of reform.[14]

While Tuckerman's group was declining a new and stronger movement to help the sailor was well under way in New York City. In 1816 the Female Missionary Society appointed the Reverend Ward Stafford as a city missionary to survey the population and determine what classes of society were most in need of religion. Stafford became interested in the large numbers of seamen who frequented the port and considered them to be among the most needy. So, on December 20, 1816, he preached to a group of sailors who were assembled for such services. This was subsequently referred to by reformers interested in the sailor as the first religious meeting in America specifically for seamen. The following spring Stafford published a report of his survey which underscored the religious needs of sailors.[15]

Among those interested in this new missionary field were Dr. Gardner Spring of the Brick Presbyterian Church and some members of his congregation. Neighborhood prayer meetings had been held at various houses on Water Street which were attended by the keepers of sailors' boarding houses and a few seamen. This evidence of interest in their devotions inspired Spring's group to hold prayer meetings especially for sailors and to enjoin other denominations to do the same.[16]

One member of Spring's congregation who was particularly interested in bringing the gospel to seamen was Captain Christopher Prince. Prior to the American Revolution Prince had been a midshipman in the Royal Navy, and during that struggle he served as a lieutenant on an American privateer. After the war he

[14] Daniel T. McColgan, *Joseph Tuckerman, Pioneer in American Social Work* (Washington, D.C., 1940), pp. 35–37.

[15] *The Sailor's Magazine*, VIII, 24–35; XII, 60; XXV (1852–53), 372; L, 171.

[16] One of the factors that is supposed to have influenced Dr. Gardner Spring of the Brick Presbyterian Church in the welfare of sailors was that a sailor saved his church from destruction by fire. On Sunday, May 19, 1811, the wind carried a burning brand into the wooden steeple of the church. While the parishioners stood watching the fire, a sailor broke through the crowd, climbed a lightning rod, and extinguished the fire. In gratitude the church voted him a $100 reward, but he never returned to claim it. See George Sidney Webster, *The Seamen's Friend. A Sketch of the American Seamen's Friend Society by Its Secretary, George Sidney Webster, D.D.* (New York, 1932), p. 2.

was active in the merchant service until his retirement from the sea in 1797. In February 1817 he held a meeting of merchants and shipmasters in his home to consider forming a Bible society devoted to the needs of the mariners. Agreement on this goal was reached, and on March 14, 1817, the Marine Bible Society was organized at a public meeting in City Hall.[17]

When the Reverend Ward Stafford's report of the spiritual needs of sailors was published that same month, a group from Spring's church already had plans for building a mariner's church. To raise funds to carry forward this project, as well as to support a preacher for the church, a new society was founded by Jonathan Little and a group of New York City businessmen. The Society for the Promotion of the Gospel Among Seamen in the Port of New York, commonly known as the Port Society, was founded in June 1818 and incorporated the following year. It was largely through the efforts of this group that the Mariner's Church became a reality and was dedicated in June 1820. For some time afterward, however, members of the Port Society found it necessary to seek out their sailor parishioners in their lodgings and in the streets and to point the way to the church. But in June 1831 it was reported that the church was filled without "special exertion."[18]

Meanwhile the Marine Bible Society sent the Reverend Stafford on a journey to awaken the country. As a result of his efforts similar societies were founded in New Haven, Portland, Philadelphia, Baltimore, and elsewhere.[19]

Stafford was back in New York and engaged in preaching to seamen when the Reverend John Allen landed in New York in April 1821 and presented him with the gift of the Bethel flag from the British and Foreign Seamen's Friend Society. The Bethel flag was first raised in the United States over the Mariner's Church in New York on Sunday, June 3, 1821. A few days later the New York Bethel Union was organized. Two weeks later the flag was hoisted on the masthead of the ship *Cadmus* in New York harbor. Two months later a Bethel meeting was held on board the U.S. frigate *Franklin*, then about to embark on a long cruise. This meeting was apparently well received by Commodore Charles Stewart, his officers, and his men.[20]

---

[17] *The Sailor's Magazine*, IV (1831–32), 253; XXV, 372.
[18] *Ibid.*, III, 338.   [19] *Ibid.*, 337.   [20] *Ibid.*, 338.

Bethel societies soon began to appear in Charleston, New Orleans, Portland, Baltimore, Hartford, and Norfolk. Within six years more than 70 societies were founded, including one at Albany, New York, for the welfare of the river- and canal-boat men. The Bethel flag also had been flown in Canada at St. John's, New Brunswick, and in Rio de Janeiro, Brazil.[21] Marine Bible societies and tract societies also grew in number. Mariners' churches had increased, and Sabbath schools were organized to give religious instruction to the children of seamen.

It soon became apparent, however, that while many of these institutions did some good, most were weak, limited, and inefficient in the scope of their operations. To overcome this limitation and to enlighten "the Christian and mercantile community" on the importance of spreading the word of God among seamen, a religious magazine for the sailor was considered indispensable.[22] The great influence of the British *Sailor's Magazine* had been noted, and it became the model for its American counterpart.

On Saturday, March 5, 1825, the Bethel Union of New York and the Society for Promoting the Gospel Among Seamen published the first issue of *The Mariners' Magazine*. Its prospectus announced that its weekly edition would bring before the reader the truth about sailors and the reader's obligations to them and to God. The editor, Reverend John Truair, added that one of the main designs of the magazine would be to make known the fact that both "the temporal interest of commercial men" and the cause of religion in general would be advanced by "christianising seamen."[23] He promised to point out the means for such a project and to give reports on the success of those means.

Truair soon proved himself to be a man of his word. In an editorial in *The Mariners' Magazine* of April 23, 1825, he proposed the formation of a society for the promotion of the spiritual and temporal interests of seamen. He asked the editors of religious newspapers throughout the country to give him their opinions of the project. Many of the editors simply republished the proposition without comment. A few approved. *The New York Religious Chronicle* pointed out that the example of the British and Foreign Seamen's Friend Society should give confidence to the planners.[24]

[21] *The Mariners' Magazine*, I, 269.   [23] *Ibid.*, 1–2.
[22] *Ibid.*, 2.   [24] *Ibid.*, 205.

The Washington, D.C., *Columbian Star* expressed surprise at the indifference exhibited. As the *Star's* editor saw it, the proposed society was similar to the American Sunday School Union and the American Bible Society, and he promised support. He added that the cause would be most effectively advanced if a circular letter were sent to every Bethel society in the country explaining the idea and its advantages and supplying a draft of a proposed constitution. Since the objects of the societies were the same, their combined efforts should enable them to produce an acceptable constitution within a short time.[25] This advice was followed. Later issues of the magazine carried a copy of the circular letter and the provisions of a constitution.

New interest in Truair's plan was awakened when he published a letter addressed to the Christian men of New York, signed by 114 masters and mates of vessels, requesting the formation of the proposed national society.[26]

The general feeling among interested parties was that the New York group should form the nucleus of the new organization. Accordingly, a public meeting was held in New York City on October 25, 1825. Former Secretary of the Navy Smith Thompson, now an Associate Justice of the Supreme Court, acted as chairman. After a number of spirited addresses in favor of the proposed society, a committee was chosen to prepare a constitution and a list of officers. The constitution of the American Seamen's Friend Society was adopted on January 11, 1826, and that same day the first officers were chosen.[27]

Smith Thompson was elected the first president, and among the society's 15 vice-presidents (not more than two of whom were to be residents of New York) were such prominent men as Philip Hone, Mayor of New York; Stephen Van Rensselaer of Albany; Thomas Napier of Charleston, South Carolina; Robert Ralston of Philadelphia; Beverly Chew of New Orleans; and Jeremiah Day, D.D., of New Haven, Connecticut. Its 30 directors (not less than 13 of whom were to be residents of New York) included four merchant captains and such men as Anson G. Phelps, James Latourette, George T. Trimble, and John B. Yates. Francis Olmstead of

[25] *Ibid.*, 210.
[26] *Ibid.*, 31–32; Webster, p. 10.
[27] *Ibid.*, pp. 14–17.

New York served as the first treasurer, and the Reverend John Truair became the corresponding secretary. Another founder worthy of note was Theodore Dwight, who helped to organize the constitutional committee.[28]

According to the constitution, any individual could become a member upon payment of two dollars annually. This provision insured the continued active participation of young women in the cause of improving the lot of the sailor. Any charitable or religious society whose object was the welfare of seamen could become an auxiliary of the society upon payment of $25, "and by the engagement to pay over, annually, its surplus funds into the Treasury of the Parent Institution." Each auxiliary was entitled to send a delegate to attend the meetings of the society and to vote for the election of officers. The Monday preceding the second Thursday in May was chosen as the date for the annual meeting in New York City.[29]

The aims of the society, as set forth in the circular letter of Smith Thompson of November 11, 1825, were as follows:

I. The establishment of reputable and orderly boarding houses in the several sea-port towns of our country, where special attention will be paid as well to the morals as to the protection of the property and civil rights of seamen. Each of the houses, when practicable, to be furnished with a reading room, and a small library of suitable books, and to be under the general superintending care of a committee.

II. Register or Intelligence Offices to be opened, where seamen of good character may have their names entered and lodgings designated, for application by ship owners and masters.

III. Savings Banks to be established in suitable places for the deposit, on interest, of such portion of the seamen's wages as they may deem expedient.

IV. The employment of agents or missionaries to traverse the coast, visit vessels and distribute Bibles and Tracts, and cooperate with the local committee appointed for that purpose, to induce seamen to resort to the boarding-houses under the patronage of the Society, and to attend places of worship.

V. The establishment of schools for the instruction, as well of adults as the children of seamen, should that be deemed expedient.

VI. To afford such aid, as the means of the institution will allow, to marine teaching establishments, and all kindred institutions, leaving them, however to manage their own concerns in their own way, except

[28] *The Mariners' Magazine*, I, 369–371.   [29] *Ibid.*

so far as interference may be consistent with the catholic spirit of this institution.[30]

For several months the Reverend Truair was employed as the agent of the society, and he visited various southern ports. He also published an address entitled "Call from the Ocean," which excited new interest in the cause of the seaman and led to the strong hope that something effective might be done to rescue him from bad companions and oppressive landlords. But no sooner had the public been aroused than Truair retired and the society's board of managers ceased their operations. Nothing further was done for nearly two years.[31]

In the summer of 1828 the Reverend Joseph Brown, the seamen's preacher at Charleston, South Carolina, was employed for a few months as the agent of the society. "A few can *begin* something that in the end will be great," said Brown. "We ought to feel that we are under an individual responsibility."[32] Some began to feel their responsibility, and slowly the society became revitalized. A reorganization followed, which led to the appointment of permanent agents. Members of the society looked upon their publication as indispensable for the work of reformation, and as the society became reactivated, its periodical changed. *The Mariners' Magazine* was replaced by *The Sailor's Magazine and Naval Journal* in 1828, and the Reverend Joshua Leavitt became the editor and first executive secretary of the society.[33]

Joshua Leavitt was a fortunate choice for both positions. The product of a New England Puritan background, his character was dominated by an unwavering faith. He was physically vigorous and had a commanding presence, and he was cheerful, witty, unselfish, and humble. But his humility did not keep him from having great confidence in his own judgment. Perhaps this confidence stemmed from the fact that he was educated both as a Congregational minister and as a lawyer. At any rate, his courage gave strength to the new society, and his editorial talents enabled him to set a high standard for its publications. His work in the society, however, was only one phase of a life devoted to reform.[34]

Some indication of the interests of the new editor, as well as of

---

[30] *Ibid.*, 301–302.   [31] *The Sailor's Magazine*, I, 310–311; III, 339.
[32] *Ibid.*, I, 67.   [33] Webster, p. 18.
[34] *Ibid.*, pp. 21–22. For a brief sketch of Leavitt's work see Charles C. Cole,

the scope of the society, may be seen from the range of topics set forth in the preface to the first volume of *The Sailor's Magazine and Naval Journal*. It treated

the whole concern of the navy, the interesting adventures of seafaring men, the particular narratives of shipwrecks, the religious experience of pious mariners, the subject of Sunday sailing, the rise and progress and success of seamen's meetings, churches, Sunday schools and worship at sea, the wrongs and oppressions of seamen, both from the government and from individuals, especially the crying grievances connected with the quarantine on navy hospital funds, the efficient introduction of the means of grace on board our ships of war, and into the army; marine schools, and the advancement of nautical sciences, all these and a thousand other incidental topics, will, with ordinary diligence, enable the Editor to furnish his readers with a rich variety of entertainment and instruction.[35]

But not every reader was entertained or instructed, if one may judge by the remarks of Nathaniel Ames, who served in the ranks of both the Navy and the merchant service. Ames supported the cause of improving the moral condition of the sailor and of encouraging temperance, but he had little use for *The Sailor's Magazine and Naval Journal*. In a book published in 1832 he expressed the opinion that it was "an exceedingly silly periodical," written "in a style too puerile, too silly for children of five years old." He asked:

Why will not these self-constituted reformers of morals reflect, if only for one moment, that if sailors are "babes in grace" they are by no means babes in common sense? Let them address seamen as though they were speaking to people who have "wit enough to go below when it rains," and their writing may have a chance to effect some good. However the vanity of seamen may be flattered by having a magazine called by their name and professedly devoted to their interests, they are by no means so easily gulled as the fabricators of this pious magazine may think; a single glance at its contents will break the charm and undeceive the most ignorant.[36]

Ames spent three years at Harvard before going to sea, and perhaps he overestimated the intelligence of his fellow sailors. But it

---

Jr., *The Social Ideas of the Northern Evangelists, 1826–1860* (New York, 1954), pp. 39–43.

[35] *The Sailor's Magazine*, I, iii.

[36] [Nathaniel Ames], *Nautical Reminiscences* (Providence, 1832), pp. 47–48.

is also true that the magazine had editorial problems for several years. The first four volumes of the magazine were issued under the editorship of Leavitt, after which he resigned to pursue another cause. He was succeeded by the Reverend Joseph Brown in 1832. Brown died a short time later, and in January 1834 the Reverend Jonathan Greenleaf took over the duties of corresponding secretary and editor.[37] During most of the succeeding years the position of general secretary of the society included the editing of the magazine. Like Leavitt the succeeding editors were all clergymen.[38] Their standards were high, and a general uniformity was maintained. But some, at least, were not unaware of their shortcomings. In the preface to the thirteenth volume, containing numbers issued from September 1840 to August 1841, the editor admitted that the magazine, "though defective in many particulars, has nevertheless accomplished much for the cause."[39] When issuing the thirty-first volume in 1859, the editor felt it necessary to make the following observation: "As to the literature of the MAGAZINE we have aimed to avoid alike the frothy and the frivolous, the leaden and the learnedly obscure."[40]

With regard to continuity and direction, the society undoubtedly profited from the long periods of service of its early presidents. Smith Thompson, elected in January 1826, served until May 1831, when the pressure of his official duties as a judge forced him to resign the presidency.[41] His successor was Adrian Van Sinderen, a New York merchant who served until 1840.[42] David W. C. Olyphant served a brief term between May and November 1840. Then came Anson G. Phelps, 1840–47; Captain Edward Richardson of the merchant service, 1847–48; Peletiah Perit, 1848–56; and William A. Booth, 1856–73. It would seem that as the society grew in strength the duties of the president became more perfunctory. The real power and direction undoubtedly came from the board of the trustees and the secretary of the society, who was also its general agent.[43]

---

[37] *The Sailor's Magazine*, XIII (1840–41), preface.
[38] Webster, p. 30.
[39] *The Sailor's Magazine*, XIII, preface.
[40] *Ibid.*, XXXI (1858–59), preface.
[41] *Ibid.*, III, 321.
[42] *Ibid.*, 332; XVI (1843–44), 163–164, 309.
[43] *Ibid.*, XX (1847–48), 345; L, 173–176.

Operations on behalf of seamen became quite extensive and interesting to the public. Agents were employed to attend to the affairs of the society and to visit various seaports. Auxiliary societies began to appear in various communities, as did a number of very active Female Seamen's Friend societies and related organizations. The second issue of *The Sailor's Magazine* carried a notice that at a future time it would print an address "to the wives of Elders and Deacons on the importance of taking a leading part in starting and encouraging enterprises of this description."[44] In 1844 the Pennsylvania Seamen's Friend Society reported that the American Seamen's Friend Society had "nearly a hundred auxiliary societies in various parts of the country, of which more than sixty are ladies' associations."[45]

One such ladies' auxiliary was founded in Concord, New Hampshire, in 1830 by 16 young women.[46] By 1841 it had about 60 members. Meetings were held every two weeks during the winter months and once a month during the summer. At such gatherings information on the wants and claims of seamen was disseminated, and articles were made to sell. The proceeds from the sales were sent to the headquarters of the society in New York. By 1841 the group had set itself a goal to double its income and usefulness each year. Just how successful it was along this line is not a matter of record. But in 1856 *The Sailor's Magazine* referred to the Concord group as "the oldest and one of the most efficient auxiliaries of the American Seamen's Friend Society."[47] Almost 15 years earlier the *Congregational Journal* indulged in some speculation on the influence of this auxiliary when it asked: "Who can tell how much influence this society silently exerted over the mind and purposes of the blacksmith boy, who is now chaplain of the American Seamen's Friend Society in Cronstadt, Russia?"[48] The reference was to the Reverend Ezra Eastman Adams, a Presbyterian minister from Concord, who spent 13 years in Europe (mainly in France) as a seamen's chaplain.[49]

It is worth noting that it was probably this group which in 1839

---

[44] *Ibid.*, I, 25–26.   [45] *Ibid.*, XVI, 164.
[46] *Ibid.*, XXVIII (1855–56), 328.   [47] *Ibid.*, XIV (1841–42), 16.
[48] *Congregational Journal*, reprinted in *The Sailor's Magazine*, XIV, 16.
[49] James G. Wilson and John Fiske, eds., *Appleton's Cyclopaedia of American Biography* (New York, 1898), I, 14.

invited a young attorney named John P. Hale of Dover, New Hampshire, to address their society.[50] Hale was later to make a name for himself in the U.S. House of Representatives and Senate as a naval reformer.

Auxiliary societies exerted great efforts to increase the funds of the parent organization. Money, raised largely through collections and sales, trickled in. A shipmaster induced his men to toss the odd change from their wages into a collection for the society.[51] Seamen of both the merchant and naval service were reported to have contributed cheerfully to such appeals. By 1833 two associations of ministers and "numerous churches" were taking up annual collections for the benefit of the society.[52] In time it also fell heir to money through the bequests of various individuals.

"Civil rights and claims of seamen are exciting unusual attention," said the society's report of 1829. Its members believed that a new era for seamen had begun. The attention of Congress had been called to the subject of marine hospitals, and the government no longer made the office of naval chaplain "a retreat for the debaucheries of broken fortune."[53] A beginning had been made, and things looked brighter for the causes of temperance, humanity, and religion.

In 1833 the society was incorporated in New York. Its report for that year stated that steps were being taken toward the building of a reading room and a mariners' museum in New York. The same issue carried the announcement that three preachers had been appointed for foreign ports.[54]

The American and British societies maintained a loose contact with each other by exchanging publications and letters and by the occasional visits of American chaplains or other interested persons to England. There were, however, a few instances of even closer operations when the societies cooperated in the financing and staffing of seamen's preachers at such places as Cronstadt, Le Havre, Rio de Janeiro, and Cape Town.

Progress was steady until the Panic of 1837. As the resources of the society were depleted it became necessary to curtail certain

---

[50] Mrs. John P. Hale to John P. Hale, Dec. 11, 1839, *John P. Hale Papers,* New Hampshire Historical Society.

[51] *The Sailor's Magazine,* I, 60.   [52] *Ibid.,* 26.

[53] *Ibid.,* V (1832–33), preface.   [54] *Ibid.,* IV, preface; V, 295, 297.

foreign and domestic operations. "Shall we strike the Bethel Flag?" asked the Philadelphia *Observer*, and added that to do so would imperil the salvation of sailors. It appealed to its readers to raise the $16,000 needed in the crisis.[55] Through the contributions of friends and some curtailment of its operations the society managed to weather this period of financial storm.[56]

As the society grew stronger it was able to step up the tempo of its protest against the living conditions of seamen. A paramount objective was the reform of the sailors' boarding houses, which in many cases were brothels. The proprietors of such places were always waiting on the dock for the crews paid off at the end of a cruise. They competed with each other in promising liquor and/or women to the sailors who would put up at their establishments. Once a sailor set foot inside such a place it was usually only a matter of time before he was broke and in debt to the landlord. In most cases the victim's only method of settling his bill was to sign on for another cruise and pay the landlord with his advance wages. If experience had not taught the hapless sailor to secure a receipt from the landlord he might find the same old bill being presented for payment when he returned. Not all landlords were as base as this, of course, but in general it was difficult for a sailor to find clean lodgings at a reasonable price in a place where his property was safeguarded.

Members of the society, believing that before any real progress could be made among seamen it was necessary to control their living conditions, attacked the problem of the boarding house in two ways: first, by inducing certain landlords to reform; and second, by raising money to build houses which would be controlled by the society. Partial success was attained in the first project, and in February 1829 it was announced that several "respectable and quiet residences" were available to seamen in New York. It was apparent, however, that it would be necessary to follow the second course also. Large boarding establishments operated by the society opened in Charleston, Portland, Boston, Baltimore, Providence, and Philadelphia, which caused an additional drain on the society's funds. In New York the experiment with a sailor's home met with

---

[55] Reprinted from the Philadelphia *Observer* in *The Sailor's Magazine*, X (1837–38), 82–84.

[56] *The Sailor's Magazine*, XI (1838–39), 297–298.

great success. Through the joint efforts of the society and the Female Bethel Union, as well as the assistance of a few volunteers who raised funds to buy furniture, the home opened in October 1837. Three years later the society was operating three houses in New York, including one for Negroes. Some 425 Negro sailors were accommodated in about a year's time.[57] By 1841 the two boarding houses for white sailors had accommodated a total of 6,000 men. Five hundred of these were reported to have become temperate, and 200 were "hopefully pious."[58]

As an adjunct to its efforts to protect the sailor's soul, the society also undertook to protect his purse. The first Seamen's Bank for Savings was opened in New York in May 1829, the first anniversary of the founding of the society itself. Similar banks were established later at Portland, Boston, New Haven, and Mobile.[59]

One of the most striking examples of the influence of the society came in 1845 when three New York marine insurance companies contributed a total of $1,750 to the society toward the upkeep of the Sailor's Home. In presenting this money they expressed their gratitude for the work the society had done. Sober seamen who saved their money were regarded as the best fitted to guard the property of others. The increase of temperate seamen in the merchant service led to the reduction of the rates for marine insurance. It was in the financial interest of these insurance companies to support such activities of the society as the Sailor's Home.[60]

By the time the society was in its seventeenth year the New York headquarters alone was spending more than $18,000 a year on the seamen's cause. Expenditures by auxiliaries throughout the country were estimated to be more than $75,000.[61]

In its nineteenth annual report, issued in 1847, the society declared that every year brought an increase in its fields of labor. Operations by auxiliaries closely connected with the society were being carried on in New Orleans, Mobile, Savannah, Charleston,

---

[57] Webster, pp. 73–74; *The Sailor's Magazine*, XI, 308.

[58] *Ibid.*, XIII, 309.

[59] *Ibid.*, XI, 40, 308; XXI (1848–49), listings inside front covers of individual issues of the magazine.

[60] *Ibid.*, XVII (1844–45), 217–220. For a comment on temperance ships by the Baring Brothers of London, see *The Mariner's Church Sailor's Magazine* (London), II (1834), 144.

[61] *The Sailor's Magazine*, XVII, 298.

Norfolk, Baltimore, Philadelphia, New York, and Boston. The same year saw some efforts at Richmond, Alexandria, Newark, Brooklyn, New Haven, New London, Providence, New Bedford, Salem, New-buryport, Portsmouth, Bath, Bangor, and other ports. Chaplains of the society labored on the inland waterways and had visited Chicago, Detroit, Cleveland, Buffalo, and Troy. In addition, there were missionaries at work on the Erie, Delaware and Hudson, Delaware and Raritan, and Morris canals. Foreign operations included the activities of the society's chaplains in Havana, Rio de Janeiro, Valparaiso, Honolulu, Le Havre, Stockholm, and Canton. But in spite of this drain on its resources, the society saw fit to reduce the price of its magazine by 50 per cent. *The Sailor's Magazine* now sold for a dollar a year, and in 1847 more than 5,000 copies were printed. A large number of these were distributed gratuitously among seamen.[62]

The year 1862 found the society operating five stations in South America, four in China, three in the Micronesian Islands, three in the Hawaiian Islands, two in France, and one each in Norway, Sweden, Belgium, Denmark, Turkey, Japan, and Caribou Island off the Labrador coast. The advent of the Civil War had cut off all reports from branches of the society within the confines of the Confederacy, but daily prayer meetings were reported on board 30 U.S. vessels of the blockading squadrons. There were also several very active and important operations in New York, Massachusetts, Maine, Pennsylvania, California, and Maryland. In New York City the society opened a second temperance boarding house for colored seamen.[63]

Such were the activities of the society in general. But how did these affect the Navy? From the very beginning no distinction was made between sailors in the merchant service, the whaling fleets, or in the U.S. Navy. It was by no means uncommon for a sailor to make alternate cruises in the Navy and the Merchant Marine. As a result, some of the enlisted men of the U.S. Navy were among the first beneficiaries of the society's efforts.

As early as 1828 *The New York Daily Advertiser* observed with pleasure "that the officers of our Navy, as well as ship-masters and seamen" contributed to the pages of *The Sailor's Magazine and*

[62] *Ibid.*, XIX (1846–47), 289–293; XI, 809.
[63] *Ibid.*, XXXIV (1861–62), 289–319, 365–366.

Naval Journal, and it hoped that others would lend their aid.[64] The very first issue of this publication carried a woodcut of a religious service on the deck of the receiving ship *Fulton.*

A naval officer writing early in 1831 declared that "at the head of the nation, and of the navy department, the cause of religion and virtue have firm friends." [65] Mention has already been made of the service rendered by ex-Secretary of the Navy Smith Thompson as the first president of the society. Samuel Southard and Levi Woodbury also served as vice-presidents of the society after their years in the office of the Secretary of the Navy.

As the society grew in strength the naval representation in its membership increased. Quite naturally, naval chaplains were among the first to be attracted to the organization and to its aims. There is, however, one case recorded where a minister in the employ of the society was drawn to the opportunities that existed in the Navy. Charles Rockwell, after receiving an appointment as chaplain of the society at Marseilles, applied to the Navy Department for passage to his post. En route to his destination he served as chaplain on a frigate, and, at the captain's urging, he decided to become a naval chaplain.[66]

Officers and chaplains often helped to spread the news of the society by distributing copies of *The Sailor's Magazine* to their crews.[67] A naval lieutenant was instrumental in establishing Bethel unions on the Ohio River in 1831.[68] Lieutenant Joseph R. Blake was an early member of the society.[69] Lieutenant William L. Hudson was active in the New York group of the society for many years.[70] In May 1831 the society elected one marine and four naval officers as directors.[71] By June 1833, 6 of the 30 directors were from the Navy and Marines. These were Captains Charles W. Skinner, Thomas Ap Catesby Jones, John T. Newton, Lieutenants John C. Long and John W. Mooers, and Lieutenant Colonel John Gamble

---

[64] *Ibid.,* I, 121.
[65] *Ibid.,* III, 164.
[66] Clifford M. Drury, I, 38–39, 58; *The Sailor's Magazine,* VII, preface.
[67] *The Mariner's Church Sailor's Magazine,* II, 4–5.
[68] *The Sailor's Magazine,* III, 340.
[69] *Ibid.,* 362.
[70] *Ibid.,* VIII, 319; XVI, 130; XVII, 289.
[71] *Ibid.,* III, 332. These were Captains Thomas Ap Catesby Jones, Charles W. Skinner, Lieutenant Colonel John Gamble, Lieutenant John W. Mooers, and Lieutenant Hugh N. Page.

of the Marines.[72] Commodore Silas H. Stringham later served as one of the vice-presidents of the society.[73] When the Philadelphia chapter of the society held its first assembly in December 1843, Commodore George C. Read acted as chairman. The other naval officers were members of a committee of ten which was charged with drafting a constitution for the Philadelphia group.[74] Three years later Commander John Marston, Jr., Commander George A. Magruder, Lieutenant James S. Biddle, and Purser Robert Pettit were serving on the board of directors of this group. Commander Magruder also acted as the secretary of the organization.[75]

News of a religious revival conducted by officers on board the sloop *St. Louis*, while on a cruise in the Pacific during 1830 and 1831, was a source of great interest to the society, as evidenced by various references to it in *The Sailor's Magazine*.[76] According to this source, the great increase of interest in religion on that ship was due to "a pious lieutenant and schoolmaster," whose labors were sanctioned by the vessel's commanding officer, Master Commandant John D. Sloat.[77] As a result of this revival three lieutenants on the *St. Louis*, John W. Mooers, Robert G. Robb, and Andrew H. Foote, wrote to the society from Callao, Peru, requesting life membership in the organization and sending the prescribed offering of $20 each.[78] In the case of Foote, at least, this was the beginning of an association with the society and its aims which lasted throughout his life, and which had a direct influence on the Navy.

Both *The Mariners' Magazine* and *The Sailor's Magazine and Naval Journal* carried news of interest to naval personnel. The latter publication announced in its first number that it would treat the "whole concern of the navy," and for a number of years its pages showed evidence of a desire to fulfill that pledge. Besides reprinting lists of officers, portions of the annual report of the Secretary of the Navy, excerpts from books by naval officers and chaplains,

---

[72] *Ibid.*, V, 297.   [73] *Ibid.*, XXV, 57.   [74] *Ibid.*, XVI, 130.

[75] *Ibid.*, XIX, 257.

[76] *Ibid.*, III, 63, 78–79, 95, 222, 228, 395.

[77] *Ibid.*, 95.

[78] *Ibid.*, 228. Two officers who were connected with other incidents in this study were also on board the *St. Louis* at this time. These were Midshipman Guert Gansevoort, a cousin of Herman Melville, who later figured in the *Somers* "mutiny," and Lieutenant John C. Long, who was interested in temperance and the abolition of flogging.

speeches, and news items, it also carried comments on congressional activity, or the lack of it, on Navy matters, and letters from men in the service. A section called "The Cabin Boy's Locker" was devoted to the activities of boys at sea in both the naval and merchant service. It did not shrink from advocating courses of action for the improvement of the public service. As early as 1830 and 1831 it carried items on flogging in the Navy,[79] and it fought for the proper control of the lash. The society's interest in boarding houses made it keenly aware of the enlistment problems of the Navy. In 1846, for example, it suggested that the Navy could be well manned with temperate men if Congress would raise the pay of the naval seaman to the level used in the merchant service. Whenever possible it publicized and encouraged all efforts to promote temperance in the Navy. Space also was devoted to such problems as dueling[80] and the selection of officers for the naval service.[81] It praised the reform efforts of chaplains, and pointed out to the graduates of theological schools the tremendous field of usefulness that awaited those who would serve in the Navy.[82]

Indeed, *The Sailor's Magazine and Naval Journal* gave its readers a virtual blueprint for reform in the Navy when in December 1830 it published the report of Edward McLaughlin, the chaplain at the Gosport Navy Yard, Portsmouth, Virginia, to the secretary of the American Tract Society. Chaplain McLaughlin wrote concerning the argument that the low class of men in the ranks of the Navy made the harsh discipline of a ship necessary. Yet such treatment served to destroy all traces of self-respect, dignity, and ambition. Under the circumstances what could be done to reclaim them? His prescription was "an enlightened and regular ministration of the gospel of Christ." This would "enlighten, reform, and liberalize officers and men."

Let there be no alcohol in any of its forms, but in the doctor's medical stores — let flogging be suppressed, and other modes of punishment substituted, and regulated by courts martial according to the crime, — give them the Bible, — the Seamen's Magazine, — suitable tracts — and back all by sending on board of every ship of the line, every frigate and every sloop of war, an enlightened, discreet, evangelical, and efficient chaplain,

---

[79] *The Sailor's Magazine*, III, 116, 281.
[80] *Ibid.*, XV (1842–43), 146–147.
[81] *Ibid.*, III, 182.
[82] *Ibid.*, 342–343, 127, 287–288; XV, 341–342.

— let the schoolmaster, in all cases, be a man of practical godliness; and then let the cabin and the wardroom countenance and encourage the Herald of the Cross — and you have the grand catholicon, which will soon change every ship's company into as moral, christian, and orderly a community as any of the country societies generally are, and under the light and power of divine truth, you will find convictions and conversions as frequent in the navy, in proportion to their numbers, as you will ordinarily in all our congregations on shore, and all this you see is practicable, and of easy accomplishment.[83]

The American Seamen's Friend Society and its allied organizations played an important part in helping to promote reforms in the conditions of service of sailors in the naval and merchant service. In agitating for the sailor's moral betterment they laid bare the rotten condition of the Navy and the indifference of many in authority. They found natural allies among the chaplains and young naval officers who sought to improve the service. This association was helpful for both. It brought religious reformers into close association with the realities of naval life, and the work of the society provided the officers and men with a respectable instrument for attacking the *status quo*. This is not to suggest that they always agreed on the best solutions, but both recognized the major problems and the need for a number of reforms. Furthermore, the naval officers could appreciate the fact that if a reform in the merchant service was important enough to cause a reduction in marine insurance rates, it might possibly be of value to the Navy.

Having thus examined the general situation in the naval establishment and the workings of an important reform group, let us now look at the activities of these humanitarians in the society, in the Navy, in the Congress, and in the country as a whole in connection with three closely related reforms. The first of these dealt with the Navy's attempts to answer the question of how to attract a superior type of American-born men into the enlisted ranks, and how to induce such men who did enlist to continue in the service of the government. The existence of this problem was an invitation to the reformers to present their case for the abolition of flogging and the spirit ration in the Navy. The story of these three interrelated problems, manpower, flogging, and temperance, forms the subject matter of the next chapters.

---

[83] *Ibid.*, III, 115–116.

PART THREE

THE MANPOWER PROBLEM

"When young men enter on board of vessels, they think them-
selves free; but when they find that they receive the treatment
of slaves, they abandon the sea, and seek other employment,
where they can enjoy the rights and exercise the duties of
citizens."

Seaman William McNally, 1839

ABUSES IN ENLISTMENT AND DISCHARGES

Throughout most of the period covered by this book the Navy suffered from a lack of seamen, and particularly of American-born seamen. This state of affairs began with the Navy itself and grew worse in the years following the War of 1812.

A British naval officer who visited the New York dockyard in 1826 gave the following description of our recruiting difficulties.

Here I had an opportunity of observing the extreme difficulty which the Americans experience in manning their navy. A large bounty is offered by the government to seamen, but it is found inadequate to induce them to enter the service in sufficient numbers. In England, no bounty is given, and sailors are at liberty to select the ship in which they choose to serve. This was found to be impracticable in the United States, in consequence of the excessive desertion; and it became necessary to fit up the Fulton as a general receiving ship, where men are entered for the service of the navy, and kept under strict surveillance. The vessel is commanded by a captain; and to such straits are they reduced for seamen, that she is completely fitted out for sea, with masts, yards, and sails for the purpose of drilling raw recruits from the inland states and converting them into sailors.[1]

This same officer also had the opportunity to observe two newly recruited sailors and was greatly surprised when the officer of the

---

[1] Frederick Fitzgerald De Roos, *Personal Narrative of Travels in the United States and Canada in 1826* (London, 1827), pp. 65–67.

recruiting rendezvous expressed satisfaction over one "wretched acquisition." But as bad as things were in New York, the Englishman wrote that it was the only place where ships could be manned. He reported that it was impossible to secure men for the Navy in Boston. "This scarcity of men is by no means confined to their ships of war; American merchantmen are well known to be principally manned by foreign seamen." [2]

Another critical view of the manpower situation at about this same period came from Nathaniel Ames, an American sailor, who claimed that many of the crew of the frigate *Brandywine* "were convicts from the New York Penitentiary, &c" and that the men of the frigate *United States* would have nothing to do with them. [3]

While both of these descriptions undoubtedly contain some exaggerations, there is ample contemporary evidence to suggest that the manpower situation was far from healthy. [4]

By the end of the War of 1812 the Navy, which seemed in danger of extinction under Jefferson, had won a new lease on life. In April 1816 Congress authorized the gradual increase of the naval force during a six-year period. But by 1820 the pro-Navy men in Congress were contending with a growing reaction to naval expansion. Attempts were made in 1821 to suspend the expansion program, and the naval appropriations were cut. Smaller ships, which were cheaper to maintain and required fewer sailors, were emphasized. The number of able seamen, ordinary seamen, and boys in the service fluctuated from 5,500 in 1815 to 3,850 in 1817 and to 4,700 in 1819. [5] In the midst of this period of reaction Smith Thompson, the Secretary of the Navy, advised the chairman of the House naval committee that it would be "unwise and impolitic" to reduce the number of men on the vessels now in service. Before any cutback was made Congress should first decide whether a small naval force was to be employed. A week later the naval committee reported

---

[2] *Ibid.*, p. 95.

[3] [Nathaniel Ames], *A Mariner's Sketches* (Providence, 1830), p. 199.

[4] *Senate Documents*, 19th Cong., 1st Sess. (Serial 125), I, Doc. 2, pp. 100–101; *House Documents*, 19th Cong., 2d Sess. (Serial 148), Doc. 2, part IV, p. 4.

[5] Sprout, pp. 88, 96–97; Smith Thompson to William Lowndes, Dec. 20, 1819, *Letters to Congress*, III, Record Group 45, National Archives (hereafter cited as RG 45, NA).

favorably on a resolution of the House to inquire into the expediency of reducing the number of seamen and boys in the Navy.[6]
Congress need not have worried, for forces were already at work which were helping to reduce the Navy. It had been difficult enough to man the Navy during the war when little of the merchant fleet was in operation. Now, in a period of expansion following the war, the difficulties increased. It was only natural that sooner or later this state of affairs would arouse the interest of various pro-Navy individuals and groups in the country. They sought to pinpoint the cause of the trouble and discussed ways in which the naval service could be made attractive to American males. Suggestions for change provoked further discussion. Little by little the whole fabric of naval life was examined for flaws. These discussions took place at a time when the spirit of nationalism was growing along with the country. It was only natural to feel that the Navy should be worthy of the country. For some, worthiness meant that the rise of the common man should be reflected in the military sphere as well as in the political and social. Reenforcing this patriotic desire was the steady growth of various reform movements. And many of these reform movements owed much of their inspiration, direction, and appeal to a revival of interest in religion during the period between the War of 1812 and the Civil War. In spreading the word of God and in attacking the evils of society, some of these reformers became aware of the methods used to secure men for both the Navy and the merchant service. Many aspects of naval life may have been hidden from them, but recruiting methods could be studied quite easily. The circumstances were such as to provide them with a natural target. They attacked what they saw, but their approach was not a negative one. They had alternatives which they claimed would solve the Navy's manpower problem. And while urging the government to enact reform legislation, they set about on their own to do what they could to improve the lot of the sailor. The activities of the humanitarians associated with the American Seamen's Friend Society have been set forth in the preceding chapter. The support given to such activities by various representatives of the maritime community not only helped

---

[6] *House Reports*, 16th Cong., 2d Sess. (Serial 57), Report 49, pp. 1–6; *Annals of Congress*, 16th Cong., 2d Sess., XXXVII, 978–982.

the humanitarian effort to survive but also increased its influence. As long as the Navy suffered from a lack of men it could not completely ignore the suggested remedies, and particularly when such remedies were introduced on the floors of Congress.

Let us now examine some of the conditions in the Navy which made it difficult to secure men, which were causes of resentment in the ranks, and which were the targets of various reformers.

Crimps and Landlords — Orders issued during the Quasi-War with France were careful to point out that no man was to be enlisted while intoxicated and that "no indirect or forcible Measures [were] to be used to induce them to enter into the service." No Negroes, mulattoes, or suspicious characters were to be enlisted. Under no circumstances was a recruit to be paid an advance until he was completely enlisted and was vouched for by a respectable citizen who would be responsible for his reporting to the ship on time. Such responsible citizens were referred to as a man's security, and they acted as a type of bondsman. At a very early date the proprietors of sailors' boarding houses acted as the security for the recruits they furnished, and they took care to see that each man reported on board ship.[7]

Thus while pains were taken to prevent fraud and to enlist good men, there are indications that a shortage of men could lead to abuses. As early as April 1798 Truxtun advised Lieutenant Rodgers that he was to open a rendezvous at the house of a Mr. Cloney in Baltimore and come to a "clear understanding" with Cloney in regard to the expense of feeding and housing recruits. Rodgers was authorized to pay Cloney "one dollar for every Seaman he procures that is healthy and able to do his duty like a man." The lieutenant was also to meet a Mr. Moore and make an agreement to pay him for every acceptable man that Moore furnished, but he was to take care that he did not pay "two people, for procuring one man." As a closing thought, Truxtun reminded Rodgers that the more men he could enlist and send without Moore and Cloney, the more money

[7] Secretary of the Navy Benjamin Stoddert to Lieutenant Henry Kenyon, Aug. 8, 1798, *Quasi-War*, I, 281–282; Captain Thomas Truxtun to Lieutenant John Rodgers, April —, 1798, *ibid.*, pp. 49–50; Secretary of War James McHenry to Captain Richard Dale, May 11, 1798, *ibid.*, pp. 72–73; Captain Samuel Nicholson's recruiting advertisement for the U.S. frigate *Constitution*, May 12, 1798, *ibid.*, pp. 73–74.

he would save the United States.[8] As time went on and sailors became harder to procure, landlords became a more and more important source of recruits, and the cost of their services was often borne by the recruit from his advance pay.[9] Every recruiting rendezvous was the center of operations for a group of men known as crimps. William McNally, a sailor-author, described them as being the twin brothers of pimps and as being as respectable as a grave robber. Crimps were either sailor landlords themselves or they worked in close association with such landlords. The crimp attempted to get men to enlist in the Navy in order that he might separate them from their advance wages. His weapon was verbal persuasion, and his most likely targets were men who were in debt. If the crimp persuaded a recruit to sign shipping articles, he induced the man to go aboard the ship just to look her over. Once on board, the crimp produced a certificate stating that the man had entered the service at the rendezvous and gave it to a naval officer. When this certificate was surrendered the recruit could not go ashore again. At this point it was not unusual for the crimp to present a bill for nearly all of the man's advance wages. These bills included such things as the cost of articles of clothing and equipment advanced, a landlord's bill, the cost of the boat passage to the ship, and a fee for standing as the man's security. It was possible for a man's friend to stand as security for his appearance, but crimps usually told recruits that they alone could act as such. The fee for this service was $4.00. Similarly, under normal conditions a boat could be rented for about 25 cents, but crimps charged a dollar. Another item on the bill was a dollar for a "shipping bowl." This was a concoction of rum, sugar, and

---

[8] Truxtun to Rodgers, April 6, 1798, *ibid.*, pp. 49–51.

[9] Secretary of the Navy Robert Smith to Master Commandant Isaac Chauncey, March 19, 1805, *Naval Documents Related to the United States Wars with the Barbary Powers* (hereafter cited as *Barbary Wars*) (6 vols.; Washington, D.C., 1944), V, 424; Sailing Master Levi Bardin to Smith, March 21, 1805, *ibid.*, p. 434; Charles Nordhoff, *Man-of-War Life: A Boy's Experience in the United States Navy, During the Voyage Around the World, in a Ship of the Line* (New York, 1855), pp. 24–27; A Fore-Top-Man [Henry J. Mercier], *Life in a Man-of-War. Scenes in "Old Ironsides" During Her Cruise in the Pacific* (Boston, 1927), pp. xxi–xxiii; James Holley Garrison, *Behold Me Once More*, ed. Walter McIntosh Merrill (Boston, 1954), pp. 19, 52, 68–69, 71–73; Lars G. Sellstedt, *From Forecastle to Academy* (Buffalo, 1904), pp. 187, 191, 206–207; Holbrook, pp. 90–91.

egg which customarily sold for twelve and one-half cents. McNally charged that this drink was "not infrequently mixed with opium or some other drug that produced drunkenness and sleep."[10] Naval officers despised crimps, but circumstances forced them to rely on them.

In the case of more experienced sailors the story was much the same. A newly discharged sailor was encouraged to put up at a certain boarding house. Here he was treated royally until his money ran out. Not infrequently he would barter away his clothes for drink. Soon afterward he was in debt to the landlord, and the only way he could pay seemed to be to enlist in the Navy and get three months' advance wages. The landlord would outfit the man, deliver him to the Navy, and claim his advance pay. The cycle would begin again when the ship returned to port. On the basis of five months' association with recruiting in New York City, McNally claimed that he had rarely seen or heard of a man receiving "more than one or two dollars out of his three month's advance."[11]

Similar exploitation of the sailor sometimes was carried on by landlords and "land sharks" while the men were still on board ship. A sailor, arriving in New York on the *Ontario* in 1817, described their activities as follows:

Scarcely had our anchor gone from the bow, before the ship was surrounded by land sharks and bad women; the latter, however were not permitted to come on board; and only a few of the former. They obtained permission only by urgently desiring to see some particular friend. As none of the crew were allowed to go on shore, the landlords went off, but soon returned with any quantity of good things, such as pies, puddings, roast beef, chickens, and also contrived to smuggle on board an ample supply of good stuff, to wash down the savory viands, notwithstanding, they were strictly forbidden against bringing any intoxicating liquor on board, the master at arms was placed in the gangway, with orders to search everything, and everybody, and "the Maine liquor law in full force," there were bottles of brandy, gin, rum, and wine enough to supply a regular bachanalian feast. Tailors and water venders came

---

[10] McNally, *Evils and Abuses in the Naval and Merchant Service, Exposed; with Proposals for Their Remedy and Redress* (Boston, 1839), pp. 19–20; *The Sailor's Magazine*, II (1829–30), 224. For a merchant service view of how men were obtained see William Sullivan, *Sea Life; Or, What May or May Not Be Done, and What Ought to Be Done by Ship-Owners, Ship-Masters, Mates and Seamen* (Boston, 1837), pp. 64, 68.

[11] McNally, pp. 19–20.

along-side; and all, knowing that the boys had between three and four hundred dollars a piece, coming to them; were very willing to trust them with any amount.[12]

Later, when bills were presented, the men discovered that they had been charged $100 for clothing. Some tried on new clothes without removing their sailor garb, with the result that seams were ripped and cloth torn. The process was repeated until the man found clothing that fitted him. But, of course, he was obliged to pay for the clothing that had been damaged. In the end the foolish sailor had little to show for his large investment.[13]

In the account mentioned above the author relates that within a week after the crew had been discharged three of his former ship-mates were in debtors prison. "Such was the manner in which man-of-war sailors were plundered in those days, before savings banks, and sailor's homes were instituted."[14]

There is no question that the sailors brought a good bit of this trouble on themselves. Their devil-may-care ways and outright foolishness made them easy targets for those who would exploit their weaknesses. But it was exactly this state of affairs that gave the reformers their cue. They looked upon the sailor as a child who must be protected from evil influences whether he wished it or not. It was only natural then that crimps, "land sharks," and prostitutes became targets of paternalistic reformers and men of religion. To protect the sailor's morals and money it was necessary to control his environment. Their solutions were temperance boarding houses and seamen's banks. Little by little these reformers began to make their influence felt among sailors. Some idea of the changes that were possible can be had from a news item concerning the dis-charge of the crews of the *Saratoga* and *Cyane*, which appeared in the Boston *Atlas* in September 1854.

Shortly after the inspection by Commodore Gregory, the crews of both vessels received their discharge; and as a large number of "land sharks" were hovering around the vessels, with a view of securing the sailors' hard earnings, Rev. Phineas Stowe, accompanied by Mr. Morrill of Amesbury, and other benevolent gentlemen, engaged the National Brass Band, and proceeded to the Navy Yard for the purpose of inducing the sailors to take up quarters at temperance boarding houses. They were well received on board ship by all classes. A flag and various

---

[12] Holbrook, p. 191.   [13] *Ibid.*, pp. 191–192.   [14] *Ibid.*, p. 192.

Japanese curiosities were presented to Mr. Stowe, and nearly 150 out of 200 on board the *Saratoga*, accompanied the apostles of temperance and humanity, the band leading the way. The procession marched through some of the principal streets of this city, to the Bethel on the corner of Lewis and Commercial streets, which had been beautifully decorated for the occasion. After listening to addresses and music they were almost all safely housed in temperance quarters.[15]

Massachusetts strengthened the hands of the reformers in 1857 by passing a law forbidding individuals to board vessels without permission, and the enticing of crew members to leave the ship.[16]

Wages, Bounties, and Advances — The wages of seamen and marines were regulated by the President according to various circumstances, principally the amount of wages paid in the merchant service. Thus, between 1798 and 1801, the able seamen in the Navy received $17.00 a month. During 1802–03 wages declined to $14.00 and later to $10.00 a month. By 1809–10 and during the War of 1812 they were usually $12.00 a month.[17] As of January 1820 the pay rate was still $12.00 for able seamen, $10.00 for ordinary seamen, and $7.00 for boys.[18] This pay scale apparently remained unchanged for the most part until 1854, and the increasing disparity between naval pay and the wages of the merchant service made it difficult to secure good men. From time to time efforts were made to overcome this disadvantage by paying bounties for enlistment, but at best this was only a stopgap arrangement.

In the beginning a bounty of $3.00 was given to every able seaman who enlisted, and $2.00 to every ordinary seaman. This gave way to the practice of advancing them two and later three months' wages, if necessary, to recruit them.[19] Sailors with three months'

---

[15] The Boston *Atlas*, Sept. 6, 1854, reprinted in *The Sailor's Magazine*, XXVII (1854–55), 84–85.

[16] Henry Farnam, *Chapters in the History of Social Legislation in the United States to 1860* (Washington, D.C., 1938), p. 248.

[17] Paul Hamilton to Representative Burwell Bassett, Feb. 22, 1810, *Letters to Congress*, I, n.p.; Master Commandant Jesse D. Elliott to Midshipman John B. Montgomery, March 20, 1815, *NR-Naval Personnel: Recruiting and Enlistments*, Box 1, RG 45, NA; Secretary of the Navy Robert Smith to Master Commandant Isaac Chauncey, March 6, 1805, *Barbary Wars*, V, 391–392.

[18] Secretary of the Navy Smith Thompson to Representative Samuel Smith, Jan. 27, 1820, *Letters to Congress*, III, 82, enclosure B, RG 45, NA.

[19] James McHenry to Captain Thomas Truxtun, March 16, 1798, *Quasi-War*, I, 43; McHenry to Captain Richard Dale, May 11, 1798, *ibid.*, p. 73;

wages to spend were a splendid harvest in the eyes of many a man in business. To many unscrupulous individuals these seamen constituted a bait too tempting to resist.

Indeed, in 1850, when Secretary Preston asked for the opinions of officers on the merits of abolishing flogging and the spirit ration, Lieutenant William D. Porter informed him that the system of advances was partly responsible for the evils affecting the sailor. Referring to the whole apparatus involving crimps, recruiting officers, and advance wages, Porter said: "It *must be seen* that this system degrades the sailor, blunts all his moral feelings and reduces him to the lowest point in human degradation, he is *sold* like a slave, *bartered* as a bale of goods & handed about from the Navy to the merchant service as fancy stocks are passed from hand to hand, therefore, Drunkenness, insubordination, theft, & desertion are the offsprings of their father *advances*." [20]

A Navy regulation issued in 1839 attempted to tighten up existing procedures. Advance wages or bounty money was to be paid only to those entitled to it. Newly recruited men were encouraged to go aboard ship as soon as possible and to receive their advance in clothing and other necessary items. When an advance was to be made, the recruiting officer was to see that the man furnished himself "with one good suit of thick clothing, two frocks or shirts, a pair of shoes, a pair of stockings, hat and handkerchief as nearly of the navy pattern as possible, or as many of these articles as can be procured with two thirds of their advance, and that the articles be sent on board with them." [21]

While this was undoubtedly a step in the right direction, it was evidently not enough. The manpower problem was alleviated in part by a reduction in force in 1844. Between 1844 and 1857, with the exception of the Mexican War period, the authorized strength of the Navy remained at 7,500 men and boys. [22] During the Mexican

---

A Fore-Top-Man, p. xxii; Secretary of the Navy Robert Smith to Lieutenant Nathaniel Fanning, June 19, 1805, *Barbary Wars*, VI, 127.

[20] Lieutenant William D. Porter to Secretary of the Navy William B. Preston, Feb. 3, 1850, *Corporal Punishment and the Spirit Ration, Reports of Officers, 1850*, No. 64, p. 5, RG 45, NA.

[21] Recruiting Service Regulations, July 1, 1839, *NR-Naval Personnel: Recruiting and Enlistments*, Box 1, RG 45, NA.

[22] *Senate Documents*, 28th Cong., 2d Sess. (Serial 449), I, Doc. 1, p. 521; Paullin, "Naval Administration, 1842–1861," p. 1457.

War the Navy was authorized a strength of 10,000, but succeeded in enlisting only 8,100 men.[23] Part of this gain was no doubt due to patriotism and to the payment of a bounty of $10.00 to every seaman and $15.00 to every ordinary seaman who enlisted. To make sure that the men themselves received this money it was paid out when they were actually on board the receiving ship.[24]

In addition to the persistent problems about seamen, the increased use of steam led to the enlistment of firemen and coal heavers. Regulations issued in 1847 authorized a pay scale of $30.00 a month for first class firemen, $20.00 for second class, and $15.00 a month and one ration a day for coal heavers.[25] Thus a new and much better paid group of men entered the Navy at the same time that the more traditional types of seamen were being sought at the old rates of pay.

The increased territorial responsibilities which resulted from the Mexican War made a naval expansion program desirable, but the discovery of gold in California led to desertions from the Army and Navy units in that area. And the gold rush economy made it virtually impossible to recruit on the West Coast. Secretary Graham was forced to recruit men on the Atlantic coast for service with the Pacific squadron.[26] Despite this situation, he felt that the United States possessed all of the elements necessary to become a great naval power, and that the Navy could be enlarged, if necessary, by drawing on the personnel of the merchant service.[27]

A plea that the wage scale for sailors in the Navy be placed on a par with that of the merchant service was made by Secretary Kennedy in 1852. He felt that this could be done either by increasing the monthly wages or by paying a bounty. In either case, the increase would make it easier to enlist good men.[28]

Congress did not enact legislation to raise the wages of sailors,

---

[23] *Ibid.*, p. 1458.

[24] Captain William K. Latimer to Commodore David Conner, July 27, 1846, *David Conner Papers*, III, Library of Congress.

[25] "Regulations Respecting the Enlistment of Firemen and Coal-Heavers," Aug. 1, 1847, *NR-Naval Personnel: Recruiting and Enlistments*, Box 1, RG 45, NA.

[26] *Senate Executive Documents*, 31st Cong., 2d Sess. (Serial 587), Doc. 1, p. 205.

[27] *Ibid.*, pp. 199–200.

[28] *Senate Documents*, 32d Cong., 2d Sess. (Serial 659), Doc. 1, pp. 321–322.

but Kennedy was allowed to pay a monthly bounty ranging from 90 cents for landsmen to $2.00 for petty officers, coal heavers, firemen, and bandsmen. This money was to be paid every six months. It is interesting to note that in his general order Kennedy felt it necessary to declare specifically that all enlisted men were to be informed of this allowance.[29]

In May 1853 Secretary Dobbin issued an order authorizing the payment of a bounty of $30.00 for every able seaman and $20.00 for every ordinary seaman who enlisted. The bounty provisions promulgated by Kennedy were to apply only to those who entered the service before June 1, 1853.[30]

Like Kennedy, Dobbin realized that an increase in wages was only a part of the solution, and he was already at work on a more comprehensive plan to improve the enlisted service, the details of which will be discussed subsequently. Let it now suffice to point out that the naval appropriation act passed on August 5, 1854, gave Dobbin the funds he requested for a pay raise. Among other things, the law stated that boatswains, gunners, carpenters, and sailmakers were to receive $700 a year if on shore duty, and $900 a year if at sea. They also received an extra 2 per cent of their base pay for every year of sea service and an additional 10 per cent of their sea pay if they served in ships carrying 400 men, or 20 per cent if on ships carrying 900 men.[31]

Soon after this Dobbin issued a general order setting forth the particulars of the new wage scale. Monthly wages now ranged from $8.00 to $10.00 for boys, $12.00 for landsmen and musicians, $14.00 for ordinary seamen, and $18.00 for seamen, to $45.00 for yeomen in ships of the line. This increase did not apply to men enlisted for duty at shore stations or on receiving ships. Men already in the service who had received a bounty under Dobbin's order of May 23, 1853, were to be charged "with such part of the Bounty as is proportioned to the unexpired time of their enlistment." This order also stipulated that in the future recruits were to be given only two months' advance pay at the time of their enlistment.[32]

---

[29] General Order, Jan. 4, 1853, *Circulars and General Orders*, II, 278, RG 45, NA.

[30] General Order, May 23, 1853, *ibid.*, pp. 287–288.

[31] *U.S. Statutes at Large*, X, Chap. 268, pp. 583, 587.

[32] General Order, Aug. 11, 1854, *Circulars and General Orders*, II, 297–298.

Pursers — No sooner was the sailor free of landlords and crimps than he fell afoul of the ship's purser. Small stores and sometimes clothing were the sailor's most immediate need, and these could be obtained on credit from the purser. From the 10 or 12 dollars a month that he earned, the sailor usually had 4 or 5 dollars deducted for such things as tea, sugar, pepper, mustard, soap, and other small stores. When shore leave was imminent he often purchased yard goods from the purser on credit in order to have some item for use in barter on shore. This combination of circumstances could easily result in a form of debt peonage where the sailor saw only a fraction of his wages.[33]

Navy pursers were paid a salary of $480 a year exclusive of rations, but the law allowed them to make a profit of from 10 to 50 per cent on goods sold to the ship's company. Luxury goods netted the purser the largest percentage of profit.[34] William McNally alleged that the cost of fancy yard goods was entered on the books by pursers as cash advanced, and that a sailor who was charged with a $200 advance might never have seen five dollars of this in cash.[35] Chaplain George Jones wrote that the purser's berth was "the best in the ship" for "in a short time, it brings wealth enough to render the man independent." He had heard that after a three-year cruise on a frigate in the Pacific a purser made $30,000.[36] McNally claimed that the purser on another frigate made approximately $58,048 during a voyage.[37] Schoolmaster Enoch C. Wines felt that the law respecting pursers was "fundamentally defective." It not only opened "a wide door to abuses, but actually courts the commission of them."[38]

There was apparently some realization of the sailor's position in regard to the purser during Secretary Southard's regime, for in 1828 he pointed out to Congress that in the merchant service the

---

[33] McNally, pp. 19–20; Roland F. Gould, *The Life of Gould, an Ex-Man-of-War's Man* . . . (Claremont, N.H., 1867), p. 172.
[34] A 'Civilian' [George Jones], *Sketches of Naval Life* . . . (2 vols.; New Haven, Conn., 1829), I, 43–44; Garrison, p. 183n.
[35] McNally, pp. 25–26.
[36] Jones, I, 43.
[37] McNally, pp. 33–44.
[38] Enoch C. Wines, *Two Years and a Half in the Navy, Or, Journal of a Cruise in the Mediterranean and Levant, on Board the U.S. Frigate Constellation, in the Years 1829, 1830, and 1831* (2 vols.; Philadelphia, 1832), I, 32.

granting of an allowance for small stores to newly shipped men helped to make easier the transition to shipboard life. He urged that similar allowances be granted to those entering the Navy.[39]

Secretary Branch reported in 1829 that recruiting difficulties would diminish if Congress would enact regulations "which would enable the seaman to obtain his little supplies of nautical comforts, at rates fixed, known and moderate, and without dread of imposition." The naval service would become popular, and time and money would be saved.[40]

If one may judge by the clippings in his scrapbook, Secretary Woodbury was also aware of some of the criticism in the ranks against pursers.[41]

Congress took up the question of compensation for pursers in 1837–38 and again in 1842. In August of the latter year a law was passed which provided for a regular pay scale for them in lieu of their former rations, allowances, *and* pay. Pursers were now paid between $1,500 and $3,500 a year, depending on the size of the ship to which they were attached. Under the terms of the new law pursers had to purchase their supplies with public funds, and they were forbidden to procure or dispose of supplies to the officers and crew for their own profit. No profit or percentage was to be charged on supplies other than that authorized by Congress.[42] The passage of this law virtually ended all complaints of exploitation by pursers. Under the terms of a law passed in 1860 pursers were henceforth to be known as paymasters.[43]

Discharges — One of the earliest grievances of sailors was the practice of keeping men in service after their term of enlistment had expired. Under the provisions of an act of 1798 the President had the power to extend the period of enlistment beyond a year if the vessel were at sea, and for ten days after its arrival in a U.S.

---

[39] *Senate Documents*, 20th Cong., 1st Sess. (Serial 167), V, Doc. 207, pp. 4–5.

[40] *House Executive Documents*, 21st Cong., 1st Sess. (Serial 195), Doc. 2, p. 40.

[41] See the letter of "A Seaman" to the editor of the *Boston Morning Post*, June 14 [?], 1834 [?], in the Levi Woodbury scrapbook marked "Clippings of Naval Affairs" [July 1833–June 1834], *Gist Blair Papers*, Library of Congress.

[42] U.S. *Statutes at Large*, V, Chap. 206, pp. 535–536.

[43] *Ibid.*, XII, Chap. 181, p. 83.

port.[44] A year later Congress stipulated that every captain was to forward to the Secretary of the Navy a list of the ship's officers and men, with their terms of service, before any of them were paid off. Those remaining on board were to be so designated.[45]

A regulation of 1800 stated that the commanding officer or proper officer delegated by him was to be present when the men were paid off "to see that justice is done to the men, and to the United States, in the settlement of the accounts."[46]

When Congress authorized the employment of an additional naval force in January 1809, the law stipulated that the men were to serve for no more than two years.[47] This law was superseded in May 1820 by one which authorized a three-year tour of duty.[48] The longer voyages of the naval vessels and the difficulties of enlisting men were both reflected in these changes. But the longer term also made the men all the more anxious to be discharged on time.

If a man's enlistment ended while his ship was still at sea, all concerned knew that there was nothing to be done for a time. Nevertheless, a sailor who found himself in such a situation sometimes resented orders and other attempts to impose discipline on him. He was inclined to feel that when his contract had been fulfilled he should have as little to do as possible until he was discharged at the next port.[49] If he was punished, he felt wronged. There was a near mutiny on the *Constitution* in 1805 over the flogging of men whose term of service had expired six months before.[50]

Sometimes difficulties presented themselves when a vessel was in port. For example, some men of the *Erie* were eligible for discharge when their ship reached Gibralter in 1825, but the commander of the garrison would not allow any men to be landed unless they were attached to a ship and their commander accepted responsibility for them.[51] In such cases the discharges had to be postponed until more hospitable shores were reached. Yet discharging men overseas was unpleasant for the Navy as well as for

[44] *Ibid.*, I, Chap. 31, p. 91.
[45] *Ibid.*, I, Chap. 25, p. 710.
[46] *Ibid.*, II, Chap. 33, pp. 48–49.
[47] *Ibid.*, II, Chap. 11, p. 514.
[48] *Ibid.*, III, Chap. 132, p. 606.
[49] Holbrook, p. 192.
[50] James Durand, *James Durand, An Able Seaman of 1812*, ed. by George S. Brooks (New Haven, Conn., 1926), pp. 32–35.
[51] Captain D. Deacon to Commodore John Rodgers, Oct. 17, 1825, *John Rodgers Papers*, correspondence, 1st Series, VI, Library of Congress.

the men themselves, and attempts were therefore made to induce them to reenlist for the duration of a cruise. If the men chose not to reenter, they were discharged at their own request.[52] When a man was discharged overseas it was usually necessary to enlist a foreigner in his place. These foreigners seldom had any attachment to the United States, or to its naval arm, and hence were no great asset. A large proportion of the insubordination and other offenses stemmed from these recruits. But with the enlistment situation the way it was, many such men could be found among our crews. "Instructions have been given to avoid them in enlistments," wrote Secretary Southard, "and it is hoped that the time is not distant, when wise *legislative enactments* will raise up an abundance of seamen, acquainted with and attached to the service, whose interests and hopes are centered in our country."[53] Unfortunately, such legislative enactments did not come about for some time, and the problem of foreigners in the Navy was a persistent one.

When a man was discharged abroad other problems were created. If he desired to return to the United States he had to purchase his passage from his hard-earned pay. If he attempted to work his way back, he might be able to secure employment on an American ship, but often he had to seek employment under a foreign flag. In the event that his money ran out before he had secured passage or employment, he became the problem of the nearest American consul. From time to time groups of these distressed seamen were brought home at government expense. The practice seems to have begun during the Quasi-War with France, when groups of American sailors were brought home from Europe. As early as January 1800, Secretary of State Pickering advised David Lenox, the American consul at London, that his salary would be increased by $500 a year to cover his services for the relief and protection of American seamen in Great Britain.[54]

By 1820 it was the general practice of the Navy Department to

---

[52] *Senate Documents*, 20th Cong., 2d Sess. (Serial 181), I, Doc. 1, p. 135.
[53] *Ibid.*, p. 136.
[54] Timothy Pickering to David Lenox, Jan. 2, 1800, *Quasi-War*, V, 29; Pickering to Isaac Cox Barnet, commercial agent at Bordeaux, April 1, 1800, *ibid.*, V, 371; Job Wall, Consul at St. Bartholomew's, W. I., to Pickering, May 14, 1800, *ibid.*, V, 515.

relieve the Mediterranean Squadron of its duties early enough for it to return home before the expiration of the terms of enlistment of the crew. Sometimes unexpected delays made extensions necessary. In that same year Commodore Stewart made his men decide whether they would be discharged abroad or reentered for nine months. Those who insisted on being discharged were paid off, and on their discharges a notation was made that they were "discharged at their own desire, and would not be entitled to any claims or provision as distressed Seamen, from Consuls of the United States in Europe." All the consuls of Europe were notified of this action, and any of these men who applied for relief were to be denied it.[55]

When faced with the possibilities of having their initial term of service extended, or of being discharged in a foreign land, it is not surprising that men shied away from the naval service. Moreover, merchant cruises were shorter and the pay was usually better. By June 1827 the Navy Department found it necessary to prepare a special circular for its recruiting officers. This was not to be posted in any public place, but was to be shown only to those who had objections to entering the service. It amounted to a promise that the government would live up to its promises regarding seamen. In sending this circular to the recruiting officers the Chief Clerk of the Navy Department called their attention to the fact "that every provision that could be expected, has been made for their [the seamen's] return home, if the period of their service should expire before the termination of the Cruise."[56]

A year later Southard's annual report revealed that the problem was still far from solved. As he saw it, the only remedies were longer enlistments for the men, or shorter periods of service for the ships. The former was against the law, and the latter would increase the expenses of the government. The Secretary believed that while "no serious evil" had as yet resulted from the overseas discharges, it had sometimes placed the officers "in an unpleasant situation, and should, as far as practicable, be avoided."[57]

[55] Secretary of the Navy Smith Thompson to Representative Samuel Smith, Jan. 20, 1820, *Letters to Congress*, III, 84.
[56] Secretary of the Navy Samuel L. Southard, Circular, June 15, 1827, *Circulars and General Orders*, I, 270–271; C[harles] H[ay], Chief Clerk, to recruiting officers, Aug. 8, 1827, *Samuel Southard Letterbook*, p. 127, New York Public Library.
[57] *Senate Documents*, 20th Cong., 2d Sess. (Serial 181), I, Doc. 1, p. 135.

Later, in a comprehensive report to the Senate on the problems of recruitment, Southard wrote that "the contract with the seaman should be scrupulously respected, and he should be discharged in his own country." This could be done by reducing the length of the cruises from three to two years. Such a reduction would increase annual expenditures by at least $150,000, but "the object is so desirable, that every effort has been, and should continue to be made to secure it."[58]

Southard's successor, John Branch, made a similar suggestion in 1829. By shortening the cruises, Branch hoped to avoid leaving men abroad and also to save the government's money.[59]

On December 22, 1830, the Senate requested Branch to supply information on what steps had been taken to relieve ships on foreign duty and to see that their crews were brought home before their enlistments expired. Branch reported that while delays in enlisting crews caused their terms to expire at different times, it was a standing order of the department that men whose terms had expired were to be given passage home as soon as possible. Currently only two ships had been away from home more than three years.[60]

One of these ships was the frigate *Java*. Later, when her crew was discharged, they sent a letter to the Secretary of the Navy commending Captains Biddle and Downes for the kind treatment they had received on board. The majority of the crew had agreed to serve another 12 months under Biddle, and they declared that the Navy would never lack seamen while it had commanders like Biddle and Downes.[61]

Congress still put off acting upon the subject, and in 1831 Secretary Woodbury recommended that it make the three-year term of enlistment begin on the actual date of a ship's sailing.[62]

In February 1832 Woodbury reported that since July 1827 the terms of about two thousand seamen had expired while they were

---

[58] *Ibid.*, 1st Sess. (Serial 167), V, Doc. 207, p. 7.
[59] *House Executive Documents*, 21st Cong., 1st Sess. (Serial 195), I, Doc. 2, p. 35.
[60] Secretary of the Navy John Branch to Senator Samuel Smith, Dec. 28, 1830, *Letters to Congress*, VI, 178–180.
[61] *The Sailor's Magazine*, III, 151.
[62] *House Executive Documents*, 22nd Cong., 1st Sess. (Serial 216), I, Doc. 2, pp. 42–43.

abroad. Of this number, about half were reenlisted. Some of those
discharged refused passage home. Over the same four-year period
these individuals amounted to 682 men, or about 170 a year. More
than half of these 170 men returned to the United States in merchant vessels or enlisted in the Navy at another port. Most of those
who remained abroad were men who had been punished or men
who had been disgraced before their shipmates, and thus were
seldom a loss to the service. Woodbury declared that his department was quite concerned about the problem of overseas discharges and that efforts were being made to correct it. These efforts
included the issuing of a circular requiring the discharge of every
sailor on the day that his enlistment expired, if he so desired; the
continuing application of the provisions of the circular of 1827
offering every discharged seaman his passage home; and the practice of the department for the past two years of calling home every
vessel before the three-year period was up. He believed that the
continued application of these measures and the previously proposed change in counting the beginning of an enlistment would
end all the difficulties. He also believed that the Navy was becoming increasingly popular, as evidenced by the facts that men had
applied for service when none were needed and that two of the five
recruiting rendezvous were closed.[63] Subsequent events, however,
served to cast doubt on the proposition that the Navy was growing
popular, and the surplus of recruits was but a temporary windfall.[64]

Congress finally enacted legislation on March 2, 1837, which
extended the term of enlistment of seamen and allowed the recruitment of boys between 13 and 18 years of age who had their parents'
consent to join the Navy. Under the terms of this act seamen were
to be enlisted for a period not exceeding five years; boys were to
serve until they reached the age of 21 years. The law provided that
when a seaman's period of service expired while he was abroad, it
was the duty of his commander to send him home in a public or
other vessel. In the event that the man had to be detained until the
vessel returned to the United States his commanding officer was

[63] Secretary of the Navy Levi Woodbury to Senator Samuel A. Foot, Feb.
16, 1832, *Letters to Congress*, VI, 293–294.

[64] *Senate Documents*, 24th Cong., 1st Sess. (Serial 279), Doc. 1, p. 331;
ibid., 2d Sess. (Serial 297), Doc. 1, pp. 460–461; Lieutenant Victor Godon,
M.D., U.S.N., to William Short, #13, Dec. 22, 1837, *Short Family Papers*,
Box 45, Library of Congress; McNally, p. 50.

obliged to report the delay and its causes to the Navy Department. Sailors so detained were still subject to the laws and regulations for the government of the Navy. But all who voluntarily reenlisted for the period until the vessel returned to the United States were to receive an additional one-fourth of their former pay for the extra service.[65]

This law virtually ended complaints about overseas discharges and service beyond the period of the original enlistment. Delays in returning home still made for some discontent, but most men seem to have been mollified by the extra money. Nevertheless, it was felt that shorter cruises would eliminate the problem. In 1856 Secretary Dobbin directed that a part of the sailing instructions to commanders of squadrons should include the provision that whenever any such commander saw that the term of enlistment of the majority of the crew of any vessel of his squadron was about to expire, then the ship was to return to the United States in time to discharge the men. Only special orders from the Navy Department or an emergency involving the honor of the flag was to justify a deviation from this rule.[66]

Secretary Toucey continued this policy of shortening cruises. He felt that such a change had long been necessary, and that it would preserve health, facilitate enlistments, make the service more acceptable to seamen, promote economy, and contribute to the increased activity, efficiency, and usefulness of the Navy.[67]

Foreigners in the Navy — From what has been said already it will be seen that the large number of foreigners in the Navy was a matter of continual concern. The habit of shipping known aliens as Americans was one of the abuses that contributed much to the arguments over impressment of our seamen. In the troubled years between 1798 and 1812 it was customary for *bona fide* American seamen to secure a legal certificate or "protection" certifying that they were citizens of the United States. But the fact that American sailors and landlords sold these protections was well known to the British, and consequently they paid no attention to the papers. The return of peace did not end these abuses. Continued use of these

[65] *U.S. Statutes at Large*, V, Chap. 21, p. 153.
[66] *Senate Executive Documents*, 34th Cong., 3d Sess. (Serial 876), Doc. 1, pp. 414–418.
[67] *Ibid.*, 35th Cong., 1st Sess. (Serial 921), IV, Doc. 11, p. 584.

fraudulent protections made it possible to ship a larger percentage of foreigners than the law allowed. Chaplain Charles Rockwell reported in 1842 that protections could be obtained by false swearing or by purchasing one from a landlord. For 50 cents a man bought a protection and a name. "Many of the seamen in our navy, ship by a new name almost every cruise."[68]

At the time of the boundary difficulties with Great Britain there was talk of the possibility of war. Great concern was felt in naval and mercantile circles about the reliability of these alien seamen in the event of war. This fear helped to stimulate discussion on what should be done to make the Navy attractive to American seamen.

When the threat of war passed away, the concern over the problem of foreigners continued. This situation made some officers favor larger marine contingents on shipboard as a possible counterpoise to troublesome foreigners. Writing on this subject in 1852 to Colonel Archibald Henderson, the Commandant of the Marines, Commander Cornelius K. Stribling declared: "It is useless to disguise the fact, that the crews of our ships are now composed mostly of foreigners and the most worthless class of our native population; with such materials to manage, a large guard of marines, is, in my judgment, highly desirable, if not absolutely necessary."[69]

The fears of some officers that this type of personnel could not be managed without flogging proved to be unfounded. But there were also fears about the effects of abolishing the spirit ration on enlistments in the Navy. By 1842 many merchant ships had ceased to distribute a ration of whisky, and the movement was growing. According to chaplains and some Navy officers, many men admitted that they joined the Navy for whisky. Some officers felt that bad as these men might be they were at least a source of manpower. If

---

[68] William Savage to Timothy Pickering, Sept. 17, 1799, *Quasi-War*, IV, 196; Captain Edward Preble to Secretary of the Navy Robert Smith, July 5, 1803, July 21, 1803, *Barbary Wars*, II, 467, 494; Ames, *A Mariner's Sketches*, pp. 15–18; Charles Rockwell, *Sketches of Foreign Travel and Life at Sea* (2 vols.; Boston, 1842), II, 387; Herman Melville, *White Jacket, Or, The World in a Man-of-War* (Boston, 1892), pp. 354–355.

[69] Commander Cornelius K. Stribling to Colonel Archibald Henderson, U.S.M.C., July 27, 1852, *Senate Documents*, 32d Cong., 2d Sess. (Serial 659), I, Doc. 1, p. 592. For an account of the Army's problems with foreigners see Francis P. Prucha, *Broadax and Bayonet*, pp. 36, 41–45.

these men were alienated, the problem of manning the Navy would be even more acute. To these arguments the reformers answered that the Navy would be better off without the low types. Abolish flogging, abolish grog, treat the men fairly and give them a worthwhile goal, and you will attract and hold better men.[70]

Those accustomed to reading the literature on naval reform in this period may well have believed that all segments of the Navy had been heard from when a self-styled foreigner named Tiphys Aegyptus produced a pamphlet in 1843. This pamphlet, called *The Navy's Friend,* was addressed to the Committee on Naval Affairs of Congress and to the public, and was based on the author's 39 months in the Navy, ending in February 1840. Aegyptus related abuses and illegal actions on the subjects of flogging, grog, seamen's accounts, abusive officers, drunken and lazy midshipmen, the neglect of divine services, and disrespect for the dead.[71]

On the subject of recruiting Aegyptus charged that between 1839 and 1842 men were enlisted in complete ignorance of the provisions of the law of 1837 which gave them one-quarter additional pay if they were detained beyond their term of service. When sailors found out about the law they were resentful about not being informed of their rights. Officers answered their protests with the statement that every man was presumed to know the law. Tiphys Aegyptus believed that every commander ought to read this act to every man before he signed on. He believed that keeping a man in service beyond his time, except for a real emergency, was worse than the operations of the press gang. Such treatment made men reluctant to enlist. During his own service he had heard Americans curse the day that they entered the Navy and declare that they

---

[70] Rockwell, II, 413–414, 416; Wines, II, 112–113; Chaplain Charles Stewart to the editor of the *New York Commercial* reprinted in *The Sailor's Magazine,* XXIII (1850–51), 30–31; Commodore Charles Stewart to William B. Preston, Mar. 11, 1850, *Reports of Officers, 1850,* No. 1; Captain Charles Morris to Preston, Feb. 6, 1850, *ibid.,* No. 2; Captain Joseph Smith to Preston, Feb. 6, 1850, *ibid.,* No. 15; Captain Robert F. Stockton to Preston, Feb. 6, 1850, *ibid.,* No. 20; Commander Robert B. Cunningham to Preston, Feb. 6, 1850, *ibid.,* No. 41; Commander Andrew K. Long to Preston, Feb. 4, 1850, *ibid.,* No. 47.

[71] Tiphys Aegyptus, *The Navy's Friend, or Reminiscences of the Navy; Containing Memoirs of a Cruise, in the U.S. Schooner Enterprise* (Baltimore, 1843), *passim.*

would never serve again unless the laws of the country were enforced in the Navy.[72]

In spite of a number of proposals the many foreign seamen in the Navy continued to be a problem throughout the period covered by this study. As late as 1859 the *New York Times* remarked that "it is even doubtful if there exist enough American seamen to man our vessels of war, let the advantages of the position be what they may."[73]

Negroes in the Navy — Closely related to the problem of aliens in the service was that of the number of Negroes in the Navy. It seems that almost from its beginning there were free Negroes in the Navy, usually acting as cooks. There is no indication that they were segregated from the rest of the crew, and integration seems to have been an accomplished fact. In view of the crowded quarters on a man-of-war it could hardly have been otherwise. Commodore Preble gave explicit instructions not to enlist Negroes,[74] but this had no lasting effect on their entrance into the service.

Some indication of their number in the Navy in this early period may be gleaned from the writings of Dr. Edward Cutbush, M.D., published in 1808. In discussing the need for exercising the men on a man-of-war Cutbush suggested that every ship be provided with two violins to supply lively music for dancing. "There will be no difficulty in procuring a 'fiddler,'" he said, "*especially* among the coloured men in every American frigate, who can play most of the common dancing tunes."[75]

The regulations for the Navy drawn up in 1818 stipulated that no slaves or Negroes were to be employed in the naval yards without the order of the Secretary of the Navy or the Board of Navy Commissioners.[76] But it appears that there were exceptions to this practice.

---

[72] *Ibid.*, pp. 30–31, 21.

[73] The *New York Times*, reprinted in *The Sailor's Magazine*, XXXII (1859–60), 104.

[74] Captain Edward Preble to Lieutenant William C. Jenckes, July 13, 1803, *Barbary Wars*, II, 479.

[75] Edward Cutbush, *Observations on the Means of Preserving the Health of Soldiers and Sailors; and on the Duties of the Medical Department of the Army and Navy: With Remarks on Hospitals and Their Internal Arrangement* (Philadelphia, 1808), pp. 126–127.

[76] *American State Papers: Naval Affairs* (4 vols.; Washington, D.C., 1834), I, 511.

William McNally declared that in spite of the law Negro slaves served as crewmen on the *Java,* and that their masters received their pay. He also charged that slaves were used in the naval yards to the exclusion of white and free colored laborers.[77]

McNally also told of a lieutenant who took great delight in flogging a cook's mate and in hearing him shout in pain. "After an act like this," he wrote, "let our northern people talk about slaves and slavedrivers." [78]

The recruiting regulations promulgated in 1839 specified that "free blacks and other colored persons" were to be entered only with the consent of the commander of the station.[79] Two months later the matter was treated again in a Navy Department circular issued by Commodore Isaac Chauncey, Acting Secretary of the Navy. This circular declared that in view of the frequent complaints made on the "number of Blacks and other colored persons" shipped in the Navy, henceforth colored enlistments would be no more than 5 per cent of the total number of white persons enlisted weekly or monthly. No slave was to be entered under any circumstances.[80]

The subject of Negroes in the naval service arrested the attention of Congress in 1842, and the House passed a resolution calling on the Secretary of the Navy to supply information. Secretary Upshur reported that the records of his department did not indicate whether the person enlisted was white or black, but he believed that the number employed was within the one-twentieth previously authorized. "There are no slaves in the Navy," said Upshur, "except only in some few cases, in which officers have been permitted to take their personal servants, instead of employing them from the crews." [81]

Congress was also momentarily distracted in 1843 by a memorial calling its attention to the fact that colored seamen arriving in southern ports were being imprisoned until their vessel sailed. Pre-

---

[77] McNally, p. 127.

[78] *Ibid.,* p. 121.

[79] Regulations of July 1, 1839, *NR-Naval Personnel: Recruiting and Enlistments,* Box 1.

[80] Acting Secretary of the Navy Isaac Chauncey, Circular, Sept. 13, 1839, *Circulars and General Orders,* I, 357.

[81] Secretary of the Navy Abel P. Upshur to John White, Speaker of the House of Representatives, Aug. 5, 1842, *Letters to Congress,* VIII, 458.

sumably this rule applied to all Negro seamen, whether naval or merchant, but most of the agitation seems to have come from mercantile groups. A congressional resolution condemning the practice was allowed to lie on the table.[82] Accordingly, the governor and the Council of Massachusetts appointed a man in Charleston, South Carolina, and one in New Orleans, Louisiana, to act as agents for the Commonwealth on matters pertaining to Negro seamen.[83] The imprisonment of these colored sailors was another element in the story of growing tensions between the North and South on the subject of slavery. Northerners believed that such imprisonments violated the rights of individuals, infringed on the commerce power of Congress, and were incompatible with national or international commercial conventions.[84] By 1851 the Charleston *Mercury* advocated the repeal of the South Carolina law and agreed that other restrictions could be made to protect the public.[85] But nothing seems to have come of this proposal.

When *White Jacket* appeared in 1850, Herman Melville's readers were introduced to a Negro slave character who was a member of the ship's company and whose master, a purser, received his wages as a seaman. Melville relates that this slave was allowed to wear civilian clothing and was almost entirely exempted from disciplinary action. He also was exempted from witnessing a flogging with the rest of the crew. As a result, this slave sailor was envied by many of the crew.[86]

In 1855 Secretary Dobbin was faced with the problem of whether the government or the owner should receive the pay balance due to a Negro slave who deserted from the Washington Navy Yard. It was decided that the money was forfeited to the government just as in the case of any other deserter.[87]

Even in the midst of the Civil War, when Captain Andrew H. Foote was trying to man his gunboats for the campaigns on the western waters, he felt it necessary to caution one of his recruiting officers that "as there are objections or difficulties in the Southern

---

[82] *Congressional Globe*, 27th Cong., 3d Sess., XII, 183, 384.
[83] *Journal of Commerce* quoted in *The Sailor's Magazine*, XVI, 165.
[84] *Congressional Globe*, 27th Cong., 3d Sess., XII, 384.
[85] *The Sailor's Magazine*, XXIII, 304.
[86] Melville, pp. 353–354.
[87] Secretary of the Navy James C. Dobbin to ?, "Slaves, enlistment of," Sept.-Oct. 1855, *NR-Naval Personnel: Recruiting and Enlistment*, Box 1.

country about colored people, we do not want any of that class shipped." [88]

This was at best but a temporary restriction which would give way before necessity. On December 18, 1862, Secretary Welles issued his contraband order. Under the terms of this circular no "contrabands" were to be enlisted in any rating higher than landsman. If found qualified and if needed in other ratings they could be advanced to coal heavers, firemen, ordinary seamen, or seamen. They could not transfer from one vessel to another except with a landsman's rating, but they could be discharged with a higher rating.[89] This order was a prelude to the increased employment of Negroes in the Navy during the Civil War.[90]

In the work of caring for the sailor and attempting to reform him the Negro seaman was not neglected. The Colored Seamen's Home in New York City, founded in 1839, averaged about 450 boarders a year from the naval and merchant service.[91] According to William P. Powell, its first director, in its first 12 years the home cared for 6,533 seamen, of which only 14 later ran afoul of the law. Thirteen of these were sentenced to the state prison for theft or assault and battery, and one was fined $25.00 "for revolt." [92] While some of these figures may be exaggerated, they do offer an insight into the growing numbers of colored seamen in the naval and merchant service.

The existence of various abuses connected with the enlistment and discharge of seamen, as well as those endured while in the naval service, were some of the reasons why Americans were reluctant to enter the Navy. While this cause and effect relationship was

[88] Captain Andrew H. Foote to Lieutenant Leonard Paulding, Sept. 17, 1861, in Richard Rush *et al.*, eds., *Official Records of the Union and Confederate Navies in the War of the Rebellion* (30 vols.; Washington, D.C.: 1894–1914), 1st Series, XXII, 337.
[89] *Circulars and General Orders*, II, 400.
[90] The role of the Negro in the Union Navy is discussed in Herbert Aptheker's *To Be Free, Studies in American Negro History* (New York, 1948), pp. 113–135, and in his article "The Negro in the Union Navy," in the *Journal of Negro History*, XXXII (1947), 169–200. The service of Negroes in the Navy from the American Revolution through the Civil War is briefly treated in Dennis D. Nelson, *The Integration of the Negro into the United States Navy, 1776–1947* (Washington, D.C., 1948), pp. 1–21.
[91] *The Sailor's Magazine*, XXI, 253.
[92] *Ibid.*, XXIV (1851–52), 486.

recognized at an early date, and was periodically underscored in the decades after the War of 1812, there was no disposition on the part of the government to eliminate such abuses in a comprehensive fashion. Long-delayed and piecemeal efforts were made to correct or minimize the most glaring causes of improper treatment but such efforts did not end the Navy's dependence on foreigners and to a lesser degree on Negroes to fill up its crews. The reliance on foreigners touched our national pride, and provided naval reformers with a constant excuse to discuss the steps that should be taken to make service in the United States Navy attractive to Americans.

TOWARD A CAREER ENLISTED SERVICE

The occasion for submitting his first annual report to President John Quincy Adams, a friend of the Navy, at the end of 1825 must have impressed Samuel Southard as an ideal time to discuss clearly some of the long-range needs of the naval service. As a holdover from the previous administration, his years of experience in the office of Secretary of the Navy gave weight to his recommendations.

Among other things, Southard reported difficulties which were encountered in enlisting the numbers of seamen necessary to man the fleet. Vessels were sometimes detained because of these shortages. Delays increased the operating expenses with no sea service to show for the money. Part of the difficulty in securing men was due to the more attractive conditions of service in our merchant marine and in the service of foreign governments.[1]

One of the means employed to overcome this reluctance of Americans to join their Navy was that of stationing at the principal recruiting stations "A vessel not calculated for the sea, but fitted up with the same comfort, and officered and governed in the same way as if in actual commission, to which the recruit can be sent, and there kept, until he can be transferred to the vessel in which he is

---

[1] *Senate Documents*, 19th Cong., 1st Sess. (Serial 125), Doc. 2, p. 100.

to sail. One or two have already been prepared for the purpose, and others will be, without delay."[2]

The advantages promised from this arrangement were that seamen would enlist more readily when assured of immediate comfort; health and discipline would be promoted; the men could be trained so that when they went on board their regular ship they would be of immediate use; such men would be employed in the naval yards, if necessary; desertions would be fewer; and when vessels returned from cruises, those whose time had expired could be discharged and immediately replaced by those awaiting assignment.

But the arrangements of the Department, however useful, must be comparatively inefficient to remove the evils suggested. The remedy rests with the power which can establish permanent regulations, which will tend both to increase the number of seamen, and bind them more permanently to our public service. This object will be found, in the progress of our Naval history, to be of high importance. Our Naval power, in all other respects, has its limit only in the will of the Nation. Our free institutions interpose a barrier to a compulsory augmentation of the number of our seamen, and a system must be devised which will ensure voluntary enlistments sufficient to meet our increasing wants. Two of the features of this system will probably be, to admit more boys, in the character of apprentices, and to enlist robust and healthy landsmen, in the interior, who will soon acquire the habits and skills of seamen, and form a most valuable portion of our force.[3]

Southard's report must have been noted with interest in some parts of Congress, for on May 20, 1826, Senator Robert Hayne of South Carolina introduced a motion directing the Secretary of the Navy to report on the difficulties encountered in enlisting seamen, the causes of same, and the measures necessary to remedy them. The measure passed, and the report was due at the beginning of the next session of Congress. The second session of the 19th Congress came and went without this report. It was not until May 23, 1828, just a few days before the end of the first session of the 20th Congress, that Southard submitted his masterful report on the recruiting situation.[4]

Among the causes of the present state of affairs Southard singled

---

[2] *Ibid.*

[3] *Ibid.*, pp. 100–101; *Senate Journal*, 19th Cong., 1st Sess. (Serial 124), p. 377.

[4] *Ibid.*, 20th Cong., 1st Sess. (Serial 162), p. 490; *Senate Documents*, 20th Cong., 1st Sess. (Serial 167), V, Doc. 207, p. 3.

out such things as wages, overseas discharges, increased merchant tonnage, foreigners, and the lack of proper hospitals. For many of the problems he had but "one adequate and appropriate remedy," namely, "such an increase of native *American* seamen as will answer every demand of our mercantile and naval service. It will not be easy, speedily, if at all, to attain this result. The process must be slow; but it is worth the sacrifice of time, convenience, and money, which it will require." [5]

Southard also put forward five proposals relative to the above goal. These were: (1) The exclusion of foreign seamen, even of naturalized foreigners, from our naval service as soon as possible. (2) The placing of a larger proportion of landsmen (inexperienced sailors) on our ships than had been customary. These men should be between 18 and 25 years of age. After one cruise of two or three years they could qualify as ordinary seamen and after a second cruise be eligible for the rank of seaman. Thereafter they would continue permanently in the United States service. (3) The enlistment of landsmen from the interior regions of the country. (4) The enactment of legislation requiring every merchant ship to carry at least one boy between 14 and 18 years of age for every 100 tons of cargo. This would provide training for the future seamen needed by both the Navy and the merchant service and would place only a small burden on the merchants involved. (5) The granting of legal authority to enlist in the Navy, with the written consent of their parents, boys over 13 and under 16 years of age who were to serve until they reached the age of 21 years; or the granting of authority to take on apprentices in the same age bracket for the same period. Southard wanted 15 to 30 of these apprentices in every naval yard, and 2 for every gun on our vessels in service. He estimated that about 1,200 would be needed and would be replaced as their terms expired. Within two years he expected that such boys could qualify for the rank of ordinary seamen; and within three years they could be rated as seamen. And all petty officers would be drawn from this class of men within ten years. [6]

According to Southard, this plan and that of enlisting landsmen from inland areas would give the Navy an annual increase of from 300 to 500 good seamen who would be attached to the service.

---

[5] *Ibid.*, p. 8. [6] *Ibid.*, pp. 10–11.

"These apprentices should be clothed in our own manufacturers — denied spirits in their rations, until they become men — educated by proper teachers in reading, writing, arithmetic, and navigation — be entitled to hospital pension and prize privileges — have a small amount of money reserved for them, and paid when their time expires, if their conduct has been good, and a premium on re-entering." [7]

Southard predicted that his plan would seem extravagant to those who had not weighed the considerations. He estimated that it would save the government $150,000 annually and "would make the navy what it ought to be in every thing — American." [8]

On the matter of an appentice system, Southard was probably influenced by the ideas of Lieutenant Matthew C. Perry, who as early as January 1824 sent a plan to the Secretary which provided for the enlistment of "a certain number" of boys a year who would serve in the Navy until they reached the age of 21. These boys were to be clothed and educated at government expense, to be denied the ration of spirits for the first two years of their enlistment, and to be promoted as high as the rank of master's mate if they were deserving. Perry believed that his plan would be a blessing to society inasmuch as it would relieve communities of a segment of the population which, for want of honest employment and parental guidance, often had recourse to crime. As naval apprentices such boys would learn discipline as well as a trade and become a credit to themselves as well as to their country. Under the arrangement then being followed boys were enlisted for a two-year period. This meant that by the time they learned the first rudiments of their trade they were discharged. If they continued to follow the sea, it was usually with the merchant service; and if they eventually returned to the Navy they had to learn discipline all over again. [9]

Perry elaborated his plan further in one of a series of newspaper articles on naval reform addressed to Robert Y. Hayne, the chairman of the Senate's naval committee, which appeared in *The Na-*

<hr>

[7] *Ibid.*

[8] *Ibid.*, p. 8.

[9] Lieutenant Matthew C. Perry to Secretary of the Navy Samuel Southard, Jan. 5, 1824, *Officers Letters*, 1824, I, No. 13 and enclosure, RG 45, NA; Paullin, "Naval Administration . . . 1815–1842," p. 636.

tional Gazette of Philadelphia on February 12, 1828.[10] Another letter was addressed to the Navy Department in 1835. He continued
his agitation until the desired legislation was enacted.[11]

While Perry was drawing up plans, Lieutenant David G. Farragut established a school for apprentice seamen on board the
receiving ship *Alert* at the Gosport Navy Yard in Portsmouth, Virginia. This was done not long after Farragut's assignment to the
Alert on November 29, 1826. When Southard inspected the naval
yard the following March, Captain James Barron, the commandant,
took him to see the class of 37 boys. So pleased was the Secretary
with their progress that he complimented the school's founder and
teacher on his work. Farragut noted the incident in his journal as
being one of the very few times he ever received a compliment from
the Navy Department or its head.[12]

Not content simply to recommend changes, Southard conducted an experiment in recruiting during the early part of 1828
in two areas far removed from the seacoast — Harrisburg and Car-
lisle, Pennsylvania. It was his contention that such recruiting
rendezvous, in addition to tapping an important supply of manpower, would broaden the base of popular support for the Navy.
When he submitted his special report to Congress in May of that
year, he admitted that it was still too early to draw conclusions
about the experiment, but it promised all that was hoped from it.
If it continued to prosper, similar rendezvous would be established
elsewhere.[13]

---

[10] Apparently eight numbered articles signed "Perry" were prepared, but
for some reason No. 3 was not printed. The apprentice system was discussed
in No. 8, which appeared in *The National Gazette* on Feb. 12, 1828. The
similarity of the ideas expressed in this piece with those sent to Southard
in a letter of Jan. 5, 1824, as well as Matthew Perry's well-known interest
in naval reform, makes the writer feel justified in attributing the series of
newspaper articles to him.

[11] Paullin, "Matthew Calbraith Perry," *Dictionary of American Biography*,
XIV (1934), 487.

[12] Loyall Farragut, *The Life of David Glasgow Farragut, First Admiral
of the United States Navy, Embodying His Journal and Letters* (New York,
1879), p. 105; Charles Lee Lewis, *David Glasgow Farragut: Admiral in the
Making* (Annapolis, Md., 1941). I, 178–180.

[13] *Senate Documents*, 20th Cong., 1st Sess. (Serial 167), V, Doc. 207,
p. 10. For an account of this experiment see H. D. Langley, "The Grass
Roots Harvest of 1828," *U.S.N.I.P.*, XC (1964), pp. 51–59.

Thus, in his annual report for 1825 and in his special report of 1828, Southard offered practical solutions to the Navy's manpower problems. Two major points in his program — the enlisting of boys as apprentices and the recruitment of men from the interior regions of the country — constituted the beginnings of a regular recruiting system. It is unfortunate that these suggestions did not receive the support they deserved, for, as we have already seen and shall see subsequently, many of the problems that he attempted to solve by means of a comprehensive plan were to trouble many future Secretaries. As it was, these proposals were not forgotten, and the agitation for them helped to set off a type of chain reaction which led to other reforms in the Navy.

Outside the government other individuals slowly became aware of the manpower situation, and from time to time comments on the dearth of American seamen in the naval and merchant services appeared in the press.

The Sailor's Magazine printed a letter to the editor from "A Yankee" which declared that it had long "been a matter of surprise to the thinking part of our mercantile community, that so little had been done towards increasing the number of American seamen." According to the law every American vessel was required to employ citizens of the United States for at least two-thirds of her total crew, but "not one half of the seamen sailing out of our ports, are Americans either by birth or citizenship." With this state of affairs affecting both the Navy and the merchant service, the "Yankee" predicted that unless something was done soon within ten years the ratio of American seamen to foreigners would be one to ten.[14]

In February 1830 the New York *Enquirer* reported that the number of able seamen in the Navy was decreasing each year and that naval officers were becoming alarmed. As a remedy it suggested that merchant ships be required by law to take on apprentices and that each warship carry two extra boys for every gun. Such a plan would not only supply future manpower needs but by withholding spirits from the boys would be the means of introducing "habits of sobriety into the navy." This, in turn, would lead to a decline of disorder and make punishments less necessary. Finally, the whole character of the service would be raised.[15] It seemed as though a

---

[14] *The Sailor's Magazine*, II, 192.   [15] *Ibid.*, pp. 191–192.

properly organized apprentice system was the panacea for many of the ills of the Navy.

It was about this same time that an agent of the American Seamen's Friend Society called on President Jackson and Secretary Branch to present a memorial urging the increase of chaplains in the Navy.[16] The Navy was in difficulty, and with various groups in the country calling for reforms in that service there was hope that something might be done. The manpower shortage might well be the means of attaining long-range reforms.

The editor of the *New York Commercial Advertiser* suggested in the fall of 1831 that the way to improve the Navy was to abolish flogging, and that anything which would make sailors feel kindly toward the service should be considered. In commenting on this item, a Philadelphia paper observed that "our gallant tars must recollect with bitterness, that most execrable practice of leaving them upon a foreign shore when their terms of service had expired; and that scarcely less reprehensible treatment which decoys them to renew their enlistment by clinking a bag of dollars, and the privilege of a week's unrestrained drunkenness in some foreign harbor." [17]

With the advent of a new administration in 1829, Southard laid aside his duties as Secretary of the Navy and assumed those of the attorney general of New Jersey. For a brief period he served as governor but resigned that office following his election as a Whig senator from New Jersey. He was back in Washington in the latter capacity when the 23rd Congress assembled in December 1833.[18]

By June 1834 it was apparent that he had not forgotten the manpower needs of the Navy, for in that month he introduced a bill to provide for the enlistment of boys in the naval service. In mid-December the bill was referred to the Committee on Naval Affairs. Southard, as the chairman of the committee, reported it out

---

[16] *Ibid.*, p. 223.

[17] Clipping from a Philadelphia paper, probably the *Philadelphia Gazette and Daily Advertiser*, undated, in the Levi Woodbury scrapbook, "Clippings on Naval Affairs, June 1831–June 1832," *Gist Blair Papers*, Library of Congress.

[18] Robert G. Albion, "Samuel Lewis Southard," *Dictionary of American Biography*, XVII (1935), 412.

promptly. It passed the Senate without amendment early in January 1835.[19]

Secretary Dickerson called attention to the importance of the bill in his annual report, and President Jackson recommended its adoption in his message to the 24th Congress in December 1835. Later that same month Leonard Jarvis, a Democratic representative from Maine, reported an apprentice bill from the House Committee on Naval Affairs. The measure was sent to the Committee of the Whole House where it lay dormant for the rest of the session. In the Senate Southard reported another bill out of the naval committee, which, by December 30, was considered by the Committee of the Whole, and on its sponsor's motion laid on the table.[20] While naval apprentice bills were pending in both houses of Congress, Southard went ahead with another plan.

In March 1836 he introduced a motion that the Senate Committee on Commerce be instructed to inquire into the expediency of an act to provide for the employment of boys in the merchant service. This led to a bill on the subject sponsored by Whig Senator Robert H. Goldsborough of Maryland, which was referred to the Committee on Commerce by a unanimous vote. Here the bill was discussed, amended, and made the subject of a special report. At the next session of Congress Alabama's William R. King, a Democrat, introduced a bill in the Senate which provided for the employment of boys "in the vessels of the United States," which also went to the Committee on Commerce by unanimous consent.[21] This bill died in the committee.

Meanwhile the Senate moved ahead with the naval apprentice measure which Southard had let lie in the Committee of the Whole. An amended bill was passed by the Senate in May 1836 and was commended to the care of the House. Jarvis, of the House Committee on Naval Affairs, reported the bill out of his committee on May

---

[19] *Senate Journal*, 23d Cong., 1st Sess. (Serial 237), p. 331; *ibid.*, 2d Sess. (Serial 265), pp. 41–42, 51–52, 71, 74. In 1832 General Alexander Macomb proposed a plan for enlisting boys to improve the quality of men in the Army; see Prucha, p. 41.

[20] *Senate Documents*, 24th Cong., 1st Sess. (Serial 279), Doc. 1, p. 331; *House Journal*, 24th Cong., 1st Sess. (Serial 285), pp. 33, 78; *Senate Journal*, 24th Cong., 1st Sess. (Serial 278), pp. 59, 70.

[21] *Ibid.*, pp. 234–235, 299, 401; *ibid.*, 2d Sess. (Serial 296), pp. 80, 181; *Register of Debates in Congress*, 24th Cong., 2d Sess., XIII, Part 2, pp. 232–233.

17.[22] It was still pending before the Committee of the Whole House when Congress adjourned in July.

Once again the President and the Secretary of the Navy recommended that a naval apprentice bill be passed. Early in the second session of the 24th Congress Southard again introduced such a measure. By the unanimous consent of the Senate it was referred to the Committee on Naval Affairs. Six days later William C. Rives, a Virginia Democrat, reported it out of that committee without amendment. The Senate passed the bill on February 21, 1837.[23]

Late in January Representative Jarvis of Maine made an unsuccessful attempt to have the Committee of the Whole House end its consideration of a similar apprentice bill. The Senate bill was sent to the House Committee on Naval Affairs on March 1, and the following day Jarvis reported it out without amendment.[24] Two attempts to amend the bill were made before the House.

Maryland Democrat Isaac McKim wanted to add sections stipulating that every American merchant vessel of at least 200 tons burden must carry one apprentice boy; those between 250 and 500 tons should have two boys; and three boys were to be assigned to all vessels over 500 tons. Failure to comply with these provisions would result in a fine of $300. McKim's amendment was rejected.[25]

The second amendment was proposed by Whig Representative George Grennell of Massachusetts. It stated that the boys were to receive instruction "in the common branches of education" for at least three months in each of the first three years of their enlistment. This education was to be under the direction of the commanding officer of the naval yard or vessel to which the apprentice was attached. Jarvis asked Grennell to withdraw his amendment on the grounds that the education of the boys would be regulated by the Navy Department. Grennell refused. He stated that since a new policy was being inaugurated he wished to make it as efficient as

---

[22] *Senate Journal*, 24th Cong., 1st Sess. (Serial 278), pp. 335, 350; *House Journal*, 24th Cong., 1st Sess. (Serial 285), pp. 828, 832, 834.
[23] *Senate Documents*, 24th Cong., 2d Sess. (Serial 297), Doc. 1, p. 461; *House Journal*, 24th Cong., 2d Sess. (Serial 300), p. 27; *Senate Journal*, 24th Cong., 2d Sess. (Serial 296), pp. 49, 63, 268, 271–272.
[24] *House Journal*, 24th Cong., 2d Sess. (Serial 300), pp. 292, 562–564; *Register of Debates*, 24th Cong., 2d Sess., XIII, Part 2, p. 1510.
[25] *House Journal*, 24th Cong., 2d Sess. (Serial 300), pp. 568–569; *Register of Debates*, 24th Cong., 2d Sess., XIII, Part 2, p. 2093.

possible. Giving the boys the education he proposed would fit them for the duties of civil life as well as for those of a sailor. The House then voted down this amendment.[26]

The naval apprentice bill was passed by the House on March 2, 1837, and signed by President Jackson that same day.[27]

Despite his long experience as Secretary of the Navy, as well as his influential position as Chairman of the Committee on Naval Affairs, and in spite of the endorsements by the President and Secretary Dickerson and the prompt action of the Senate on three occasions, it took Southard 32 months to get his apprentice bill passed – a measure which he had recommended nearly nine years before! The stumbling block was the House of Representatives.

The naval committee of the House (which was predominantly northern in composition) seemingly had little interest in a naval apprentice bill unless there was a similar measure for the merchant service. Once such a bill was under way in the Senate, Jarvis, of the House naval committee, seemed quite willing to have the House pass the Senate's naval apprentice bill without amendments. Indeed, Jarvis and others successfully resisted the attempts to add provisions relating to the merchant service or to make the Navy's educational responsibilities more specific.

The bill finally passed simply authorized the enlistment with parental consent of boys between the ages of 13 and 18 years, who were to serve until they reached the age of 21 years. Other sections of the law extended the term of enlistment of the regular class of sailors to five years and dealt with the problem of detaining men beyond their term of service and of returning them to the United States.[28]

If keeping the bill simple made it easier to pass, it also laid the foundation for future difficulties. Within a short time Navy officers found it necessary to explain to parents that the receiving vessels or naval yards where the apprentices were collected were not intended to be similar to the facilities at West Point. Furthermore, the purpose of the program was to produce trained sailors, not midshipmen! The Navy regulations governing the apprentice pro-

---

[26] *Ibid.*

[27] *House Journal*, 24th Cong., 2d Sess. (Serial 300), pp. 592, 603; *Senate Journal*, 24th Cong., 2d Sess. (Serial 296), pp. 315, 321, 323, 326.

[28] *U.S. Statutes at Large*, V, Chap. 21, p. 153.

gram made this quite clear, but it would seem that many parents had little factual knowledge of the program.[29]

To meet this need and to help the harried recruiting officers *The New York American* printed the regulations in the fall of 1838. In Washington *Niles Register* did the same.[30]

These regulations were quite comprehensive and offered an opportunity to implement the law to the fullest possible extent.

In addition to meeting the aforementioned age requirements, apprentices were required to have a parent sign their shipping articles, or, if this were not possible, to execute duplicate certificates of assent before a justice of the peace or other magistrate. One of these copies went to the Secretary of the Navy; the other was sent to the commander of the receiving ship to which the boy was to be sent. Under no circumstances were the parents or the boy to receive any advance pay. Clothing and other articles necessary for comfort were to be issued to them when they arrived on board the receiving ship.[31]

At the time of their enlistment apprentices were to be rated as either second or third class boys, "according to their age, size and qualifications." Pay for a third class boy was $5.00 a month; $6.00 a month for a second class boy; and for those promoted to first class, $7.00 a month. None of this money was to be paid to the apprentice until he was discharged, except for clothing, necessities, and "small expenses" while on liberty. If his rating would allow it, a boy could allot a small amount of his pay to his parents. But he must have at least $6.00 a month for himself.[32]

In the event that a boy possessed special talents to be a boatswain, a gunner, or a master, this fact was to be reported to the Secretary of the Navy, and the boy's commanding officer was to give him all the proper facilities for instruction.[33]

Commanders of vessels in which apprentices served were to instruct them in reading, writing, and arithmetic, and to employ them in duties which would give them a thorough knowledge of seamanship and best qualify them for the duties of seamen and petty officers. They were never to be required or permitted to at-

---

[29] *Niles Register*, Sept. 8, 1838, p. 24.
[30] *Ibid.*   [32] *Ibid.*
[31] *Ibid.*   [33] *Ibid.*

tend the officers as waiters or servants whenever there were "other persons" present who could properly perform such service.[34]

Apprentices were eligible for promotion to vacancies in the ship's company, but their advancement was to be gradual and regular: from third to second and first class boys, then on to landsmen, ordinary seamen, seamen, and petty officers. Similarly, if they were guilty of misconduct or a neglect of duty, they were subject to a reduction in rank.[35]

The apprentice boys were not to be allowed to draw the spirit ration nor to receive tobacco. Instead they were "to be encouraged and required, if possible, to abstain from the use of both." [36]

When discharged after his full term of service, an apprentice was to receive a certificate setting forth his service and time in each rating. It was also to contain an evaluation of his conduct, qualifications, and merits.[37]

If a former apprentice wished to reenter the Navy, he was to show this certificate of good conduct to the recruiting officer, who, if there were no objections on the grounds of health or other reasons, was to give the man preference over the recruits without previous service.[38]

At the expiration of their service, or at the time of their regular discharge, the apprentices were to receive the amount of wages due to them.[39]

Finally, it was pointed out that these regulations were subject to alteration and modification, as the Secretary of the Navy saw fit, and it was to be understood that they formed no part of the agreement between the United States and the other parties as set forth in the shipping articles.[40]

Long before the act was passed it was pointed out by individuals both in and out of the Navy that it would be dangerous to expose young boys to the bad example of older men. Concern also was voiced over giving the boys the ration of spirits. To avoid these pitfalls it was proposed that the apprentices be isolated and trained on special ships with handpicked crews.[41] Others made more gen-

[34] *Ibid.*   [36] *Ibid.*   [38] *Ibid.*
[35] *Ibid.*   [37] *Ibid.*   [39] *Ibid.*
[40] *Ibid.*
[41] *Army and Navy Chronicle*, II (June 1836), 358–359; III (July 1836), 34–36; *Senate Documents*, 25th Cong., 3d Sess. (Serial 340), III, Doc. 223.

eral suggestions that the Navy put its house in order before the boys were put aboard ships.

The Navy agreed that the boys should not have the spirit ration, and there seems to have been a genuine attempt to implement the previously mentioned regulations on the subject. As for keeping the boys separate from the regular crews, the Navy established school ships at the principal naval yards: the *Hudson* and the *North Carolina* at New York; the *Columbus* at Boston; and the *Java* at Norfolk.[42]

The press, particularly in New York City, gave enthusiastic support to the apprentice experiment, and it seemed well pleased with the progress of the boys.[43] But difficulties were in the making.

In effect the school ships were little more than receiving ships. Here boys ran the risk of being exposed to the bad example of some of their sailor teachers, or of other sailors due to their proximity to the naval yard, as well as of boys from their own ranks. Furthermore, once they had learned the rudiments of being a sailor, they saw active service on regular Navy ships. Captain Matthew C. Perry reported in 1839 that the boys on his school ship gave less trouble and were more dependable than the regular sailors. But he also admitted that the utmost vigilance of the officers was necessary to keep the boys from deserting and going into New York City.[44] Chaplain Charles Rockwell, who had 15 or 20 boys under his care during the course of a cruise, wrote that there were "few situations in which I would not place a boy, sooner than on board a man-of-war."[45] Similar feelings were expressed by the *Boston Journal* in March 1842. It argued that the apprentice boys must be separated from the regular seamen, placed on board their own ship, and instructed by a group of carefully chosen officers and seamen. It added that

if due attention was paid to the moral education of these apprentices, if parents had assurance that their sons would be subjected to no immoral

---

[42] Paullin, "Naval Administration . . . 1815–1842," pp. 630–637.

[43] A Gentleman of New York, *Remarks on the Home Squadron, and Naval School* (New York, 1840), pp. 17, 19–20, 22–27, 29–37.

[44] William E. Griffis, *Matthew Calbraith Perry: A Typical Naval Officer* (Boston, 1887), pp. 437–438.

[45] Charles Rockwell, *Sketches of Foreign Travel and Life at Sea* (2 vols.; Boston, 1842), II, 384–385.

influences, until their characters were fixed, we should find no difficulty in increasing the number of apprentices to almost any extent. But as long as the present system continues, who can wish to see a lad separated from virtuous associates at his school . . . and placed in that Pandemonium, the birth-deck [sic] of a receiving ship, there to remain long enough to be inducted into the vices of the most disgusting character — for, to the youthful mind, vice often assumes an aspect more alluring and fascinating than virtue, and its lessons are apt to remain indellibly [sic] stamped upon the heart.[46]

As clear and as well intentioned as the recruiting regulations were, they were apparently not well enough known, or perhaps not applied evenly enough to insure the success of the experiment. Between 1839 and 1844 about 1,500 apprentices were enlisted in the Navy.[47] Some of these boys turned out quite well, but in general the apprentice program was a disappointment. The reasons given are varied.

In the beginning it was said that the sons of good families enrolled as apprentices in the belief that they could earn a commission as a midshipman within a short period of time. When time proved otherwise, the seeds of discontent were sown. Discontent soon found its outlet in demands for discharge. When two of the apprentices on a ship were appointed midshipmen, the demands for releases grew louder and acquired political backing. Before long the pressure on the Secretary of the Navy was too great to be resisted. Large numbers of the boys were discharged; others deserted.[48]

Later it was said that the plan failed because the apprentices were recruited from large cities and came into the service with the vices of "wharf rats." Only a few were able to elevate themselves. Moreover, the majority of these boys were said to have been of

---

[46] *Boston Journal* quoted in *The Sailor's Magazine*, XIV, 223.

[47] David Henshaw to Representative Henry C. Murphy, Jan. 31, 1844, *Letters to Congress*, X, 183–184.

[48] White, *The Jacksonians*, p. 248; Paullin, "Naval Administration . . . 1815–1842," pp. 636–637; T[homas] G[oin] to James K. Paulding, Dec. 28, 1839, *Martin Van Buren Papers*, XXXVII, Library of Congress; Lieutenant S. Godon to William Short, Nov. 16, 1843, *Short Family Papers*, Box 45; Secretary of the Navy John Y. Mason to Representative William Parmenter, April 4, 1844, *Letters to Congress*, X, 214; Captain Stephen B. Luce quoted in Benson J. Lossing, *The Story of the United States Navy for Boys* (New York, 1880), pp. 375–378.

foreign birth or parentage, and this factor was at odds with the plan to build a force of native American seamen.[49]

The apprentice system also suffered as a result of the publicity attending the *Somers* affair of 1842. The *Somers* was a school ship engaged in carrying out an educational cruise for apprentices between Africa and the United States. During that cruise her commander, Captain Alexander Slidell Mackenzie, hanged a midshipman, a petty officer, and a seaman for a conspiracy to commit mutiny. Eleven other men, including at least one apprentice, were placed in irons to await trial. The incident, which was exciting enough in itself, became even more so when it was learned that the unfortunate midshipman was the son of the Secretary of War! Before the case was finished, the press and a good deal of the populace were convinced that three innocent men had been sacrificed because of the suspicious mind of one officer. Recent research has not altered this view despite the fact that Mackenzie has never lacked defenders.[50]

By the end of 1845 Secretary Bancroft reported that the apprentice plan had not been completely successful, but he believed that its failure was due to "defects of arrangement, and not from the system itself." He hoped "to revive it in a simple, unpretending form," and eventually to increase the number of qualified seamen. In the meantime he was happy to report that good men were being obtained from the merchant service.[51] Unfortunately, Bancroft left office before his plans for a revitalized apprentice program could be carried out. It remained for Secretary Dobbin to revamp the program in 1855, after which it operated fairly successfully on a selective basis down to the Civil War.

---

[49] The *New York Times* reprinted in *The Sailor's Magazine*, XXXII, 103; Rockwell, p. 384.

[50] A recent work on the *Somers* affair is Frederic F. Van de Water, *The Captain Called It Mutiny* (New York, 1954). Mr. Van de Water is a descendant of a 17-year-old sailor who was imprisoned on board the *Somers* by Captain Mackenzie. See also Leon David, "An Episode in Naval Justice," *Case and Comment*, LXII (1952), 20. Secretary Upshur's involvement in the controversy is described in Claude Hall, *Abel Parker Upshur*, pp. 164–171. For a selection of documents pertaining to the case see Harrison Hayford, ed., *The Somers Mutiny Affair* (Englewood Cliffs, N.J., 1959).

[51] *Senate Documents*, 29th Cong., 1st Sess. (Serial 470), Doc. 1, pp. 653–654.

Closely related to the apprentice system was the plan for a home
squadron and boys' naval school. Under this plan boys from poor
families in the larger cities would be saved from lives of idleness
and crime by enlisting them as naval apprentices. Once they had
received their preliminary training on board a receiving ship they
would be assigned to a vessel of the home squadron. These vessels,
whose crews would be made up of boys, were to patrol our coasts
in order that the boys might practice seamanship. Such ships also
would be available to lend assistance to merchant vessels in distress.[52]

The outstanding advocate of this plan was Thomas Goin, a
notary and shipping broker with the firm of Goin, Poole and Pentz
of New York, who had long been engaged in the hiring of seamen.
His work made him keenly aware of the fact that there was a high
percentage of foreigners in the Navy, and he attempted to do something to remedy this situation. According to later newspaper accounts, he brought the idea to the attention of Congress, where a
bill passed the Senate but died in the House as a "consequence of
the 'panic' of 1832."[53] Neither the *Register of Debates* in Congress
nor the printed journals of the House and Senate substantiate this
statement. Goin's measure may have been the one identified as a
bill relative to naval schools which Pennsylvania's John C. Wat-
mough, a "Whig" member of the Committee on Naval Affairs,
reported to the House in January 1832. But this bill simply authorized the President "to increase the benefits of instruction now in
course at New York and Norfolk, and extend the usefulness of the
same to the navy yard at Charlestown, Massachusetts." Six thousand dollars was to be appropriated for this purpose. After a first
and second reading this bill was referred to the Committee of the
Whole House of the State of the Union where it apparently died.[54]

In any case, by 1835 Goin was in communication with Secretary
Dickerson concerning the scheme. Under Goin's supervision Henry
Eckford, the marine architect and shipbuilder, built a model of a

[52] A Gentleman of New York, pp. 15–16, 19.
[53] The *New York Herald* quoted in A Gentleman of New York, p. 20.
[54] *House Journal*, 22d Cong., 1st Sess. (Serial 215), p. 234; H.R. 305,
22d Cong., 1st Sess., Jan. 24, 1832, RG 233, NA; *Biographical Directory of
the American Congress*, 1774–1927, comp. by Ansel Wold (Washington,
D.C., 1928), p. 1673. "Whig" refers to a member's allegiance after the Whig
party was formally organized in 1834.

corvette of the type recommended for the home squadron. Goin entrusted the model to Captain A. D. Crosby of the merchant service, who presented it to Dickerson in Goin's name in the fall of 1835. The Secretary accepted the gift with thanks, placed it in a conspicuous place in his office, and assured Goin that it was admired by all the men skilled in shipbuilding who had seen it.[55] In December of that same year, in a reply to a letter from Goin, Dickerson referred to the project as a means of training officers and stated that it must be examined by the Navy Board before it could be adopted by the department. If the subject was to be brought before Congress, the department would be glad to furnish information concerning it.[56]

Late in 1836 Goin had a conversation on the subject with Representative John McKeon of New York just before the latter was to depart for Washington. Shortly after this he sent the congressman a petition from the merchants of New York City urging the establishment of a school ship at that port. McKeon presented this petition to the House in January 1837.[57]

At Goin's request Representative Ely Moore of New York in the winter of 1837 called up the notary's memorial relating to the home squadron and naval school in the Committee on Naval Affairs, which presumably made a favorable report on it.[58] But Congress apparently dealt with the proposals in a piecemeal fashion.

On December 22, 1837, Congress passed an act authorizing the President to cause "any suitable number" of the government's vessels to cruise along the coast during the winter season "when the public service will allow it," and to relieve distressed navigators.[59]

---

[55] Secretary of the Navy Mahlon Dickerson to Thomas Goin, Sept. 1, 1835, quoted in A Gentleman of New York, pp. x–xi. According to a later newspaper report, Eckford refused $40,000 for the model and presented it to Goin. A "British Agent" offered Goin $2,700 for the model of the school ship. See A Gentleman of New York, p. 24.

[56] Secretary of the Navy Mahlon Dickerson to Thomas Goin, Dec. 31, 1835, quoted in A Gentleman of New York, p. xi.

[57] Representative John McKeon to Thomas Goin, Jan. 21, 1837, Aug. 6, 1839, quoted in A Gentleman of New York, p. xi.

[58] Representative Ely Moore to Thomas Goin, Aug. 19, 1839, quoted in A Gentleman of New York, p. xii. I have found no record of these proceedings in the *Register of Debates* in Congress, the *House Journal*, or the *Congressional Globe*.

[59] *U.S. Statutes at Large*, V, Chap. 1, p. 208.

By this time the apprentice program had been enacted, but Goin continued to work for a regular home squadron and naval school. If this were done, the only reward he sought was the appointment as agent for this home squadron school, with the privilege of naming his own associate. This associate was an unnamed man who had formerly been associated with the press in New York City and who had written newspaper articles for Goin urging the adoption of his school and squadron system.[60] A number of these articles, as well as correspondence on the subject, were published in book form in 1840 under the title *Remarks on the Home Squadron, and Naval School.*

In the preface of this work an attempt was made to bring home to the reader the fact that the boy apprentices required a special type of handling. The management and manner of instruction in the various ships and naval yards should be as uniform as possible. Discipline should be "as parental as is consistent with good order." No punishment should be resorted to that is "in the slightest degree degrading to the individual," and expulsion should be considered as the greatest disgrace. Everything should be done "to encourage a high spirit of independence," and to stimulate that chivalry which will make him face danger and death when his country's call requires it. For "where the spirit is broken by corporal punishment, or by degrading menial offices, the moral influence of the School Ship is lost, and high spirited boys will become reluctant to enter." [61]

Congress finally authorized an appropriation for a home squadron on August 1, 1841. It was to consist of two frigates, two sloops, two small vessels, and two armed steamers.[62] This was to be about as close as Goin could get to seeing his scheme adopted. The Home Squadron lasted until the outbreak of the Civil War, but it was an operation of the regular naval force.

Meanwhile Captain Matthew C. Perry had been looking for

---

[60] T[homas] G[oin] to Secretary of the Navy James K. Paulding, Dec. 28, 1839, *Martin Van Buren Papers*, XXXVII, Library of Congress. Goin was given the rank of master in the Navy on Nov. 23, 1839. See Edward W. Callahan, ed., *List of Officers of the Navy of the United States and of the Marine Corps, from 1776 to 1900* (New York, 1901), p. 222.

[61] "Introductory Remarks," in A Gentleman of New York, p. x.

[62] *U.S. Statutes at Large*, V, Chap. 4, pp. 438–439.

some way to dramatize his success in training apprentices. He wanted to send a crew of them on a long voyage under picked officers. The launching of the brig *Somers* in April 1842 provided him with an ideal vessel. After a conference with Secretary Upshur, it was arranged that the ship would take a crew of apprentices on a cruise to Africa. Perry's brother-in-law, Commander Alexander Slidell Mackenzie, was given the command of the ship. Two of Perry's sons, Matthew C., Jr., and Oliver Hazard, were assigned to the ship as sailing master and captain's clerk, respectively. The crew numbered 120 men, 9 of whom were ordinary seamen and 99 apprentices.[63]

As has already been noted, the cruise of the *Somers* ended in tragedy. Mackenzie's subsequent court-martial brought out the fact that there had been a good bit of flogging on board the ship, though in the case of the boys a lighter version of the cat-o'-nine-tails and a light rope, or colt, were used.[64]

But of more importance was the way in which the alleged conspirators had been treated. Public attention was directed to the fact that Mackenzie's actions constituted an abuse of authority and a flagrant disregard for the forms of law. Three men had been executed without a trial! The commander's acquittal by a Navy court-martial helped to advertise the fact that there was much that needed overhauling in that service.[65]

Those who were shocked by the *Somers* incident, and who sought reasons for the failure of the apprentice program, would have done well to contemplate the words that Navy veteran William McNally published in 1839. McNally was especially irked by the reports of past Secretaries which indicated that the Navy was popular with seamen. It was far from the truth, he wrote. Most Americans joined the service only as a last resort, and foreigners were attracted to it only because of pay. He estimated that there were about 120,000 seamen in the United States, and it was only

[63] Griffis, pp. 438–439; Van de Water, p. 38; David, "An Episode in Naval Justice," p. 20.

[64] Van de Water, pp. 48–52.

[65] *Ibid.*, pp. 130–148; David, "An Episode in Naval Justice," p. 25; Fletcher Pratt, *The Navy: A History* (Garden City, N.Y., 1941), pp. 236–238. President Tyler refused to sign the verdict of this court martial and Mackenzie did not get another command until the Mexican War. He died in 1848.

with the greatest difficulty that the Navy could get 3,000 men annually. "Say, fellow citizens," asked McNally, "can the government be popular which is opposed by nineteen-twentieths of the people?" He criticized past Secretaries for deceiving Congress as to the true condition of the Navy until it was almost too late. Evils had been entrenched so long that it would take many years to eradicate them. McNally pointed out that when citizens feel that they have been wronged they appeal to Congress for a redress of grievances. Citizens also petitioned Congress "for the abolition of slavery in the southern states"; but they do not know that their seamen "are in a worse condition than the swarthy brood of Africa." [66]

While waiting for the bright tomorrow which he hoped the apprentice system would bring, the Secretary of the Navy still faced the problem of manning the ships then in service. In an effort to attract more men, Secretary Paulding authorized the payment of a bounty of $30.00 for every seaman who entered the Navy. This was given in lieu of advance wages. McNally considered the plan foolish because men shipped from necessity, and as the amount of bounty was less than the three months' advance, there was less of an inducement to enlist.[67]

On July 1, 1839, a little more than two years after the adoption of the apprentice system, new regulations governing the recruiting service were issued. No radical changes were introduced, but the aim seemed to be to tighten up existing procedures. Several points in these rules offer interesting insights into the recruiting conditions of the day.

The regulations stated that the commanding officer of a rendezvous was expected to be in daily attendance "morning and evening and to personally question the persons offering to enter, examine their qualifications and determine whether they may enter or not and in what capacity or rating." No landsman over 25 years of age was to be enlisted unless he had a knowledge of a mechanical trade, and even then he must be under 30 years. To be shipped as an ordinary seaman a man needed at least two years' experience. Five years' experience was needed to qualify for the rank of seaman.

---

[66] McNally, pp. 18, 50, 52–53.
[67] *Ibid.*, p. 60.

Shipping articles were to be read to each man before he signed them. No one was to sign them while intoxicated. Officers were forbidden to enter any person known to have been convicted of a felony. Advance wages were to be paid only to those entitled to receive them. Newly recruited men were to be encouraged to go aboard ship as soon as possible and to receive their advance in clothing and other necessary items. When an advance was made, the recruiting officer was to see that the man furnished himself "with one good suit of thick clothing, two frocks or shirts, a pair of shoes, a pair of stockings, hat and handkerchief as nearly of the navy pattern as possible, or as many of these articles as can be procured with two thirds of their advance, and that the articles are to be sent on board with them." [68]

Such regulations were surely a step in the right direction, but to the humanitarians and other reformers it seemed like a very small step. The persistence of complaints about conditions in the Navy could not fail to give an interested citizen the impression that virtually the entire naval establishment needed overhauling. But with various groups agitating for pet reforms, he might well be confused as to what to do first. Congress seems to have suffered from such confusion from time to time, and in the midst of such a dilemma could be easily influenced to postpone consideration of a particular matter at hand. But in spite of the diversity of these calls for reform, nearly all of the agitation touched a central theme — a theme that later generations would call morale.

The editors of *The Sailor's Magazine* believed that a new day began for the Navy when flogging was abolished in 1850. It was their conviction that a better class of men would now enter the service and many of the personnel problems would decrease.[69]

This spirit of confidence was not shared by naval officers such as Commander W. F. Lynch. He opposed corporal punishment but felt that three things should have been done before flogging was abolished. These were (1) the reintroduction of the apprentice system; (2) a pay increase for the crews and the exclusion of

[68] Recruiting Service Regulations, July 1, 1839, *NR-Naval Personnel Recruiting and Enlistments*, Box 1.
[69] *The Sailor's Magazine*, XXIII, 83.

foreigners from our ships; and (3) an increase in the Marine guards on board ships.[70]

Secretary Kennedy felt obliged to devote a large segment of his report for 1852 to the subjects of the recruitment, organization, and discipline of seamen. Much concern was felt by the Secretary about reports of disorder that allegedly resulted from the abolition of flogging without providing a substitute. He asked for a corrective measure.[71]

On the subject of manpower he pointed out that the legal limit of 7,500 men was insufficient to discharge existing obligations, and he asked for an increase of 1,500 men.[72]

As a means of holding good men in the Navy, Kennedy proposed that at the end of a voyage every commanding officer submit to the Secretary a muster roll of his men with remarks on their deportment. Those whose conduct made them valuable to the service were to be specially designated, and the Secretary would submit their names to the President. Before being discharged every man singled out for praise would receive a parchment certificate, signed by the President, commending him for his conduct. Those awarded this certificate would sign a book on board the ship and be designated as registered seamen of the United States Navy. Registered seamen were to be entitled to such privileges as (1) the right to wear a special badge designated by the Navy Department; (2) an additional dollar a month for every five-year period of service; (3) the privilege of resigning their posts any time after three years of service unless on a cruise; (4) exemption from corporal or degrading punishments (minor infractions were to be punished by stopping rations; punishment for major infractions would be as a court-martial directed); (5) a furlough for every three-year period of service to enable them to make "one or more voyages in the merchant service, not extending, without special permission, to more than six months"; and (6) as far as convenient, petty officers were to be drawn from the ranks of the registered seamen.[73]

---

[70] Commander W. F. Lynch to Brevet Brigadier General Archibald Henderson, U.S.M.C., July 30, 1852, *Senate Documents*, 32d Cong., 2d Sess. (Serial 659), Doc. 1, pp. 602–603.

[71] *Ibid.*, pp. 312–314.

[72] *Ibid.*

[73] *Ibid.*, pp. 315–318.

It was also Kennedy's hope to enlist a limited number of boys who would serve until they reached the age of 21. Each ship could have its quota, and the rules governing these boys would be laid down by the Navy Department. Kennedy pointed out that the proposed system would create a more effective naval force and hinted that it could be implemented at once. "There already exists power in the Executive to adopt nearly the whole of its details." But it might be proper to submit it to Congress in order to give the measures the force of law. This was especially true in regard "to the establishment of the registry which constitutes the groundwork of the plan."[74]

Kennedy's ideas deserved more attention than they apparently received, and recruiting remained a problem. Two months after taking over the Navy Department, Secretary Dobbin issued an order authorizing the payment of a bounty of $30.00 for every able seaman, and $20.00 for every ordinary seaman who enlisted. The bounty provisions promulgated by Kennedy were to apply only to those who entered the service before June 1, 1853.[75] Dobbin knew that money alone would not build a strong enlisted force, and like his predecessor he set about planning a long-range program.

As Dobbin saw it, permanent enlistments would be encouraged and the character of the enlisted personnel would be raised if they were given a goal to strive for. He suggested that at the end of a cruise the sailors be given an "honorable discharge" which would be considered as a leave of absence with pay if they reenlisted within a certain length of time. Officers would submit lists of those honorably discharged to the Navy Department where a registration list of regular Navy men would be compiled. He reminded Congress of Kennedy's worthy proposals and suggested that a pay increase would supply an additional incentive. First class seamen should be paid as much as they could earn in the merchant service. Bounty payments had been used as a temporary measure and would be ended soon.[76]

Dobbin also called the attention of Congress to the fact that his

---

[74] *Ibid.*, p. 318.
[75] General Order, May 23, 1853, *Circulars and General Orders*, II, 287–288.
[76] *Senate Documents*, 33d Cong., 1st Sess. (Serial 692), III, Doc. 1, pp. 314–318.

predecessors had long urged the adoption of a new code of Navy regulations, and the need was still acute. He emphatically opposed the restoration of flogging but urged congressional action to legalize a substitute. Lazy seamen could be punished by forfeiting pay, by confinement, and by a reduction in rations. The forfeited pay of laggards and deserters would constitute a "merit fund" which would be divided among the faithful sailors at the end of a cruise. Meritorious seamen also would be rewarded with liberty and shore privileges.[77]

In July 1854, Dobbin outlined his plan for a comprehensive wage increase to George S. Houston, the Chairman of the House Committee of Ways and Means. Under the present wage rates, Dobbin said, it was not possible to man the Navy. It was absolutely necessary to raise the pay in order to place the service "on a footing with the private enterprise of the Country" and "to present stronger inducements" for men to enter. He proposed an addition of 33⅓ per cent to the present rates and included this increase in his estimate of expenses for the coming year.[78]

Dobbin got his raise, and in his annual report, written at the end of 1854, he expressed the gratitude of the Navy for what had been done. He urged "with deep solicitude" the adoption of his earlier suggestions in regard to discipline, the honorable discharge, and an increase in the Navy. He pressed for a reorganization, for an additional 2,500 men, and for a modified apprentice system.[79]

Appeals from the Navy Department were not new, but Dobbin had reason to be optimistic. Slowly Congress was turning out some important naval legislation. This was no doubt due in part to the existence of a crisis between the United States and Great Britain during 1855–56. At any rate, the cause of naval reform took a step forward on March 2, 1855, with the passage of an act to provide for more efficient discipline. Among other things, this law provided for the honorable discharge system, for leaves of absence, for a reenlistment bounty, and for summary court-martial procedures. This law was then implemented by Dobbin's general order of

---

[77] *Ibid.*
[78] Secretary of the Navy James C. Dobbin to Representative George C. Houston, July 13, 1854, *Letters to Congress*, XII, 474–475.
[79] *Senate Documents*, 33d Cong., 2d Sess. (Serial 747), II, Doc. 1, pp. 393–396.

April 7, outlining the procedures to be followed in reenlisting men with honorable discharges.[80]

Three days before this, on April 4, Dobbin issued a circular authorizing the payment of a bounty of $15.00 to all ordinary seamen and $20.00 to all able seamen who enlisted for three years' service within the next 60 days.[81] Dobbin was doing his best to get the new system under way on as broad a basis as possible.

Commenting on these bounty provisions, *The Sailor's Magazine* observed that men could be secured in this way but they would be neither the best nor the second best men. The better types would and should not enlist where "they will be exposed to the degrading influence of the grog tub." If Congress would remove this, parents and guardians would feel that their boys were "comparatively safe" in the Navy.[82]

Dobbin also went forward with plans for the new apprentice system. Regulations issued on April 14, 1856, specified that the boys must be between the ages of 14 and 18 and were to be rated as second or third class boys according to their age and abilities at the time of enlistment. As soon as practicable, boys were to be advanced in ratings after passing an examination. Their pay ranged from $8.00 per month for third class to $10.00 per month for first class. One-quarter of this monthly pay was to be put aside for the boy until the end of his enlistment. In addition, he also drew money for the spirit ration which was forbidden to him. No apprentice was to be allowed shore leave in a foreign port unless accompanied by a petty officer or a "steady and exemplary seaman." By these and other rules the Navy Department hoped to safeguard the environment of its young charges and eventually to raise the caliber of its entire enlisted force.[83]

By the end of 1855 Dobbin was able to report that while enlistments were not as numerous as desired, the department was having

---

[80] Sprout, pp. 144–145; *U.S. Statutes at Large*, X, Chap. 136, pp. 627–629; *Circulars and General Orders*, II, 306–308.

[81] No copy of this circular has been found, but the above information is in a letter of Secretary of the Navy James C. Dobbin to Purser W. B. Stockton, August 30, 1855, in NR-*General Orders, Regulations, etc., Relative to Recruiting for the U.S. Navy*, Box 1, RG 45, NA.

[82] *The Sailor's Magazine*, XXVII, 283.

[83] *Circulars and General Orders*, II, 309–313; *The Sailor's Magazine*, XXVIII, 49–51.

no difficulty in meeting its commitments. In the six months preceding the passage of the act establishing the honorable discharge only 896 men had been enlisted. Six months after it was passed, 2,816 men had been signed on. Dobbin willingly admitted that other factors may have combined to produce this result, but a gain of 1,920 men was certainly worth noting. Nor was this all; this gain was made at a time when the large naval powers of Europe were very active in recruiting and when the higher wages and shorter cruises of the merchant service offered keen competition.[84]

Dobbin also reported his satisfaction over the working of the apprentice system. Five hundred boys were enlisted, and the department had another one hundred applications on file. But he intended to move cautiously and to pick the boys as carefully as possible. Officers of the Navy expressed their approval of the boys' progress. Commodore Hiram Paulding no doubt echoed the sentiments of many of the reformers when he wrote Dobbin that he hoped the system was "but a beginning of a new order of things in the navy," and that eventually it would be manned by men "conspicious for their energy and cheerful subordination," as well as for their love of the flag.[85]

Lieutenant William Porter was equally enthusiastic. "I am of [the] opinion that nothing more is wanted to place our navy in the most perfect state of discipline as regards the men." Knowledge of the punishments for violating the regulations and of the reward of an honorable discharge made them do their duty well. Crews were allowed shore leave at every port and with one or two exceptions returned to the ship clean and sober. Most of the offenses committed on board his ship were not serious, and summary courts-martial were necessary only three times.[86]

In view of this happy state of affairs Dobbin again urged that the Navy be expanded to a force of ten thousand men.[87]

A year later Dobbin's report contained news of the continued good effects of the recent naval legislation. He was happy to point out that the records of his department confirmed the fact that there

---

[84] *Senate Executive Documents*, 34th Cong., 1st and 2d Sess. (Serial 812). Doc. 1, p. 15.
[85] *Ibid.*, pp. 16–17.
[86] *Ibid.*, p. 17.
[87] *Ibid.*

had indeed been an improvement in the number and character of the seamen. Now and then there was still a complaint from men detained on foreign stations beyond their time, but sometimes these detainments were necessary, and, if so, the men were paid for their extra time. Nevertheless, he believed that the cruises should be shortened to two years, and he had issued orders to that effect.[88]

The supply of apprentices was still greater than the demand. Dobbin believed that the gradual improvement of this system was "the surest *means* of making a *radical improvement*" in the Navy, and the only mode for incorporating a fair percentage of native-born Americans into the service. As a means of encouraging the apprentices he advised the passage of a law giving the President the authority to appoint annually ten of the "most meritorious" apprentices as midshipmen at the Naval Academy.[89] Such an act would appeal to many Americans as being in keeping with the best of our traditions. Here were the potentialities of the success story of the rise of a poor boy to the station of a distinguished officer.

On the last day of the Pierce administration Congress authorized an increase in the enlisted strength of the Navy by one thousand men. Dobbin's successor, Isaac Toucey, apparently had no difficulty in securing the men, but he increased the proportion of landsmen and boys on ships in an effort to overcome the shortage of Americans and to train inexperienced hands. The experiment with two-year cruises was continued partly as an economy measure and partly as a means of stimulating enlistments. Toucey favored the building of a larger naval force and the improvement of its shore facilities, but for a time the effects of the panic of 1857 induced him to be content with urging only the immediate needs of the service.[90]

In spite of everything the naval force was kept busy. In his report for 1858 Toucey boasted that "at no period when we were not

---

[88] *Senate Executive Documents*, 34th Cong., 3d Sess. (Serial 876), Doc. 1, pp. 414–416.

[89] *Ibid.*, p. 416.

[90] *U.S. Statutes at Large*, XI, Chap. 3, pp. 243–244; *Senate Documents*, 35th Cong., 1st Sess. (Serial 921), IV, 584; *ibid.*, 2d Sess. (Serial 977), IV, 8–9; *ibid.*, 36th Cong., 2d Sess. (Serial 1080), III, Part 1, p. 5.

actually engaged in war has the navy been more actively employed than during the past year."[91]

The Navy's experience with the new apprentice program had been so pleasant that a similar plan was tried in the Marines. A proviso in the appropriation act passed in June 1858 authorized the Marine Corps to enlist boys between the ages of 11 and 17, with their parents' consent, to serve until they were 21 years of age.[92] More and more the naval service was staking its future on the youths that it could train as it saw fit.

In 1859 the *New York Times* proposed that each year from two to four boys between the ages of 14 and 16 be taken into the service from each congressional district to serve as naval apprentices. When they reached the age of 21 they would be appointed "third class United States seamen" by the Secretary of the Navy. These appointments would be given on the same terms as officers' commissions, namely, during the pleasure of the appointing power or during good behavior. A seaman could resign his appointment, but a court-martial would be necessary to deprive him of it. At the end of a cruise he would have a leave of absence at reduced pay. The plan would, in general, be parallel to the rights granted to officers. Third class seamen, ordinary seamen, and seamen would be paid $15.00, $17.00, and $19.00 a month, respectively. Promotions to the positions of petty officer and warrant officer would be made from the ranks.[93]

In replying to this article an individual who signed himself "Viator" suggested that the advancement of apprentices should not be limited to the ranks of petty or warrant officer but that the highest stations in the Navy should be open to the boy who could qualify. "Viator" believed that a system of schools should be established for the education of those who had ability and merit. Here these gifted boys would learn such things as languages and international law. He predicted that if this plan were followed, within "less than half a generation there will be a set of men and officers that will be full of the spirit of the service."[94]

---

[91] *Senate Documents,* 35th Cong., 2d Sess. (Serial 977), IV, 16.

[92] *U.S. Statutes at Large,* XI, Chap. 153, pp. 318–319.

[93] The *New York Times,* reprinted in *The Sailor's Magazine,* XXXII, 104–105.

[94] *The Sailor's Magazine,* XXXII, 143.

When the Civil War began, the strength of the Navy was 7,600 men. After his call for volunteers for the Army, Lincoln decreed that the Navy be increased by 18,000 seamen who were to be enlisted for one to three years' service. Naval rendezvous were opened in all of the principal seaports, and one-year enlistments were offered to recruits. Men responded to their country's need. With one or two exceptions ships were manned almost as fast as they were armed and equipped. And even the delays never extended beyond three days. Secretary Welles proudly reported that "at no period of our history has the naval force had so great and rapid an increase, and never have our seamen come forward with more alacrity and zeal to serve our country." [95]

The recruiting rendezvous on the Atlantic coast and the Great Lakes made special efforts to attract fishermen and those engaged in coastal trade by means of a one-year enlistment. Instead they found themselves deluged with inexperienced men, many of whom were recent immigrants. This was particularly true in New York City. Reports of inefficient crews operating from there soon reached the ears of Secretary Welles. The result was the issuing of an order, applicable to the New York rendezvous alone, curtailing the enlistment of inexperienced men. A few days later a similar order forbade the enlistment of any more landsmen at Philadelphia. Both orders represented attempts to bring unemployed but experienced American mariners into the Navy. [96]

On July 24, 1861, Congress authorized a temporary increase in the Navy. This was followed by the act of August 5, authorizing additional enlistments. Under the terms of this act the Secretary was allowed to enlist for three-year terms or for the duration of the war the number of able seamen, ordinary seamen, and boys that "he may judge necessary and proper" to place the Navy on an efficient basis. [97] The Navy had come a long way. After having heard Secretary after Secretary plead for an increase in the force,

---

[95] Report of the Secretary of the Navy, *Senate Executive and Miscellaneous Documents*, 37th Cong., 1st Sess. (Serial 1112), pp. 92–93, 2; R. N. Scott et al., eds., *The War of the Rebellion: A Compilation of the Official Records of the Union and Confederate Armies* (130 vols.; Washington, D.C., 1880–1901), II, 146.

[96] Secretary of the Navy Gideon Welles to Speaker of the House Galusha A. Grow, July 13, 1861, *Letters to Congress*, XIII, 371–372.

[97] *U.S. Statutes at Large*, XII, Chap. 13, pp. 272–273; Chap. 50, p. 315.

Congress now authorized the Secretary to determine its proper size.

Under the pressure of the war Congress passed several acts designed to bring the Navy up to date. On July 5, 1862, a Naval Reorganization Act set up specialized bureaus. The establishment of the Bureau of Equipment and Recruiting was a tardy recognition of the needs and special problems of those engaged in manning the fleet. Flag Officer Andrew H. Foote, the first head of this bureau, was a man who had long been active in the cause of temperance in the Navy. The relationship of the grog ration to the Navy's manpower problems as it appeared to temperance reformers has been noted from time to time in this chapter. It was, then, rather appropriate that nine days after it established the recruiting bureau, Congress ended the spirit ration.[98]

The act of July 16, 1862, establishing and equalizing the grades of naval line officers, also contained some interesting provisions in regard to enlisted men. Seamen who had distinguished themselves in battle or by "extraordinary heroism in the line of their profession," might be promoted to acting master's mates or forward warrant officers, "as they may be the best qualified," providing they had the recommendation of their commanding officer, and the approval of the flag officer and the Navy Department. Men so promoted were to receive "a gratuity of one hundred dollars and a medal of honor" prepared by the department. This same law also provided that the President be allowed to make three appointments a year to the Naval Academy from the boys enlisted in the Navy. These boys must not be over 18 years and must have at least a year's service, six months of which was spent at sea.[99] Thus it came about that the suggestion of Secretary Dobbin became law. By making it possible for some men and boys to move from the ranks to officer grades, Congress had taken an important step in raising the sights, the goal, and the morale of the enlisted man. It is true that these laws applied to very few men, but holding out the possibility of commissions for even a few in the ranks was an important beginning.[100]

---

[98] Ibid., Chap. 134, pp. 510–512; Chap. 164, p. 565.

[99] Ibid., Chap. 183, pp. 584–585.

[100] In 1859, when a deficiency in the number of midshipmen allowed by law affected the discipline of the Navy, Toucey rated about 160 enlisted

Unfortunately for the Navy, the early rush to recruiting stations did not last. Service in the Navy did not hold the same appeal that Army service did. Regimental competition for recruits and the payment of state bounties often made it possible for a would-be recruit to secure very good terms. So many qualified sailors entered the Army that it eventually became necessary to transfer some of them to the naval service.[101] But in spite of shortages the Navy under Secretary Welles accepted its responsibilities and gave a good account of itself.

It is not within the scope of this book to relate the Navy's Civil War service. That has been done several times. It is rather to point out that by 1862 a great improvement had taken place in matters pertaining to enlisted personnel. The Navy's chronic shortage of men during most of the period covered by this work forced the Secretaries, the officers, and other interested individuals to study ways in which the situation might be improved. The rise of the humanitarian spirit in the late 1820's led to a critical examination of many aspects of nautical life by militant reformers. And though Navy people might disagree with the solutions proposed by the various reformers, they could not escape the fact that it was exceedingly difficult to man the Navy as it was then being run. The continued shortages of men and the bad publicity surrounding some courts-martial or abuses made the Navy vulnerable to charges that flogging, the spirit ration, exploitation, and poor pay kept worthwhile men from the service. As long as the Navy was short of men, the reformers had a lever to use for their cause. Attempts to remedy abuses in regard to discharges, to small stores, and to pay helped to make the continuance of flogging and the spirit ration all the more glaring. This was particularly true when the temperance spirit gained great headway in the rest of the country and when the growing antislavery spirit led to an increased interest in the conditions of labor of the Negro. Once this was done, the naval reformers had a telling point when they charged that the sailor was

seamen and landsmen as master's mates to do the duties of midshipmen. See Toucey's report in *Senate Executive Documents*, 36th Cong., 1st Sess. (Serial 1025), III, Doc. 2, p. 1142.

[101] *Official Records of the Union and Confederate Navies in the War of the Rebellion*, 1st Series, I, 9, 24–26; Howard K. Beale, ed., *Diary of Gideon Welles* (3 vols.; New York, 1960), I, 498–499, 545–548.

debased by liquor and flogged like a slave. The story of this movement against flogging will be related in the next chapter.

When the Secretaries, the officers of the Navy, and Congress
came to see that the future of the service depended on enlisting
American boys and training them for careers in the fleet, the naval
reformers won an important foothold. Virtually everyone agreed
that the apprentices should be isolated from bad influences and
governed by special rules. All agreed that the boys should not
draw the spirit ration. The humanitarians argued that the Navy
should put its house in order before taking in young boys. Proposals by Secretaries and officers to separate midshipmen and
apprentices for special training was a tacit admission of this. But
separated or not, the apprentice boys were less likely to receive the
severe floggings that the older hands did, and their exposure to
harsh discipline at an early age would make them less troublesome
as men. Flogging would eventually become necessary only in rare
instances. This idea went hand in hand with the arguments of
officers that foreigners received most of the punishments on board
ship. When the Navy staked its future on the youth of America, it
paved the way for the eventual abolition of flogging and grog, and
on the way gradually transformed the rank and file of individual
ships and yards into the nucleus of a career service.

**PART
FOUR**

THE QUEST FOR HUMANE DISCIPLINE

"Flogging a seaman was never productive of any benefit: if he is a bad man, flogging will not make him any better — if a good one, it will ruin him; for no man who has any pride, can feel otherwise than a slave, after he has been treated as one."

Seaman William McNally, 1839

THE USE AND ABUSE OF CORPORAL PUNISHMENT

ORIGINS AND BACKGROUND

The use of the lash as an instrument of punishment goes back to ancient times. The Mosaic law, the Gospels, and the annals of Rome testify to its use in a variety of forms. Its use on board ships probably stems from the fact that slaves were used to row the ancient galleys. At a later period danger, poor food, irregular pay, and harsh living conditions made it difficult to recruit good seamen, and ship complements often were filled from the dregs of society. During the reign of King Henry VIII of England one of his captains, Sir Peter Carew, described the crew of one ship as "a sort of knaves whom we could not rule." Letters from captains in the time of Elizabeth I reflect the troubles that they had with the "loose rable" [sic] and "common rogues" that were drafted on board. These men were savagely punished for every offense by flogging, keel-hauling, tongue scraping, or by being hung up with weights around their necks. Many of these punishments, such as flogging and keel-hauling, had no formal authorization under the law but were carried out under the orders of various commanders and had come to be considered as customs of the sea.[1]

---

[1] Charles N. Robinson, *The British Tar in Fact and Fiction; The Poetry, Pathos, and Humor of the Sailor's Life* (New York, 1909), p. 54.

During the rule of Cromwell there was a compilation by Parliament of the instructions of admirals in command. These first "Articles of War" were approved in 1661 during the reign of Charles II. The preamble of this act reads: "For the Establishing Articles and Orders for the Regulating and better Government of His Majesties Navies, Ships of War and Forces by Sea." It was "the first legislative code for the enforcement of discipline and punishment of offences in a standing navy, and the first positive enactment of military law to be found in the statute-book." [2] These rules were in force until 1749 when Parliament repealed them by the passage of a new set of articles. The new rules were entitled: "An Act for amending, explaining, and reducing into one act of Parliament, the laws relating to the government of his Majesty's ships, vessels, and forces by sea," and they became effective on December 25, 1749. This act was notable in that it contained many death penalties.

Neither the act of 1661 nor that of 1749 mentioned the lash or specifically authorized flogging. This authority was contained in various "Regulations, and Instructions" and "Rules of Discipline" which were issued from time to time after 1731 by the Lord High Admiral or by Commissioners acting in his name. These instructions were intended to make up for deficiencies in the acts of Parliament. Some time after the passage of the act of 1749 these additional instructions contained specific authority to flog seamen.[3]

British maritime rules and regulations were well known among the shipping interests in the 13 American colonies. English Common Law was the foundation of their legal codes. Thus, in October 1775, when the Continental Congress, acting on George Washington's suggestion, decided to establish a naval force for service during the American Revolution, it was but natural that they turned to British precedents for their regulations. The legal background of John Adams proved quite valuable when, as the head of the naval committee, he was called upon to draw up the laws that would govern the Continental Navy. His raw materials were the act of 1661, the act of 1749, and the "Regulations and Instructions Relat-

---

[2] Theodore Thring and C. E. Gifford, *Thring's Criminal Law of the Navy, with an Introductory Chapter on the Early State and Discipline of the Navy, the Rules of Evidence, and an Appendix Comprising the Naval Discipline Act and Practical Forms* (2d ed.; London, 1877), p. 42.

[3] Leo F. S. Horan, "Flogging in the United States Navy: Unfamiliar Facts Regarding Its Origin and Abolition," *U.S.N.I.P.*, LXXVI (1950), 970.

ing to His Majesty's Service at Sea, established by His Majesty's Council" which contained "Rules of Discipline and good Government to be observed on Board His Majesty's Ships of War." The latter source had gone through 11 editions as of 1772. The act of 1749 was then still in effect in the British service, but because it was quite verbose, Adams was inclined to borrow very little from it. The act of 1661, however, was quite succinct, and it appears that 14 of the articles of the Continental Navy were based on this source. Eighteen articles, including the authority to flog, were based on the British "Rules of Discipline." John Adams' version of this authority stated that "no commander shall inflict any punishment upon a seaman beyond twelve lashes upon his bare back with a cat of nine tails; if the fault shall deserve a greater punishment, he is to apply to the Commander in chief of the Navy, in order to the trying of him by a court-martial, and in the mean time he may put him under confinement." [4]

These articles were debated paragraph by paragraph in the Continental Congress and accepted. In December 1775 they were promulgated as the "Rules for the Regulation of the Navy of the United Colonies" which were in force throughout the American Revolution.

British and American disciplinary practices were also influenced by a series of mutinies in the British Navy in 1797. The first of these mutinies took place in April among the seamen of the Channel Fleet at Spithead on the south coast of England. A modern naval historian has described it as "a sit-down strike, the first of its kind," masterminded by unknown leaders who possessed great talents of leadership and organization.[5] Considering that it took place in the midst of the warfare growing out of the French Revolution, it was doubly dangerous. But the mutineers in presenting their demands soon made it clear to the authorities that they were still patriots, and promised that if a French force appeared the mutiny would end. Other interesting aspects of the mutiny were the discipline and restraint of the mutineers and the conservatism of the demands.

---

[4] *Ibid.*; "Rules for the Regulation of the Navy of the United Colonies," quoted in Gardner W. Allen, *A Naval History of the American Revolution* (Boston, 1913), II, 686–695.
[5] Michael Lewis, *The History of the British Navy*, Pelican edition (Harmondsworth, 1957), p. 186.

They asked for a pay raise (to a shilling a day thus putting them on the same basis as the Army); for back pay; for the end of short weights by ship's pursers; that they be served vegetables instead of flour when in port; that men be given shore leave within a limited boundary when a vessel was in harbor; that the sick be better cared for; and that the wounded continue to draw their pay until they were cured and discharged. The mutiny at Spithead ended when Lord Howe, the commander of the Channel Fleet, promised a redress of their grievances and a royal pardon for the mutineers. The sailors eventually got their chief demands, and troublesome officers who were responsible for some of the men's irritation were transferred.[6]

A second and much more serious mutiny took place in May 1797 among the seamen of the naval force in the Thames River estuary at The Nore in southeastern England. It was led by Richard Parker, a man who had the talents of a demagogue and who was influenced by the ideas of Thomas Paine. Parker had twice held a midshipman's commission in the Royal Navy which he lost through insubordination. He had also been a schoolteacher and had served time in debtors' prison before being caught up in the Royal Navy again as a result of Prime Minister William Pitt's Quota Act of 1795. Under Parker's leadership the mutiny at The Nore took on a political as well as economic and social tone. Patriotism and restraint, so evident at Spithead, were missing at The Nore. Mutineers made trouble in the neighboring towns, and there was talk of taking the ships over to the French. With press gangs, the Quota Acts, and impressments bringing men into the Royal Navy, and with poor pay, hazardous employment, and harsh discipline to contend with, there was much to foster discontent. Yet these conditions were not new and many of those exposed to the rigors of a sailor's life led equally hard lives on shore. Furthermore, changes were already on the way as a result of the Spithead mutiny. As the mutiny dragged on more and more seamen became disenchanted with Parker and his colleagues and deserted the cause. Parker

---

[6] G. E. Mainwaring and Bonamy Dobrée, *The Floating Republic: An Account of the Mutinies at Spithead and The Nore in 1797* (London, 1935), pp. 3–118; Conrad Gill, *The Naval Mutinies of 1797* (Manchester, 1913), pp. 3–93.

surrendered to the authorities and was subsequently hanged with 29 others.[7]

The third mutiny took place in September 1797 on board the British frigate *Hermione* while she was cruising off Puerto Rico. Brutalized by frequent and severe floggings, the crew rose up and killed their captain and nine other men. The ship was turned over to the Spanish authorities and was later recaptured from them by the British. Reward posters for the mutineers of the *Hermione* were posted throughout the Caribbean and the United States. A search for the guilty men went on for a decade. At least seven of the *Hermione's* men subsequently served on American merchant ships. One enlisted in the United States Navy but was turned over to British authorities. By 1806 the last one of the 24 men hanged for mutiny had been executed. Another man was transported, two turned King's evidence, and three were acquitted. But more than 100 others, including one American and some leaders of the mutiny, were never caught. This was a matter of concern in both the American and British naval circles. From a British point of view, another disturbing bit of news came from Lord McDonald following his visit to the United States in 1800. McDonald reported that many Americans were elated by the news of the mutinies in the fleet and on board the *Hermione*, and attributed them to the work of Americans who had been impressed into the British service. He also wrote that members of Congress, including ex-Representative John Marshall who was then serving as the Secretary of State, had argued that impressed American seamen had a right to mutiny.[8]

There were other incidents of mutinous behavior in the British Navy during this period, and an insubordinate spirit prevailed until 1800 when it was stamped out. Nevertheless, the uprisings

---

[7] Mainwaring and Dobrée, pp. 121–245; Gill, pp. 101–258, 261–296, 299–358. Brief accounts of the mutinies at Spithead and The Nore may be found in Michael Lewis, *The Navy of Britain*, pp. 301–304, and in his work *A Social History of the Navy, 1793–1815* (London, 1960), pp. 124–127; Christopher Lloyd, *The Nation and the Navy: A History of Naval Life and Policy* (London, 1954), pp. 163–166; Dudley Pope, *The Black Ship* (Philadelphia, 1964), pp. 124–125.

[8] Pope, *passim.* Pope's book is a detailed study of the mutiny on the *Hermione*, its causes and results. The substance of the debates in the House of Representatives may be found in the *Annals of Congress*, 6th Cong., 1st Sess., X, pp. 511–512, 515–518, 531–532, 542–547, 548–578, 583–622. The remark of Marshall's referred to is on pp. 616–617.

had shown the authorities that seamen could and would unite to alleviate their grievances. The British sailor began to be treated with more respect and consideration. This approach to the men was reenforced by the example of such officers as Vice Admirals Horatio Nelson and Cuthbert Collingwood, who taught their juniors how to command.[9]

Soon after a regular American Navy came into existence Captain Thomas Truxtun, U.S.N., received word that several mutinous assemblies of seamen had taken place in 1798 on board the frigate *Constellation.* Truxtun responded by issuing an order which reviewed the pertinent regulations that were binding on all. He promised that he was always ready to hear complaints and to remedy injustices. As for the rules, he reminded the men of the United States Navy that: "The Seamen of Great Britain have sat [sic] such an Example of Infamy, that the Marine Laws of the United States, England, France, Spain, and Holland, as well as the Rest of the Maritime Powers of Europe, have been, and will still be made more severe in Consequence thereof." [10] Truxtun's firm but fair stand prevented any disorder.

The United States Navy was strongly influenced by the ideas of Truxtun, a strict disciplinarian. On the subject of punishments he wrote that

too great a disposition to punish where we have the power is not necessary either to facilitate business, or to keep alive good Subordination (The punishment among refractory Men Cannot be dispenced [sic] with) provided the deportment of an Officer is Correct, and where his temper is unhappily inclined, he Should Strive to Check it, as much as is Consistent with the Character of a Gentleman, for that Character Shoud [sic] never be Separated from the Officer.[11]

It deserves to be pointed out that there was relatively little flogging on board his ship.

While Truxtun was building *esprit* and discipline, Congress enacted three laws that were important to the subject of flogging in the Navy. The first of these was the act of July 1, 1797, which stated that the Navy was to be governed by the rules and regulations of 1775. By this action the Congress of the United States, like the

[9] Lloyd, p. 165; Lewis, *The Navy of Britain,* p. 304.
[10] *Quasi-War,* I, 157.
[11] *Ibid.,* p. 14.

Continental Congress before it, gave a legal sanction to the practice of flogging sailors. This was an action which no English Parliament had taken up to that time.[12]

In March 1799 Congress enacted a new set of naval regulations. These "Articles for the Government of the Navy" contained two changes in regard to the practice of flogging. The earlier regulations provided that any seaman who was guilty of swearing, cursing, or blasphemy was to wear a wooden collar or some other badge of disgrace. A man guilty of drunkenness was to be put in irons until sober. Article three of the regulations of 1799 stated that anyone guilty of "profane swearing, or of drunkenness" should be "put in irons until sober, and then flogged if the captain shall think proper." Under this act Congress authorized flogging for specific offenses for the first time.[13] A year later the article noted above was amended to read "put in irons until sober, or flogged" to prevent double punishment for the same offense.

Article four of the regulations of 1799 provided: "No commander, for any one offense, shall inflict any punishment upon a seaman or marine beyond twelve lashes upon his bare back with a cat of nine tails, and no other cat shall be made use of on board any ship of war, or other vessel belonging to the United States — if the fault shall deserve a greater punishment, he is to apply to the Secretary of the Navy, the commander in chief of the navy, or the commander of a squadron, in order to the trying of him by a court martial; and in the mean time he may put him under confinement." [14] The "other cat" referred to in the articles was the refinement of some British naval officers who made cats of wire or pickled regular ones in brine.

On April 23, 1800, Congress again amended the regulations of the Navy. The new "Act for the better government of the navy of the United States" authorized punishment by flogging for such offences as "oppression, cruelty, fraud, profane swearing, drunkenness, or any other scandalous conduct, tending to the destruction of good morals." Such offenses as sleeping on watch, performing an assigned duty negligently, or leaving a station before being relieved could be punished by death if the sentence of the court-martial

---

[12] Horan, "Flogging in the United States Navy . . .," p. 971.
[13] *Ibid.*
[14] *U.S. Statutes at Large*, I, Chap. 24, p. 709.

ordered it. If the offender were a seaman or noncommissioned officer, however, he might be placed in irons or given 12 lashes at the
discretion of the captain. A commander of a ship was forbidden to
inflict more than 12 lashes except under the sentence of a court-
martial; and a court-martial was forbidden to inflict more than
one hundred lashes, "for any one offence not capital." The law also
stated that no commanding officer was to "suffer any wired, or
other than a plain, cat-of-nine tails, to be used on board his ship."
Officers who commanded by accident, or in the absence of the commanding officer, were forbidden to order any punishment except
confinement, and were to give an account of this when their commander returned.[15]

Thus, in 1800 Congress gave to naval courts-martial the legal
right to flog a man with a cat-o'-nine tails up to one hundred lashes.
These articles on flogging were to remain in force for 50 years, and
the act of 1800 was not again revised until 1862. It was against these
regulations that most of the pre-Civil War agitators for various
types of naval reform contended. Each of the aforementioned laws
also contained specific instructions on the amount of alcohol that
was to be given to each man as a part of his daily ration. For many
naval reformers this issuing of liquor to sailors and the punishing
of them by flogging had a cause and effect relationship.

All of the aforementioned political, military, and legal considerations had a bearing on the type of discipline that was established in
the American Navy at the time of its birth. In both the Revolution
and the Quasi-War with France the Navy was established out of
necessity and at a time when the fighting was already in progress.
The needs of war called for strict discipline and instantaneous
obedience. The most important leaders of the early Navy had either
served in the British Navy or were civilians who were well versed
in maritime and admiralty law. At the time that the Navy was
established under the Constitution, the government was controlled
by the Federalist faction, which supported all naval measures despite the Hamilton-Adams split. The Federalists were great ad-
mirers of England and of the English method of doing things. This
predisposition to favor things English, plus the English heritage of
the colonies, as well as the fact that Britain was the greatest sea

---

[15] *Ibid.*, II, Chap. 33, pp. 45–46.

power, all tended to make us lean heavily on English practice in establishing a Navy for the United States. In addition, most of the seamen and officers were recruited from the coastal areas — areas of Federalist strength.

There was a feeling among the officers of the newly established Navy that the discipline of the Continental Navy had been much too lax. Truxtun and others felt that strict discipline was necessary in order to build a reliable fighting force, and they took steps to bring this about. Their task was made easier by the cooperation of the President, the Secretary of the Navy, and the Federalist majority in Congress. Our early naval officers and some of the politicians were concerned over the French Revolution and the way it had affected the French Army and Navy. They resolved that no such notions of *égalité* would find their way into the newly founded Navy. They took what they considered to be the best of British practice and modified it to suit American circumstances. The Federalist Congress enacted laws that would promote discipline and safeguard justice. Under a high type of naval officer such as Truxtun they hoped that there would be no abuse of authority. They prepared for the future by building ships, training young officers under experienced men, and establishing traditions of service and duty. They did their work well. The foundations which they laid endured in spite of the dislike of the Jeffersonians for a standing navy. The hostility of this group to most things naval no doubt prevented any realistic appraisal of the needs of the service, and, as a result, perpetuated abuses which began to excite public attention after the War of 1812.

ANTIFLOGGING AGITATION

Since flogging was sanctioned by law from the very beginning of the United States Navy, and since vivid descriptions of the practice helped to arouse public opinion against it, some notice of the ceremony and the instruments seems in order.

At the sound of the boatswain's pipe calling "All hands witness punishment, ahoy," the entire ship's company would assemble at the gangway on the spar deck. All the officers and midshipmen stood together near the mainmast; the first lieutenant and the ship's surgeon stood a little in advance of the group. The marines were drawn up in formation with fixed bayonets. The rest of the crew gathered about the area wherever there was room. When all were assembled, the captain would emerge from his cabin carrying a sheet of paper on which the offenses were listed. At an order from the captain the master-at-arms would escort the prisoner or prisoners to the scene. The charges and the rules of the Navy that affected the case were read. The prisoner was then questioned about the charges. Since a large percentage of the flogging was for drunkenness, the questioning usually resolved itself into an attempt by the captain to discover the source of the beverage. But whether the offense was drunkenness, fighting, or attempting to desert, seamen rarely implicated a shipmate. In cases where the man tried to defend his action he was often cut short by the captain. There also were cases reported where men were flogged without even knowing their offense. On rare occasions some captains would dismiss a man after hearing his defense. For most men, however, being reported by an officer was tantamount to guilt, and punishment was sure to follow.

When the questioning was over, the captain prescribed the number of lashes to be given by the boatswain. The prisoner was then stripped to the waist and his shirt laid loosely over his shoulders. Quartermasters prepared gratings for the punishment. These gratings were square frames of barred woodwork which were sometimes placed over the hatches. When a punishment was ordered, the quartermasters would place one of these gratings flat on the deck and close against the bulwarks. The quartermaster would then bind the prisoner's feet to the cross bars of the gratings. The prisoner's hands were raised above his head and tied to hammock nettings or rails overhead.

While all this was going on, the boatswain stood by and removed a cat-o'-nine tails from its special bag. If more than one man was to be punished, a fresh cat was brought for every prisoner. When the prisoner was secured, the master-at-arms, on a signal from the captain, removed the shirt from the victim's shoulders. At the captain's order the boatswain stepped forward, combed the tails of the cat with his hand, swung it around his neck and brought it down with his full force on the bare back of the prisoner. The efficiency of the boatswain was gauged to some degree by the quality of the notes that he blew on his whistle and the way that he swung a cat. As he whipped, the master-at-arms counted aloud the number of lashes. When the prescribed number were administered, the prisoner was cut down and returned to duty.

Some men were known to have taken 12 lashes without uttering a sound. It was said that old seamen became hardened to it. Others, particularly first offenders, suffered horribly. The lash was said to feel like molten lead on the bare back. The ship's surgeon did what he could for the victims, but often men were incapacitated for several days. The surgeon stood by during all floggings to see that the man was able to bear the lash. This was particularly true in cases where courts-martial would prescribe more than a dozen lashes. If the surgeon believed that a man could stand only a part of his punishment, the prisoner was cut down and made to stand the rest of his lashes at a time when his back was healed.

The plain cat-o'-nine-tails referred to in the regulations of 1800 consisted of nine small hard twisted cords of cotton or flax about eighteen inches long which were fastened to a wooden handle. At the end of each cord there was a hard knot or a pellet of lead. Small cats or "kittens" were sometimes used for flogging boys.

Another method of disciplining men for minor offenses was flogging with a "colt." The "colt" was a small, hard, twisted rope about the diameter of a man's forefinger and approximately three feet in length. These frequently were carried in the caps of deck officers and boatswain's mates and were used to "start" men in various duties of the ship. When a man was punished with a "colt," he was supposed to be whipped through his clothing. There were, however, instances where "colts" were used on the bare backs of seamen. The delegation of power to "colt" to subordinates by the captain was, of course, a direct violation of the rules and regulations of the Navy.[16]

In cases where more than one ship or a squadron was serving together in foreign waters, court-martial sentences of more than 12 lashes were sometimes carried out by the practice of "flogging 'round the fleet." This involved the carrying of the prisoner around

---

[16] Descriptions of floggings may be found in Holbrook, p. 85; A 'Civilian' [George Jones], I, 33–35, 50, 64, 214–216; Nordhoff, pp. 138–141; Rockwell, II, 407–410; Sellstedt, 137–138; Melville, pp. 127–132; George E. Belknap, "The Old Navy," *Naval Actions and History, 1799–1898* (Boston, 1902), p. 21. For a graphic analysis of the effect of a flogging see Pope, pp. 332–333.

the harbor in a small boat and inflicting a portion of his sentence at the side of every ship and in the presence of its crew. Such a spectacle was believed to be a good example to the seamen and to promote good discipline. The phrase and the practice were borrowed from the British, and in that service it was usually equivalent to a death sentence. We know very little about the practice in the American Navy, but it is said to have been used on rare occasions. For example, it is stated that in 1804, while a United States fleet was blockading Tunis, a court-martial held on board the frigate *Constitution* sentenced one John Graves to receive 300 lashes for desertion by being "whipped through the fleet."[17]

The men of the Marine Corps found themselves in a strange dual situation in regard to flogging. While on shore they considered themselves bound by Army laws and regulations which, after May 1812, prohibited flogging. But they were under Navy regulations while at sea and hence were liable to be flogged.[18]

The first recorded comment that flogging might not be the ideal type of discipline for the Navy came from an officer whose leadership contributed much to building its discipline — Captain Thomas Truxtun. Writing to the Navy Accountant in 1801 about his last cruise, Truxtun noted that he had saved the government a considerable amount of spirits. This was the result of his practice of punishing those guilty of offenses by stopping their daily ration of rum. Since most of the disciplinary problems on board were the result of drunkenness, stopping a man's grog "answers the purpose intended much better than public flogging, and is more humane, and not so degrading to man."[19]

Another early criticism of flogging in the American Navy came from a naval surgeon. In 1808 Dr. Edward Cutbush published a work on the means of preserving the health of soldiers and sailors in which he urged commanders to use "almost unlimited severity" to keep the men from indiscriminate sexual intercourse with women and from intemperance. But he also declared: "Though I confess myself an advocate for strict discipline, I by no means think

[17] *Durand*, p. 26.

[18] Edwin McClellan, *History of the U.S. Marine Corps* (1st ed.; Washington, D.C., 1925), I, Chap. 18, p. 19.

[19] Truxtun to the Navy Accountant, May 20, 1801, *Quasi-War*, VII, 230–231.

that corporal punishment is correct for *trifling* crimes, unless the delinquent be *incorrigible* by other means; but whatever the penalty be, that is attached to certain crimes, *that* penalty ought to be absolutely and justly inflicted; and *the necessity for it* will most assuredly *be less* frequent."[20] Rough treatment of men makes them despondent, inactive, and predisposes them to disease, Cutbush wrote. "Good *treatment* and indulgence to seamen cannot be too strongly inculcated." It would make men enter the service and make them do their duties "with alacrity and promptness." "Hence, with a man of sense, strict discipline will always be accompanied with indulgence and humanity, and they will regularly go hand in hand with it."[21]

A protest from a man in the ranks appeared in 1820 in *The Life and Adventures of James R. Durand.* Written by Durand himself, the narrative covers the period 1801–15, during which time he served in the U.S. Navy and was impressed and forced to serve seven years in the British Navy. Speaking of his service in the American Navy in 1804, he says: "I have seen a man hauled up and made to receive eighteen lashes for a crime no more serious than spitting on the quarter deck. Such outrages on human nature ought not to be permitted by a government which boasts of liberty."[22]

Other works published later in the nineteenth century and various letters and journals of the period tend to bear out Durand's descriptions of the hard life of the sailor and the fact that there were frequent violations of the laws of the Navy by various officers. By the end of the War of 1812 it was apparent that changes were necessary in the regulations of 1800. The correspondence of Secretary Crowinshield with various congressmen reflects this need. While there is no reference to flogging, the general subject of discipline seems to have been discussed. At any rate, in April 1818, the Secretary, with the assistance of the Board of Navy Commissioners, issued a set of "Rules, Regulations, and Instructions for the Naval Service." These rules outlined in great detail the duties of every commissioned and noncommissioned officer on a ship. Insofar as flogging was concerned, these regulations stated that captains were

---

[20] Cutbush, pp. 19–20. [22] Durand, p. 18.
[21] *Ibid.*, pp. 130–131.

to be bound by the act of 1800 and that they should supervise the punishment. They also stated that no men should be given long periods of confinement, except when awaiting a trial by court-martial, "nor be deprived for more than a week at a time of their grog, nor punished by a reduction of their allowance of provision, nor exposed for punishment to any uncommon hard work or services, to exposures that may endanger their health, or to any kind of torture, for any offense committed."[23] These rules were communicated to the House of Representatives but apparently never were acted upon. Nevertheless, they were generally observed in the Navy during the period of this study.

The year 1820 was notable in that it marked the beginning of discussions in Congress on the subject of flogging. On December 6, Samuel A. Foot, a Democrat from Connecticut, presented a resolution to the House requesting that the Committee on Naval Affairs be instructed to inquire into the expediency of abolishing flogging and also to provide a means of punishment for any naval officer or enlisted man who gave or accepted a challenge to a duel.[24]

Democratic Representative Samuel Smith of Maryland, a former major general of the militia and a defender of Baltimore in the War of 1812, said the measure as he understood it would destroy the efficiency of the Navy. Foot pointed out that the resolution proposed only an inquiry. Corporal punishment already had been abolished in the Army in 1812, and this inquiry would establish whether or not it should be continued in the Navy. At that point Smith moved to lay the resolution on the table, and his motion passed.[25]

Two days later Foot suggested that his resolution be reconsidered. A negative vote prevented this, and the House went on to consider problems relating to the admission of Missouri to the Union.[26] So ended the first attempt to have Congress reexamine the Navy's methods of punishment.

It is perhaps fitting to point out here that Foot had some acquaintance with the sea. As a successful shipping merchant in

---

[23] *American State Papers: Naval Affairs*, I, 520.
[24] *House Journal*, 16th Cong., 2d Sess. (Serial 47), p. 55.
[25] *U.S. Annals of Congress*, 16th Cong., 2d Sess. XXXVII, 506.
[26] *Ibid.*, p. 531; *House Journal*, 16th Cong., 2d Sess. (Serial 47), pp. 59–60.

the days before the Embargo, he occasionally made voyages in his own ships. Before his election to Congress he had been active in a movement for a new state constitution for Connecticut and had served in the legislature.[27] He had already manifested an interest in care for the deaf and dumb, and within a decade both he and his son, Andrew Hull Foote, were to express interest in the American Seamen's Friend Society and its work.[28]

In May 1826 Secretary Southard wrote to Richard S. Coxe, an attorney in Georgetown, D.C., asking him "to prepare and furnish to this Department, a digested System of Rules and Regulations for the government of the Navy, calculated to enforce discipline, and afford a precise definition and description of offences, and the regular administration of justice in the service." He added that there was no legal authorization for this work and that Coxe would have to run the hazard of not being paid, but that the department wished that "fit compensation" be made.[29] The writer has been unable to find any record of Coxe's report on this work, or any proof that he decided to undertake this task.

The following year Southard reported to President Adams that while the discipline, economy, and efficiency of the service were worthy of commendation, many evils that had been noticed in the past still existed. Those which were within the power of the Executive were removed, and the rest awaited legislative action. He felt that it was improper for him to present again his views on such needs as the "want of a regular organization; of a code of criminal law and regulations," but that duty impelled him to express his conviction that "discipline, economy, and efficiency" would be promoted by "judicious legal provision."[30]

One of the most interesting accounts of conditions in the Navy during this period is George Jones's *Sketches of Naval Life, with Notices of Men, Manners, and Scenery, on the Shores of the Medi-*

[27] Jarvis M. Morse, "Samuel Augustus Foot," *Dictionary of American Biography*, VI (1931), 498.
[28] *Annals of Congress*, 16th Cong., 1st Sess., XXXV, 885; *The Sailor's Magazine*, III, 98, 329; IV, 64.
[29] Secretary of the Navy Samuel L. Southard to Richard S. Coxe, May 26, 1826, *Samuel Southard Manuscripts*, Library of Congress. Coxe often acted as judge advocate for the government in court-martial cases. See H. W. Howard Knott, "Richard Smith Coxe," *Dictionary of American Biography*, IV (1930), 487–488.
[30] *Senate Documents*, 20th Cong., 1st Sess. (Serial 163), Doc. 1, p. 213.

terranean, which was published in 1829. Jones was a chaplain and schoolmaster on board the frigates *Brandywine* and *Constitution* during the years 1825 to 1828. He states that in winter a flogging generally took place every nine or ten days, while in the summer flogging was very rare. The reason was that in the summer the men had few opportunities for getting liquor. Drunkenness was a main cause of flogging. Jones felt that many men in the Navy would be assets to society if it were not for their addiction to alcohol. But unlike many chaplains he was not completely opposed to the daily ration of liquor given to the crew. If the men had to drink, it was much better that they drank in the disciplined environment of a warship than on shore.[31]

On board the *Constitution* it was a custom to confine the culprit for a week or two before bringing him before the captain. Some men were set free after this hearing, and occasionally a whole group would be pardoned, but most cases ended with a flogging at the gangway. Jones listed the various types of infractions and the customary punishments as follows:

Desertion — trial by court martial: the punishment severe.
Drunkenness — confinement in the brig or coal hole, either in single or double irons: perhaps gagged in the bargain: then usually a dozen before all hands.
Half corned — confinement from one to five days.
Sleeping on watch — half a dozen with the colt.
Not answering to name, } do.
when called on watch — }
Having dirty clothes; leaving clothes
lying about deck; sky larking (i.e., } grog stopped.[32]
engaging in rough play) at improper times — }

Jones admitted that in spite of the regulations a captain could multiply the charges against a seaman, but he himself knew of only one case where more than the legal dozen lashes were applied. He admits that he was sickened by the flogging that took place on the ship, particularly on Sunday, but he felt that it was a very necessary part of naval discipline. He also felt that the right to inflict the lash should be extended to the officers of the deck as they were the best judges of its need.[33]

As for the reactions of the seamen to flogging, he tells two stories.

---

[31] A 'Civilian' [George Jones], I, 214–215.   [32] *Ibid.,* p. 215.
[33] *Ibid.,* pp. 215–216.

First, he admits that there were men of "fine sensibilities" who "formed the best part of the crew" to whom a flogging was "a serious injury for life." He tells of a hard character who wept when he talked about flogging. Second, he tells the story of a conversation with an old sailor who was flogged one day for drunkenness and who was caught in the same condition on the following day. Instead of flogging him again the first lieutenant talked to him about his offense. The sailor, according to Chaplain Jones, declared that his feelings were hurt more by this talking to than "all the punishment in the world." "Talk'n is sometimes more punishment than flogg'n," said the sailor.[34]

Jones's mixed emotions on the subject of flogging apparently were not shared by Chaplain Edward McLaughlin, whose letter on the subject was printed in the December 1830 issue of *The Sailor's Magazine*. McLaughlin suggested that flogging be suppressed and other modes of punishment substituted; that there be no alcohol in any form on the ships (except medical supplies); and that an efficient chaplain be placed on every ship.[35]

In the spring of 1830 the New York *Daily Sentinel* ran a series of articles on "Abuses in the Navy" which were noted by *The Sailor's Magazine*, as were comments against flogging from various sources.[36]

Another early protest against flogging came from Chaplain Charles S. Stewart in his book, *A Visit to the South Seas*, published in 1830. Stewart wrote: "This mode of punishment is deemed by many indispensable on board a man-of-war; and it may be so — but as yet I am far from being reconciled, in feeling, to the necessity. To me there is an indignity and degradation in it, which seem inconsistent with the high-toned principles and spirit of Americanism; and independent of all other consideration, I never witness it without being tempted to ask Paul's question to the centurion, 'Is it lawful for you to scourge a man that is a Roman?'"[37] This protest was reprinted in *The Sailor's Magazine* in August 1831.[38]

---

[34] *Ibid.*, pp. 216–217.
[35] *The Sailor's Magazine*, III, 116.
[36] *Ibid.*, II, 280–281; III, 281.
[37] Charles S. Stewart, *A Visit to the South Seas in the U.S. Ship Vincennes, During the Years 1829 and 1830; With Scenes in Brazil, Peru, Manilla, Cape of Good Hope, and St. Helena* (2 vols.; New York, 1831), I, 30–31.
[38] *The Sailor's Magazine*, III, 367.

When the "Eaton Malaria" affair led to the resignation of Jackson's original cabinet, Levi Woodbury of New Hampshire became the Secretary of the Navy in May 1831. Woodbury was an able, industrious, and humane administrator. Furthermore, he had gained some knowledge of Navy matters as a result of his service on the naval committee of the Senate. Turning his attention to the relationship between liquor and punishments, he issued a circular on June 15, 1831, which stated that if any man in the Navy voluntarily relinquished his spirit ration he would receive payment for its value. Woodbury followed up this order by another circular on September 26, 1831 which declared that

till Congress deem it proper to alter the existing laws concerning punishments in the navy, and whenever those laws allow a discretion in the choice of punishments, the first resort, in the case of offences by seamen, is recommended to be always had to pecuniary fines, badges of disgrace, and other mild corrections, rather than to the humiliating practice of whipping; and that never on the same day, by punishing, under an officer's own authority, the two offences at once, should the stripes, limited by law, be exceeded in number, or be inflicted otherwise than in the presence and under the sanction of the commanding officer of the vessel or station.[39]

During that same month he issued an official circular which declared that subordination and authority were to be maintained "by humanity and kindness on one hand, and respect and implicit obedience on the other."[40]

Secretary Woodbury also issued a general order to commanders of naval yards directing them and the two other officers next highest in grade at their yards to inspect any vessel returning to the yard from a cruise, noting its "internal regulations and arrangements, discipline, health, and accomodations of her officers and men, and any other particulars deemed useful to the service." Reports on these inspections, together with the commander's opinions, were to be forwarded to the Secretary of the Navy.[41]

---

[39] *Circulars and General Orders*, I, 289. This circular is also reproduced in the annual report of the Secretary of the Navy; see *Senate Documents*, 21st Cong., 1st Sess. (Serial 216), Doc. 2, Appendix M-2, p. 265.

[40] Circular, September 1831, printed in *Rules of the Navy Department, Regulating the Civil Administration of the Navy of the United States* (Washington, D.C., 1832), p. 35.

[41] *House Executive Documents*, 21st Cong., 1st Sess. (Serial 233), Doc. 2, p. 229.

In the fall of 1831 the subject of naval discipline was brought to the President's attention by John Randolph of Roanoke. It all began when Randolph was sent on a diplomatic mission and traveled from Virginia to Russia on board the sloop-of-war *Concord* under the command of Master Commandant Matthew C. Perry.

Randolph was a strong-willed individual with some very definite ideas on the rights of men. While in Congress he had been instrumental in abolishing the use of the lash in the Army. He felt that the spirit of the militia man was such that he could not brook such a punishment. Now, as a representative of the State Department, he had some definite ideas about his own rank and importance in relation to that of the commander of the ship.

This was Perry's first command, and he had very definite ideas about the need for better naval training for officers and men. One indication of this was his request for a chaplain who would be competent to act as schoolmaster for the midshipmen. Now that he had a ship he was anxious to test his theories. American naval officers of the nineteenth century were inclined to be very touchy about matters of command and jurisdiction, and one can imagine that this might be particularly true in the case of a first command. When two such strong-willed individuals were thrown into close association for several weeks, the stage was set for trouble.

The first few weeks of any such voyage were spent in breaking in the newly shipped men. Before this adjustment was completed a considerable amount of flogging generally took place. Such was the case on board the *Concord*. During the course of the voyage between Hampton Roads and Portsmouth, England, Randolph observed some floggings and was so sickened by the spectacle that thereafter he fled to his cabin whenever one was in the offing. It was during this period that he apparently clashed with Perry over the management of the men, for Randolph says that he spent the time between England and Russia confined to his cabin, and chiefly to his bed. At any rate, at the end of his mission he wrote to Jackson that the scenes he had witnessed "were so revolting, that I made up my mind never to take passage again on board a vessel of War — at least with a newly shipped crew." The spectacle "surprised and shocked" his Negro slaves. He asserted that there was more flogging in three weeks on board the *Concord* than in seven years on the plantation among the same number of slaves. If he were in Congress, he would feel obliged to introduce a bill to abolish flogging in the Navy.[42]

Randolph's charges against Perry reached the Navy Department and prompted an inquiry. Perry and his officers sent a joint letter to the Secretary explaining their side of the story. This letter apparently satisfied the President and the Secretary, and the matter was dropped.[43] Perry's countercharges of interference would certainly hold much weight with any military man.

As far as discipline was concerned, Perry probably was no better and no worse than most of the American naval officers of the period. Nevertheless, it is interesting to compare Randolph's charges with a sailor's recollections of Perry as a lieutenant on board the *North Carolina* in 1824 under Commodore John Rodgers. James H. Garrison, the brother of William Lloyd Garrison, the abolitionist, wrote this memoir about 1840, but it was not published until 1954. Writing some 16 years after the events, he described several instances of Perry's cruelty. According to Garrison, Perry cursed, struck, and kicked men. "I have seen him come along the gangway and knock down men, giveing [sic] them a black eye, and then punish them for haveing [sic] same." Two men who were caught urinating on the deck were punished by stopping their grog, giving them 13 lashes each, and by ordering the master at arms to take them to the head and "fill their face and eyes with the excrescence of man and to rub it well in." [44]

On May 19, 1832, Congress passed an act authorizing the revision and extension of the Navy's rules and regulations. Under the terms of this law the President was to constitute a board of naval officers who, with the aid of the Attorney General, were to revise and enlarge the regulations in order to adapt them to the present and future needs of the service. These rules were then to be presented to Congress for enactment into law.[45]

---

[42] John Randolph to President Andrew Jackson, Oct. 24, 1831, in John Spencer Bassett, ed., *Correspondence of Andrew Jackson* (Washington, D.C., 1929), IV, 363–364; Edward M. Barrows, *The Great Commodore: The Exploits of Matthew Calbraith Perry* (Indianapolis, Ind., 1935), pp. 106–108.

[43] *Ibid.*

[44] Garrison, pp. 81–82, 85. The editor of this work, Walter McIntosh Merrill, believes that Garrison's accounts of cruelty apparently were inspired by his reading of William McNally's book, cited *supra*, p. 76 (see also pp. 153–154). See Merrill's comments, p. viii and notes on p. 87.

[45] *U.S. Statutes at Large*, IV, Chap. 80, p. 516.

Considering what had thus far been done, Woodbury evidently felt that a good start had been made toward improving conditions in the Navy. In his annual report for 1832 he declared that "corporal punishment has been less common and less necessary."[46]

A valuable addition to the naval literature of the period was made when Enoch Cobb Wines published his reminiscences of *Two Years and a Half in the Navy* in 1832. Wines served as a schoolmaster on board the frigate *Constellation* during the period 1829–31. These years gave him an opportunity to observe a great deal about the government of a man-of-war, and to contemplate changes. Wines said that the most common punishment was flogging, but the severest, from the men's point of view, was stopping their grog. He speculated about an officer's right to deprive a man of his grog any more than any other part of his ration. When a sailor was deprived of his grog and received no money for it, Wines wondered if he might not recover damages in a civil court. It was an academic question, of course, for sailors did not take such problems to court. Stopping a sailor's grog was a frequent occurrence, wrote Wines, and most men would rather be flogged than lose their liquor.

The schoolmaster believed that there was a great need for uniformity in the discipline administered on naval ships. He felt that flogging was carried on to an unnecessary extent, and that it should be done only by an order of a court-martial. He favored limiting the power to use the "colt" to the captain and first lieutenant. Some system of "honorable distinctions" should be used to reward men who had distinguished themselves by their faithful performance of duty. Those who violated their trust should suffer "some notorious disgrace." If this were done, it would no longer be necessary to frighten men into doing their duty.[47]

The subject of illegal and improper conduct by individuals in the naval service engaged the attention of the House of Representatives in January 1833. Representative William Hogan, a Jackson Democrat of New York, presented several resolutions to inquire into alleged abuses in the Navy. These were referred to the Committee on Naval Affairs which, in turn, requested an opinion from

---

[46] *House Executive Documents*, 21st Cong., 1st Sess. (Serial 233), Doc. 4, p. 47.
[47] Wines, I, 64–65; II, 108, 110.

Secretary Woodbury as to whether legislation was required to correct these abuses. Woodbury replied that no further legislation was necessary since corrections could be made by the Navy Department acting through courts-martial and courts of inquiry. Whereupon Chairman John Anderson, a Democrat from Maine, speaking for the committee, announced its concurrence with Woodbury's views and entered "their protest against any such future proceeding through the medium of this House, against either the naval or military officers of the Government," and asked that they be discharged "from all further consideration of the subject."[48]

The reference to the military men had to do with the efforts of Army officers to restore flogging in that service. Congress had passed laws in April and May 1812 which forbade punishment by the lash in the militia and Army, respectively. In the case of the militia, Congress prescribed specific substitutes, such as stopping up to one-half of a month's pay for a first offense, or being confined under guard on half rations for up to ten days. It also stated that this law would expire at the end of two years. The prohibition against flogging in the regular Army remained and was incorporated into subsequent regulations. Many Army officers regarded the abolition of flogging as detrimental to the service. As a substitute the Army punished men by "cobbing" or paddling them with a board or strap. And despite the prohibition, corporal punishment was inflicted, especially in out of the way posts. In 1828 a lieutenant colonel of an infantry regiment was courtmartialed and punished for flogging a private so severely that he was disabled for nine days. The Army finally induced Congress to pass an act in March 1833 which allowed it to flog men convicted of desertion by a general court-martial. For other breaches of discipline the Army resorted to a variety of punishments. These included stopping part of a man's pay, giving him extra duty, restricting him to the post, forcing him to sit astride a sharp edged wooden "horse" for periods of time, obliging him to carry weighty objects, and confining him in the guardhouse. The guardhouse had two types of rooms. One was an open room where men guilty of minor offenses were confined. The other type was a small cell

---

[48] *House Reports*, 22d Cong., 2d Sess. (Serial 236), Report No. 77.

measuring 8 x 3 x 3 feet, designed to prevent the culprit from standing upright. These were used for men guilty of more serious crimes. In the Army as in the Navy most of the punishments were for offenses that resulted from drunkenness. The tendency to resort to whipping persisted in spite of the law, and Congress was obliged to reenforce the prohibition in laws passed in 1861 and 1872.[49]

Meanwhile, complaints about what was happening in the Navy kept cropping up. The New York *Daily Advertiser* discussed naval discipline in 1835, and the item was reprinted in the *Army and Navy Chronicle*. The *Chronicle* also carried four articles relating to naval discipline between January and April 1839.[50] The annual reports of Secretary Dickerson contained only general remarks about discipline and implied that all was well.[51]

From 362 representatives of the maritime industry in New England came a long memorial urging Congress to discontinue the spirit ration in the Navy. They argued that evidence showed that the greatest amount of insubordination and mutinies at sea could be traced to the daily ration of liquor furnished to seamen. This ration had been successfully eliminated in the armies of Great Britain and the United States, as well as from most of the American merchant service. The ration was more injurious in the Navy than in private ships for the crews were subjected to greater dangers and to severer discipline. The elimination of grog would prevent the ruination of young boys who would enter the Navy under the newly launched apprentice program. West Point cadets were not allowed liquor, why should it be served in the Navy?[52]

It was during the early part of Secretary Paulding's term of office that William McNally published his book on the evils and abuses in the naval and merchant services. He believed that the public was

---

[49] *U.S. Statutes at Large*, II, Chaps. 55 and 86, pp. 707, 735; IV, Chap. 68, pp. 647–648; XII, Chap. 54, p. 317; XVII, Chap. 316, p. 261; William Addleman Ganoe, *The History of the United States Army* (New York, 1924), pp. 129–130, 173–175, 262; Francis P. Prucha, *Broadax and Bayonet*, pp. 40, 44–51; *Army Life on the Western Frontier* (Norman, Okla., 1958), pp. 107–133; John S. Hare, "Military Punishments in the War of 1812," *Journal of the American Military Institute*, IV (1940), 225–239.

[50] *Army and Navy Chronicle*, I (1835), 299; VIII (1839), 73–74, 92–93, 140–141, 234–235.

[51] *Senate Documents*, 23d Cong., 2d Sess. (Serial 266), Doc. 1, p. 33; *ibid.*, 24th Cong., 1st Sess. (Serial 279), Doc. 1, p. 330.

[52] *Ibid.*, 25th Cong., 3d Sess. (Serial 340), III, Doc. 223.

unaware of the conditions that existed on our ships. The sailors had few persons who would speak for them. Members of Congress might be willing to do something if they had the facts. To remedy these deficiencies McNally presented case histories of abuses, complete with the names of ships and the officers involved in tyrannical conduct.[53]

On the subject of flogging McNally cites several cases in which the legal limit of a dozen lashes was exceeded. He states that on board the *Delaware* the "cats" were put in brine before being used. He reports that a man was flogged through the fleet in 1829 in accordance with the order of the captain of the *Warren*. Of his own service on board the *Fairfield* he says: "I do not believe that a single day elapsed that punishment, by flogging, did not take place, — at least, for the nine months that I remained on board, I can answer for the fact." Elsewhere he said: "Never let American citizens in the northern states rail at slavery, or the punishment inflicted on slaves, or say that it is wrong, so long as their own sons, their own flesh and blood, their own seamen, their own free citizens, and the men to whom they look for protection in case of war, are daily subject to the same treatment as the slaves, whose degraded situation in the southern states calls forth, so justly, the warmest sensibilities of the heart and nature of philanthropists."[54]

McNally's book was a startling exposé of the abuses practiced in the Navy, not only in regard to punishments, but also in connection with enlistments, clothing issues, rations, pay, and courts-martial. He hoped that an aroused and informed people, acting through their elected representatives, would remedy these evils.

In his annual report of 1839 Secretary Paulding called attention to the fact that a board of naval officers, acting in accordance with the law of May 19, 1832, had revised and extended the rules and regulations of the Navy. These changes had long since been communicated to Congress, but nothing had been done to enact them into law. Believing that changes were still needed, Paulding directed the Board of Navy Commissioners to revise the old regulations with a view to adapting them to the laws then before the Congress and to take advantage of the results of experience. As of November 1839 the board was still at work on the project. Despite

[53] McNally, pp. iii, 97, 98, 100, 101, 106, 123, 127.
[54] *Ibid.*, pp. 87, 106, 128.

the many interruptions in their task Paulding was hopeful that he would have a revised system ready to send to Capitol Hill before the end of the first session of the Twenty-sixth Congress. He believed that with some modification the law of 1800 would still be used to form a system which, "if administered with a firm, steady, temperate perseverance," would sustain the Navy.[55]

Paulding also issued an order to commanding officers directing that punishment by flogging should be employed strictly in accordance with the law and always in the presence of the captain. They were also to make reports to the Navy Department on the amount of punishment administered for infractions of discipline.[56]

An editorial in the New York *Evening Star* of January 18, 1840, praised Paulding's action as follows:

This order is not only conceived in proper spirit of humanity, but is likewise policy, as good seamen are unwilling to join our navy, from an abhorrence of the system of tying up a free citizen and flogging him like a convict. The subject has probably been brought to the immediate consideration of the Secretary from having seen it asserted in a Portsmouth paper that a gentleman saw twenty-five hundred lashes inflicted on board a United States line-of-battle-ship one morning before breakfast. Without crediting this statement, various considerations pressed upon the Secretary the necessity and importance of taking some measures to abridge such practices in the future.[57]

The *Star* then reprinted some material from the Norfolk *Herald* relating to the arrival of the United States sloop-of-war *Vandalia* after a long voyage in the Gulf of Mexico, under the command of Uriah P. Levy. The *Herald* remarked that Commander Levy had kept his ship in prime condition without frequent use of the lash, and that it felt that Levy owed it to the service to impart his secret. The story behind the remarkable cruise, said the *Herald*, is that Commander Levy was a veteran of 28 years' service in the Navy both as a seaman and as an officer. He believed that too little care was given to the comfort, morals, health, and character of the seamen. On board the ships that Levy commanded he introduced his own system of discipline. For example:

---

[55] *Senate Documents*, 26th Cong., 1st Sess. (Serial 354), Doc. 1, pp. 537–538.

[56] *Circulars and General Orders*, I, 342–343.

[57] New York *Evening Star*, Jan. 18, 1840, reprinted in the *Army and Navy Chronicle*, X (1840), 54.

When a sailor is drunk, instead of his being taken in charge by an officer and handed over to the master-at-arms, and put under a sentry's charge in irons, and the next day flogged for using abusive language when drunk, the officer was not permitted to have intercourse with him; his messmates were directed to take charge of him, and he was immediately placed in his hammock and lashed securely. The next day he was sober, and at work, under reprimand from his captain, instead of being in irons and punished at the gangway, and then placed a week on the sick list in consequence of exposure in the brig. This produced the best moral effect. The habitual drunkard had a wooden bottle painted black and lettered "punishment for drunkenness," hung round his neck and locked securely, which he wore night and day: this fretted and worried the sailor as a disgrace, and it seldom occurred twice to the same person.[58]

The *Herald* noted several other substitutes for the lash that were employed by Levy, such as making men who were guilty of fighting drink a tin pot of sea water; and the use of a wooden collar, badge, and separate messing mangers for men guilty of petty theft.[59]

The *Evening Star's* editorial, including the material taken from the Norfolk *Herald* on Levy's substitutes, was reprinted in full, without comment, in the January 1840 issue of the *Army and Navy Chronicle*.[60]

Early in February a memorial was presented to Congress by the "Seamen of the United States" calling for the correction of eight abuses practiced in the American service. One of these eight was concerned with the practice of flogging, and the memorialists asked that the law authorizing the lash be repealed. They added that "the lash is for slaves, your petitioners were born free, yet they are subject to treatment the most degrading, which is not the case on board the merchant ships of any Christian nation except the United States."[61] While it is obvious that this petition was presented by merchant seamen, many of the abuses about which they spoke were similar to those suffered by sailors in the Navy.

Conditions under which the seamen of the Navy lived were described in a very frank and revealing manner in a book by William M. Murrell, entitled *Cruise of the Frigate Columbia Around the World*, which made its appearance in 1840. He tells of men receiving 12 lashes for such trivial offenses as having dirty pots and pans, failing to close the door of a toilet, and "talking on the fore

[58] *Ibid.*   [59] *Ibid.*   [60] *Ibid.*
[61] *House Executive Documents*, 26th Cong., 1st Sess. (Serial 364), Doc. 54.

yard, to another man, *upon a point of duty.*" [62] The author himself
received 12 lashes for failing to mark a piece of clothing properly
and again when he accidentally spilled ink on the deck. Murrell
did not hesitate to mention the names of the officers on board the
Columbia who had been most flagrant in the abuse of authority.
But while he did not hesitate to condemn unjust punishment,
Murrell did not favor the complete abolition of flogging. He
believed that some offenses, such as stealing, deserved punishment
by flogging.[63]

The year 1840 also saw the appearance of one of the most famous
narratives of life at sea, Richard Henry Dana's *Two Years Before
the Mast*. Dana's book contains a very moving account of a terrible
flogging which took place on board the brig *Pilgrim* in the year
1839. When the punishment was over, he thought of the situation
in which he and others were placed in as living under tyranny, and
he "vowed that if God should ever give me the means, I would do
something to redress the grievances and relieve the sufferings of
that poor class of beings, of whom I was then one." [64] Dana's work
was widely read, and his pledge was fulfilled beyond his expecta-
tions. His words added to the growing literature of protest on the
subject of flogging. But in spite of his vow Dana had a slight change
of heart at the time that he was finishing his book. In his last chapter
he again speaks about flogging and says that when the proposition
is made to abolish it entirely at once, and to prevent the captain
from using it under any circumstances, "I am obliged to pause, and,
I must say, to doubt exceedingly the expediency of making any
positive enactment which shall have that effect." [65] Such mixed
opinions on the practice no doubt helped to delay concerted action
to abolish the lash and firmly establish a system of humane punishments. Certainly these opinions by such men as Dana and Murrell
must have confused those who wanted *some* change, and it undoubtedly played into the hands of those officers in the Navy who
wanted *no* change.

[62] William Meacham Murrell, *Cruise of the Frigate Columbia Around the World, Under the Command of Commodore George C. Read, in 1838, 1839, and 1840* (Boston, 1840), pp. 176–177, 198–199, 206–207.
[63] *Ibid.*, pp. 35–36, 137–139.
[64] Richard Henry Dana, *Two Years Before the Mast* (New York, 1907), pp. 107–108.
[65] *Ibid.*, p. 380.

Between 1840 and 1843 there appeared a series of articles in
The Southern Literary Messenger which dealt with conditions in
the Navy. These articles were signed "Harry Bluff," who was later
identified as Lieutenant Matthew F. Maury, U.S.N. While he
made no reference to the practice of flogging, he pointed out that
incompetent officers in positions of authority were ruining the discipline of the Navy. He states that year after year official reports
continue to be made to the public that "the most rigid economy,
perfect management, and wholesome discipline" prevail, and that
under the circumstances naval officers have become instruments
for deceiving the public.[66] Maury's articles helped to keep alive
the idea that all was not well in the Navy. Their appeal was
strengthened by the fact that they appeared at the time that the
Maine boundary was being discussed with Great Britain. There
were those who felt that the problem could lead to war, and if so,
then the Navy should be ready to meet the emergency. Even after
the Webster-Ashburton Treaty was negotiated, *Hunt's Merchant's
Magazine and Commercial Review* declared that all the problems
with England were not settled, and there was still the possibility
of war.[67]

In May 1841 the Secretary of the Navy, George E. Badger,
admitted that "the opinion seems to have become general, as well
in the service as in the nation at large, that a thorough reorganization of the navy is demanded by considerations connected with
the defense and honor of the country." Badger agreed with this
opinion but warned against "haste and inconsideration." Before
the next session of Congress met he hoped to submit a "well
digested system of reform."[68]

But while men talked and wrote of naval reform in general terms,
the voices of those who cried out against flogging were not stilled.
In 1841 a pamphlet appeared in New York City under the title
An Exposition of Official Tyranny in the United States Navy by
Solomon H. Sanborn, late of the U.S. Navy. In it Sanborn men-
tions the last annual report of the Secretary of the Navy which
contained a complaint about the shortage of competent officers and

---

[66] Harry Bluff [Matthew F. Maury], "Scraps from the Lucky Bag," p. 793.
[67] "The Navy and the Late Treaty," *Hunt's Merchant's Magazine and
Commercial Review*, VIII (1843), 56.
[68] *Senate Documents*, 27th Cong., 1st Sess. (Serial 390), Doc. 1, p. 63.

seamen and attributed it to the high wages of the merchant service. This, Sanborn says, is only a part of the story, for one of the principal causes of the unpopularity of the Navy is the flagrant violations of its laws. He then sets forth case histories of violations which he witnessed during four years of service. Sanborn records several gross violations of the law that limited the number of lashes, and he names the ship, the man punished, and in several cases, the officer responsible for the abuse. He praises the humane efforts of the Secretary of the Navy, but says that officers are ignorant of the laws and show a disrespect for the orders of the Secretary. He says that if the "humane principle" of the Secretary of the Navy were carried out, the "odious system of flogging" abolished, and the officers set an example of respect for the law by the administration of strict justice, then the moral character of the seamen would be elevated.[69]

The moral character of the seamen also was a concern of the chaplains of the Navy. Their accounts of their travels and of life aboard ship contain much valuable information on the Navy and its disciplinary practices. Such an account is that of Chaplain Charles Rockwell, whose *Sketches of Foreign Travel and Life at Sea* was published in Boston in 1842. After describing some of the punishments inflicted on board his ship, he says that "every benevolent mind" will ask if "this cruel and degrading punishment" can be dispensed with in the Navy. He tells us that the scenes he has witnessed have forced him to "think much and feel deeply" on this point, and concludes that "severe and summary punishment" is necessary to restrain the sailors. As for himself, he would not risk service on board a man-of-war "where the crew were not restrained from crime, and impelled to duty by the fear of corporal suffering." At the same time he called for the end of the spirit ration.[70]

The conduct of Commander Levy during the cruise of the *Vandalia*, which had been praised by the Norfolk *Herald* and the New York *Evening Star*, was brought under the review of a naval court-martial in April 1842. Lieutenant George Mason Hooe charged Commander Levy with "scandalous and cruel conduct, unbecoming an officer and a gentleman" in ordering a substitute

[69] Solomon H. Sanborn, *An Exposition of Official Tyranny in the United States Navy* (New York, 1841), p. 6.
[70] Rockwell, II, 409, 412–417.

for corporal punishment. The substitute punishment involved one John Thompson, variously described as from 16 to 18 years of age, who was put on report for mimicking an officer of the ship. Commander Levy, not wishing to flog the boy, devised a more appropriate punishment. He ordered the boy tied to a gun, his trousers lowered, and a small quantity of tar (described by some witnesses as the size of a dollar and by others as the size of a man's head) applied with oakum to his backside along with a half dozen parrot feathers. The court-martial found Levy guilty and sentenced him to be dismissed from the service. When the findings of the court were sent to President John Tyler, he did not agree with the sentence and mitigated it to suspension for 12 months. Tyler stated that Levy's action was entirely within the spirit of Secretary Woodbury's circular, which recommended the substitution of badges of disgrace in place of flogging whenever practicable. He believed that the tar was a badge of disgrace which was borne only a few minutes, drew no blood, and caused no harm. Tyler said that while it was true that some men would prefer to be lashed than to wear a badge of disgrace, he did not consider the badge more cruel than corporal punishment. But he also admitted that "Levy erred by resorting to an entirely disgraceful punishment" and that "in order to protect the service from its repetition in the future he should be punished." Nevertheless, Levy's motives were good, and he was not deserving of the extreme sentence of the court.[71]

The *Somers* affair brought the subject of naval discipline and the powers of commanding officers into sharp focus. An anonymous pamphlet entitled *The Cruise of the Somers: Illustrative of the Despotism of the Quarter Deck; and the Unmanly Conduct of Commander Mackenzie*, declared that there was "a very remarkable amount of flogging" of the *Somers'* "seasick, homesick crew of boys." "There was, to say the least, a determination to try what the lash would do in the way of discipline." The author also wrote that many men felt that the right to flog was out of harmony with the spirit of the age.[72]

---

[71] "Record of the Proceedings in the Case of Commander Uriah P. Levy . . . ," pp. 84–85, *Uriah P. Levy Manuscripts*, Library of Congress.

[72] Anonymous, *The Cruise of the Somers; Illustrative of the Despotism of the Quarter Deck; and the Unmanly Conduct of Commander Mackenzie* (3rd ed.; New York, 1844), pp. 6–7, 13.

The flogging situation was again called to public attention by the publication of a pamphlet called *An Inquiry into the Necessity and General Principles of Reorganization in the United States Navy, with an Examination of True Sources of Subordination,* by an "Observer," which appeared in 1842. The Observer, John Murphy, called attention to the fact that in spite of the appeals from the public, the press, the President, and the service itself, a reorganization of the Navy had not taken place. The author proposed to show how the existing naval organization was inefficient and inconsistent with the American character. He did not pretend that "cats" and "colts" were unnecessary for the discipline of the type of sailors then available. But the error lay in bringing the system of government down to the lowest type of men rather than elevating their character. Murphy called for a system of rigid and uncompromising discipline in which the degree of punishment increased with the rank and responsibility of the guilty men.[73]

Many of these criticisms were given additional weight when Secretary Upshur submitted his annual report for 1842. Upshur reported that in view of 20 years of "stepmother care" by the government and "an imperfect system of laws and regulations" as a substitute for public opinion, it was not surprising that abuses existed in the Navy. "It was established without plan, and has been conducted upon no principle, fixed and regulated by law. Left, to get along as well as it could, the wonder is that it retains even a remnant of the character which it won so gloriously during the last war."[74]

Secretary Upshur was interested in improving the lot of the enlisted men, but, unfortunately, his thoughts on this subject took form slowly. For this reason and in spite of his ability, his contribution to the abolition of flogging was very small. Nevertheless, the steps that he took to improve the service gave encouragement to many in the Navy and undoubtedly gave heart to those who would improve disciplinary practices. In the fall of 1843 Upshur was promoted to Secretary of State, and seven months later he and his

[73] An Observer [John Murphy], *An Inquiry into the Necessity and General Principles of Reorganization in the United States Navy, with an Examination of True Sources of Subordination* (Baltimore, 1842), pp. 7, 11, 46.
[74] *Senate Documents,* 27th Cong., 3d Sess. (Serial 413), I, Doc. 1, pp. 544–545.

successor in the Navy Department were killed by the explosion of
a naval cannon on board the *Princeton*.

Another piece of reform literature made its appearance in 1843
under the title *The Navy's Friend*. In it one Tiphys Aegyptus re-
counted abuses that occurred during his 39 months of service.
The pamphlet is addressed to the public and especially to the Committee on Naval Affairs and others who are unaware of the defects
in the Navy. He condemns commanders who allowed young midshipmen "to execrate the crew in the most violent manner." "It was
this abuse, more than anything else, that induced me to write this
pamphlet." He says that officers frequently disregarded the rules
of the Navy and were confident that no seaman would trouble
himself to report them.[75]

On the subject of flogging Tiphys Aegyptus declares: "I do not
mean to say, and I cannot with justice, that punishment by flogging
can be done away with." But he condemns tyranny and recklessness
in the use of the lash. He considered a certain lieutenant on his
ship better fitted to be a slave driver than an officer. He praises
Captain Louis M. Goldsborough for being one of the few officers
who, when a prisoner is brought before him in a court, reads the
law violated and asks for the man's defense. Other commanders,
says the author, very often have a man flogged without the victim
knowing the reason. He considers that the only way to stop the
abuse of flogging is to have a board of inspection visit each ship and
question the men on their general treatment.[76]

Tiphys Aegyptus also calls attention to the neglect of divine services, the embezzlement of public stores, the disrespect of the dead
on board ship, the drunkenness of officers and men, the improper
medical care, and other abuses. He asks:

How it is that, since the Hon. Secretary, A. P. Upshur, managed the pen,
there have been a great many corrections made? It is because he begins
to find out some of the many *little difficulties* that exist between officer
and man, and every body, the landsmen as well as the marine, esteem
him. My pen will not enable me to express his great activity, knowledge
and patriotism. Not a Navy afloat dares boast of a man like him. Every
man that hears his name praises him highly, and from all the general
reports and speeches I have read, I esteem, honor and respect him.[77]

---

[75] Tiphys Aegyptus, pp. 27–28.   [76] *Ibid.*, pp. 11, 33.
[77] *Ibid.*, p. 28.

Upshur's successor in the Navy Department was David Henshaw, who in November of 1843 suggested that since drunkenness was a frequent cause of punishment, the spirit ration ought to be abolished. But Henshaw was in office only seven months and apparently had little opportunity to follow up his suggestion.[78]

After Commodore Lawrence Kearney returned to the United States from a 42-month cruise in the *Constellation*, his crew printed a letter in a newspaper thanking him for his kind treatment during the voyage. *The Sailor's Magazine* publicized the event under the heading "No Need of Flogging in the Navy," and concluded the article with a statement that this was "valuable proof of the superiority of kindness over force, in the government of men."[79]

The close relationship between the abolition of grog and of flogging to the cause of naval reform was illustrated again in the deliberations of Congress. When the annual naval appropriation bill was under discussion in the House, Daniel King, a Whig representative from Massachusetts, offered an amendment to it prohibiting the spirit ration and paying money in lieu of it. His amendment passed by a vote of 75 to 49. King's amendment was followed by one from John P. Hale, a New Hampshire Democrat, calling for the abolition of flogging in the Navy and Marine Corps and the repeal of all laws that authorized it. This proposal, submitted on May 23, 1844, at first drew only 53 affirmative and 39 negative votes and thus fell short of a quorum. After a reminder from the chairman the vote was taken again, and the amendment passed 67 to 63.[80] Again, on June 3, Hale returned to the subject and proceeded to give a long discourse on flogging, bolstered by quotations from documents. The reading of such material was strongly opposed by Charles J. Ingersoll, a Pennsylvania Democrat, who repeatedly called Hale to order. Four days later, before the appropriation bill finally passed the House, Hale's amendment was again upheld, this time by a vote of 85 to 57. This victory was accomplished in spite of the efforts of Hale's New Hampshire colleague and fellow Democrat, John R. Reding, who pressed for an adjournment when the measure was due to be voted on and who, after the

---

[78] *Senate Documents*, 27th Cong., 1st Sess. (Serial 390), Doc. 1, p. 63.
[79] *The Sailor's Magazine*, XVI, 378.
[80] *Congressional Globe*, 28th Cong., 1st Sess., XIII, 618.

vote, tried unsuccessfully to have it reconsidered.[81] Within 15 days Hale had gathered 18 votes for his measure. The outlook was hopeful.

In the Senate Richard H. Bayard, a Delaware Whig, moved to strike out the provision on flogging as well as the one on the spirit ration. The Senate agreed to this. When the Senate's action on these amendments was put to the Committee of the Whole House, the latter body upheld the eliminations, the vote on flogging being 63 to 58. That evening the House voted on concurring with the amendments of the Committee of the Whole, and Hale won another victory. The House refused to agree to the elimination of the flogging amendment, the vote being 54 yeas and 87 nays.[82] The action of the House on these and other amendments made it necessary to appoint a conference committee of which Hale was a member. In the end, following the report of this committee, the House receded from its position, and the appropriation bill passed without any reference to flogging or spirits.[83]

Hale had lost his amendment but had begun to build for himself a great reputation for being a friend of the sailor. He was neither the first nor the last influential figure to be interested in the abolition of flogging. But he was persistent, hardheaded, and opportunistic. In his speeches he could be pompous and irritating, and in an instant dissolve the chamber into laughter with some dry remark. If he was not the best spokesman for the cause, he was at least *a* spokesman. And he was in an influential position. Furthermore, he did not have to depend on books or reports for his information on the Navy. His brother-in-law, Thomas Lambert, served as chaplain in the Navy from 1834 to 1856. Hale and Lambert were on close terms and corresponded with each other.[84]

Lambert had a unique background which gave him additional insights into the Navy's problem and a circle of influential friends. While beginning his freshman year at Dartmouth he received and accepted an appointment to West Point. Illness made it necessary

---

[81] *Ibid.*, pp. 639, 651.
[82] *Ibid.*, p. 691.
[83] *House Journal*, 28th Cong., 1st Sess. (Serial 438), pp. 1143, 1156, 1162, 1167.
[84] For examples, see letters of Hale to Lambert, May 20, 1836, Feb. 24, 1837, and Dec. 19, 1847, in the *John P. Hale Papers*.

for him to leave the military academy in 1829, and he began the study of law in Portsmouth, New Hampshire under Levi Woodbury. In 1832, after Woodbury joined President Jackson's cabinet as Secretary of the Navy, Lambert was admitted to the bar. Sometime later he became interested in religion and in the naval chaplaincy. In 1834 Jackson appointed him a chaplain in the Navy prior to his ordination in the Episcopal Church. He had charming personal qualities, and his circle of friends included Woodbury, John C. Calhoun, Henry Clay, Daniel Webster, Lewis Cass, Thomas Hart Benton, Edward Everett, many naval officers and religious leaders.[85] Lambert also kept a diary, which is the earliest known extant diary of an American naval chaplain. Like most diarists Lambert made observations about the men and events with which he came into contact; in his case this included Navy men and naval events. His entries show, for example, that as early as 1836 he often had difficulties with Commodore Jesse D. Elliott in relation to religious services.[86] Hale undoubtedly heard a great deal about conditions in the Navy from Lambert, and Lambert's connections may well have helped Hale.

And this was not all. There is a letter in Hale's papers which indicates that in 1839 he wrote to Secretary of the Treasury Levi Woodbury, a fellow New Hampshire man and ex-Secretary of the Navy, and endeavored to secure a discharge for his brother, then a deserter from the Navy. Woodbury referred the matter to Secretary Paulding who, in turn, curtly informed Hale that nothing could be done until the deserter returned.[87] If the abuses in the naval service were items of common talk in this period, ideas on "what's wrong with the Navy" were surely favorite topics in the Hale and Lambert households. Even before Hale's election to Congress, and four and one-half years before he introduced his antiflogging measure, he was invited to address a New Hampshire group of the American Seamen's Friend Society.[88] His reputation as a reformer was soon to grow.

---

[85] *Boston Daily Advertiser*, Feb. 5, 1892; *The Boston Herald*, Feb. 5, 1892; *Concord Evening Monitor*, Feb. 6, 1892.

[86] Drury, I, 56–57.

[87] Secretary of the Navy James K. Paulding to Senator John P. Hale, Oct. 10, 1839, *John P. Hale Papers*.

[88] Mrs. John P. Hale to Senator John P. Hale, Dec. 11, 1839, *John P. Hale Papers*.

He was already proving to be a thorn in the side of the Navy Department. In December 1843, during a discussion of a bill authorizing the President under certain circumstances to direct the transfer of appropriations to the Navy, Hale asked for an investigation of naval spending. He charged that the Navy was now spending more money in peacetime than it had during any year of the War of 1812, when it was winning glory. The next day he followed up these remarks with a speech on retrenchment in the Navy.[89]

The laudable nature of the antiflogging measure could easily be lost sight of when it was recalled that in January 1844 Hale introduced a bill to abolish West Point.[90] This could not help but make him seem an irresponsible radical to many officers in the military and naval services.

After the defeat of Hale's amendment the next move of the House of Representatives appears to have been the outgrowth of a compromise reached with the Senate in the Conference Committee. On January 11, 1845, the Committee on Naval Affairs sent a resolution to the Secretary asking what substitute, if any, could be used in place of flogging without endangering naval discipline. Near the end of February Secretary Mason replied that he knew of no substitute. He mentioned the laws which regulated the punishment by flogging and prevented its abuse. He reported that quarterly returns of punishments from ships were carefully examined, and that he was gratified to see how rare punishments were in some vessels. Mason directed the attention of the House to the fact that the great body of seamen considered flogging necessary and did not consider it a degradation. But he added:

It is true that the infliction of corporal punishment is revolting to the great body of the American people; and it is because of this feeling that it might be dispensed with on the shore stations within the United States, where citizens are frequently employed. This, I think might be advantageously done by a regulation of the department; but I feel constrained to express the opinion that it cannot be dispensed with on ship-board

---

[89] *Congressional Globe*, 28th Cong., 1st Sess., XIII, 71, 75.
[90] *Ibid.*, p. 205. This idea did not originate with Hale. Petitions for abolishing West Point, submitted by groups in Connecticut, were presented in Congress by Representatives Thomas H. Seymour and George S. Catlin in December 1843 and February 1844, respectively. See *House Journal*, 28th Cong., 1st Sess. (Serial 438), pp. 108, 345.

without injury to the discipline of the service, endangering the safety of our ships of war, and making necessary a system of punishments far more oppressive and cruel to those in whose behalf sympathy has suggested the modification.[91]

When George Bancroft became Secretary of the Navy in March 1845, he turned his talents to the task of rehabilitating the Navy by raising its standards and morale. He was responsible for the establishment of the Naval Academy at Annapolis, Maryland, as a place to train midshipmen for future command responsibilities. He further improved the leadership of the Navy by making promotion depend solely on merit and not on years of service. Bancroft also attempted to put an end to the casual flogging of seamen by officers. In his annual report, submitted at the end of 1845, he declared that the "former customs" of delegating the power of the lash to subordinate officers was "a flagrant violation of the will of Congress and the people." "The men have rights, and must be protected in them. Experience shows that discipline is never so good, as when the commanding officer sets the example of subordination by obedience to the laws of his country."[92]

In this connection it is interesting to note an article on the Navy, submitted under the name "Afterguard," which appeared in the newly launched *United States Nautical Magazine* in July 1845. Afterguard identified himself as a "plain 'blue jacket'" with more than 30 years of service in the Navy. It was his contention that since the War of 1812 naval discipline had relaxed and insubordination had grown. Discontent and negligence flourished as a result of the long period of peace and the lack of exciting employment.

In connection with these, we have the more liberal and extended ideas of freedom, which at present prevail throughout the civilized world, by which man has learned to value himself more highly than in the days of yore, (if I may so express myself, when speaking of the extension of republicanism,) the above causes have lead to the change in affairs, military and naval; and the question now is, how they may be remedied, — I answer by the most simple method in the world. Give the navy a sound and wholesome code of regulations, let each man know his place, reward the meritorious, and punish the offenders.

---

[91] *House Executive Documents*, 28th Cong., 2d Sess. (Serial 466), IV, Doc. 157.

[92] *Senate Executive Documents*, 29th Cong., 1st Sess. (Serial 480), Doc. 2, p. 654.

Afterguard condemned the practice of some Presidents of remitting sentences of officers who were court-martialed.[93]

On the subject of flogging Afterguard asked that it be done only by order of the ship's commander and suggested that no man be punished "until at least six hours" after his offense to prevent any punishment while in a state of anger. The editor of the magazine, Lieutenant T. Augustus Craven, U.S.N., commented that "Afterguard's hints are very acceptable, and well worthy of attention." [94]

Throughout this period articles appeared from time to time in the newspapers denouncing the abuses in the practice of flogging. One such article in a Boston paper of 1847 stated that flogging was brutalizing and horrifying and asked: "What is the Secretary of the Navy about, that he does not lift up his powerful voice in denouncing the *torture of the lash*?" [95] This item was reprinted in a book opposing the use of corporal punishment in schools and families. Lyman Cobb, the author of this book, made references to the horrible floggings which took place in the British Army and Navy and to the movement against corporal punishment in both Great Britain and the United States.[96]

By 1848 the work of informing the public on the evils of corporal punishment, and the relationship of drunkenness to it, was well under way. Widespread public interest in the cause of total abstinence for the whole country had declined, but it was still an issue in the Navy, at least as it applied to the daily ration of spirits. One thing that stood in the way of a more complete renunciation of the grog ration was the fact that many men kept it as a type of insurance against being flogged. A man guilty of a minor offense might be punished by stopping his grog for a brief period. If he had already elected not to draw his grog, the usual alternative was to flog him. Faced with such a choice it is not surprising that the men preferred to hold on to their spirit ration. Therefore, if flogging was abolished it would not only be the beginning of a more

---

[93] Afterguard, "Our Navy, Economy, and Good Order," *United States Nautical Magazine*, I (1845), 307, 311, 313.

[94] *Ibid.*, pp. 311–313.

[95] Quoted in Lyman Cobb, *The Evil Tendencies of Corporal Punishment as a Means of Moral Discipline in Families and Schools, Examined and Discussed* (New York, 1847), p. 83.

[96] *Ibid.*, pp. 9, 57, 83n, 28–29n.

enlightened approach to discipline, but also give additional encouragement to voluntary renunciations of grog.

Past experience had shown the reformers that a proposal to
abolish flogging would have a difficult time clearing the Congress,
and especially in the Senate. Nevertheless the ground was being
prepared for another attack. The literature of protest had been
widely distributed. Opinions for and against the practice had been
forming in the minds of the public, and were being noted by the
politicians. More and more the attacks on flogging added a dimen-
sion to the problem that was absorbing the best minds of the
nation: the question of Negro slavery. Attempts by southerners to
point out how well off the Negro slaves were also served to point up
how poor the lot of the common sailor was in comparison — at least
insofar as punishment was concerned. Southerners tended to
oppose attempts to outlaw the use of flogging in the Navy, and
their actions reenforced the abolitionist stereotype of the lash-
wielding master. To some northerners the speeches of southerners
in Congress looked like an effort to defend two forms of tyranny —
slavery and corporal punishment. This type of identification was
not only a useful propaganda device, but it also served to relate the
antiflogging movement to the larger political issues of the day.

Some of the writers who felt that flogging was a necessary evil
had described its horrors so well that many of their readers came
to an opposite conclusion. Accusations that the authority to punish
was grossly abused were increasing. It was a subject which lent
itself to emotion, and emotion led to political action. The naval
committees of Congress tried in vain to dodge or bury the problem. It was not a party issue, but Democrats were being numbered
increasingly among those who sought to abolish, or at least curb,
the use of the lash. The antiflogging groups needed a leader in
Congress to push the issue through to victory. Such a leader was
now at hand.

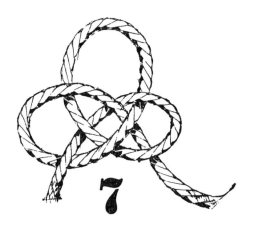

THE END OF FLOGGING

In February 1849 Senator John P. Hale of New Hampshire predicted to his colleagues that they would see the end of flogging in
the Navy during the course of the year. He based his prediction
on his observation of the way that public opinion was moving on
this question. Hale proved to be a poor prophet insofar as predict-
ing the date of such an event was concerned, but not about the
fact that the end was in sight. To better comprehend his role in
these events it is necessary to shift this narrative back a few years.

Near the end of his term in the House, during the Twenty-eighth
Congress, Hale suggested a limitation of the area open to slavery in
the event that Texas joined the Union. He refused to vote for the
annexation of Texas, although instructed to do so by his state
legislature. Later he denounced the annexation before his constituents. For such views and actions he was read out of the Democratic party in February 1845. Returning home after his term in
Congress, he helped the Whigs and Independent Democrats to
gain control of the New Hampshire Legislature in 1846. He won a
seat in that house and served as its speaker. He then ran for the
United States Senate and was elected as the first antislavery man
to that body. On March 4, 1847, he took his seat as a freshman
senator.[1]

---

[1] *Congressional Globe*, 30th Cong., 2d Sess., XVIII, 512; William A. Robinson, "John Parker Hale," *Dictionary of American Biography*, VIII (1932),

Nearly a year and a half passed before he again attacked the practice of flogging. It was near the end of the session and the Senate chamber contained only a fraction of its legal occupancy. Those that remained were trying to get through the remaining business with as little delay as possible. They were discussing the naval appropriation bill on July 21, 1848, when Hale offered an amendment prohibiting flogging and abolishing the spirit ration. His fellow senators were in no mood to pursue the topic. Too few members rose to his call for the yeas and nays to continue it. Undaunted, Hale proceeded to address the Senators on the merits of his amendment. When he finished, the amendment was rejected, having been supported by about five men.[2]

Why was there so little interest in the measure? Among other things, Hale's timing was off. It was Friday. It was also July, and in Washington Julys are often uncomfortable. The Senate attendance was small and its spirit impatient. The rights of sailors could not compete with *mal de fin de session.*

On this same day, however, the Senate did pass a resolution calling on the Secretary of the Navy to submit copies of the reports of punishments inflicted on the various ships of the naval force. One week later Secretary Mason transmitted the returns. These showed that during the year a total of 424 men had been punished on the 16 ships of the Navy in the service. Of this total, 278 cases had received the legal limit of 12 lashes.[3]

These figures whetted the congressional appetite for statistics, and on August 3 reports were requested for the years 1846 and 1847. This request was a part of the naval appropriation act, so that it now became the duty of the Secretary to submit similar reports of punishments every year thereafter. Secretary Mason forwarded the figures "so far as received" in February 1849.[4]

A perusal of these figures offers a splendid insight into the daily life and living conditions of the Navy in this period. They also

105–107; Ansel Wold, comp., *Biographical Directory of the American Congress,* p. 1045; Richard H. Sewell, *John P. Hale and the Politics of Abolition* (Cambridge, Mass., 1965), pp. 1–88.

[2] *Congressional Globe,* 30th Cong., 1st Sess., XVII, 983; *ibid.,* 2d Sess., XVIII, 488, 506.

[3] *Senate Executive Documents,* 30th Cong., 1st Sess. (Serial 510), Doc. 69.

[4] *U.S. Statutes at Large,* IX, Chap. 121, p. 271; *Senate Executive Documents,* 30th Cong., 2d Sess (Serial 531), Doc. 23.

show the rather wide range of offenses that were punished by flogging. Most of the entries on every ship are concerned with drunkenness, fighting, desertion, and insubordination. Unless otherwise indicated, the lashes are with the cat-o'-nine tails. Here, then, is a cross section of some of the offenses punished during 1848–49.

Smuggling cigars from ship to shore	12 lashes with the cats
Drunkenness and mutinous conduct	12 lashes
Profane language	11 lashes
Having another's shirt	8 lashes with colt
Fighting	12 lashes with colt
Throwing belaying pin at boatswain's mate	12 lashes with cats
Smoking after 10 P.M.	8 lashes with the colt
Throwing soapsuds in the eyes of captain of afterguard	6 lashes with the colt
Cursing sentry on post	12 lashes with the cats
Beating colored man	12 lashes with cats
Doubling grog tub	12 lashes with colt
Circulating false reports	12 lashes with cats
Swindling	9 lashes with cats
Skulking	9 lashes with cats
Hallooing on gun deck	8 lashes with cats
Selling clothes	9 lashes with cats
Missing muster	8 lashes with cats
Scandalous conduct	12 lashes with cats
Filthiness	8 lashes with cats
Letting block fall from aloft	12 lashes with cats
Kicking man on quarter deck	8 lashes with cats
Stealing liquor from spirit room	12 lashes with cats
Taking indecent liberties with boy in hammock	12 lashes with cats
Endangering ship with fire	12 lashes with cats[5]

Glancing over the above selection, the reader may wonder about the small number of punishments for homosexual activities. Such problems did exist, of course, but precise evidence of them is scarce. One of the reasons for this is that the subject was repulsive to most sailor authors, and they either ignored such topics completely or gave them a brief treatment. For example, sailor Jacob Hazen described the school ship *Columbus* in 1839 as "a den where some two hundred boys are collected together, exposed to

---

[5] *House Executive Documents*, 31st Cong., 1st Sess. (Serial 576), Doc. 26, *passim*.

every kind of sinful vice — where swearing, gambling, cheating, lying, and stealing, are the continual order of the day; where drunkenness, obscenity, and self-pollution, stalk unrestrained; and where crimes abound of even so deep and black a dye that it fires the cheek with shame to name them, and which yet escape the just punishment their heinousness deserves. . . ."[6]

This account suggests that the offenses were ignored, but other evidence indicates that when homosexual acts were discovered, the participating parties were discharged from the Navy. An example of this procedure may be found in the journal of another sailor, F. P. Torrey. He noted that in January 1841 two men were discharged from the crew of the *Ohio* "for a crime hardly ever committed, and as the officers of the ship will not disgrace the criminal calendar trying them, I will not sully this page by describing it; but it would have been as well to make an example of the wretches."[7]

The restraint noted by Torrey was not characteristic. It was more common to punish the men before discharging them. Nevertheless, it seems likely that the offenses for which such punishments were administered were not always accurately described in the records. How often this happened and what circumlocutions were used it is impossible to say. If we assume, for instance, that a punishment for a homosexual offense was entered in the log as one for drunkenness, then all attempts at analysis become impossible. If, on the other hand, we assume that regulations and habit made for keeping an accurate log, and if we assume that when there was no desire to put down the bald truth a close equivalent might be used, then we can speculate about the amount of homosexuality discovered in the Navy. Virtually all of the printed returns show that most captains reported crimes in a brief but straightforward way.

The report submitted to Congress for the years 1846–47 showed that 60 vessels administered a total of 5,936 floggings. Of this total five are clearly homosexual offenses: three attempts at sodomy; one case of "Improper conduct, too base to mention"; and one case of "Filthy and unnatural practices." In addition, four cases of "Indecency" and one of "Obscenity and immoral conduct" were punished by 12 lashes. Six other offenses which caused the culprits

---

[6] Jacob Hazen, *Five Years Before the Mast* . . . (Chicago, 1887), p. 227.
[7] F. P. Torrey, *Journal of the Cruise of the United States Ship Ohio* . . . (Boston, 1841), p. 86.

to suffer 12 lashes, and which *may* possibly refer to homosexual offenses, are one case each of "Filthy conduct," "Gross misconduct to boys," "Scandalous conduct and fighting," "Improper conduct ashore," "Improper conduct on a berth deck," and "Disgraceful & riotous conduct." If one were to assume that the 12 lashes given for filthiness represented instances of homosexual conduct, and this seems unlikely, then an additional seven cases might be noted. Therefore, the broadest possible interpretation of the entries would make the total number of punishments for homosexual offenses 22 out of 5,936. A more likely total would appear to be about eight.[8]

The situation is much the same in the first report for 1848. Out of 424 floggings, there is only one clear cut homosexual case. If we assume that filthiness and indecency are circumlocutions, this adds only four more cases (two for each offense) to the total.[9]

The next phase in the story took place on January 18, 1849. On this day the House was considering the compensation of the Secretary of the Navy and of the clerks in his office. An Ohio Democrat, William Sawyer, proposed an amendment which made it the duty of the Secretary to publish an order abolishing flogging. Samuel F. Vinton, an Ohio Whig, made an attempt to stop this on the grounds that it was not a condition germane to the Secretary's receiving his salary, but the Speaker ruled it in order. The House then accepted the amendment by a vote of 79 to 36.[10]

Meanwhile, at least one naval officer was doing all that he could to stop this movement. Alarmed by the action of the House, Captain Samuel F. Du Pont came to Washington to enlist senatorial support. He felt that he was on strong ground. The recent punishment returns showed that there had been little flogging on his ship. Nevertheless, he did not believe that the lash could be completely outlawed. His arguments were set forth in a letter to Whig Senator John M. Clayton of Delaware.

Du Pont thought that the antiflogging reformers labored under three major misapprehensions. The first was that there was a great deal of flogging in the Navy. The captain denied this. The punish-

---

[8] *Senate Executive Documents*, 30th Cong., 2d Sess. (Serial 531), Doc. 23, pp. 92, 97, 118, 231, 219, 238, 266, 337, 138, 291, 213.
[9] *Ibid.*, 1st Sess. (Serial 510), Doc. 69, passim.
[10] *Congressional Globe*, 30th Cong., 2d Sess., XVIII, 295.

ment was rarely used, he said, and then only after all moral influence had failed.[11]

The second mistaken notion was that most men were flogged for offenses against the officers. Not so, wrote Du Pont. Nineteen-twentieths of the floggings were "for the protection of the sober, honest, hard working portion of a crew, (a class always composing a large majority of every American man of war). . . ."[12]

The third erroneous assumption was that naval officers opposed the abolition of corporal punishment. They did not, said Du Pont, but they wanted to be provided with an effective substitute.[13]

He called the Senator's attention to the procedure followed by Great Britain in response to public and Parliamentary concern over the amount of corporal punishment in the armed forces. After a long and patient study by a royal commission, some changes were made. But it was found that flogging could not be completely eliminated.[14] Du Pont wanted a congressional committee to make a thorough investigation of punishments. Then, if changes were needed, Congress could enact them.

What would happen if Congress abolished flogging without giving the officers some other power to punish? Du Pont predicted that law and order would vanish. As soon as the abolition order was read on board any ship in the Pacific, the crews would seize the vessel and head for the California gold fields.[15]

Clayton's reaction to this letter is not known, but it would seem that the captain had an influence on the Senator and on some of his colleagues.[16]

A few weeks later, on February 9, Senator Hale presented to the

---

[11] Captain Samuel F. Du Pont to Lieutenant Garrett J. Pendergast, Jan. 2, 1849, *Wintherthur Collection* (Samuel F. Du Pont Papers), Eleutherian Mills Historical Library, Wilmington, Delaware; Captain Samuel F. Du Pont to Senator John M. Clayton, Jan. 24, 1849, *John M. Clayton Papers*, III, Library of Congress.

[12] *Ibid.*

[13] *Ibid.*

[14] For a report of the Royal Commission of 1835–36, see Scott Claver, *Under the Lash: A History of Corporal Punishment in the British Armed Forces* (London, 1954), pp. 232–256.

[15] Du Pont to Clayton, Jan. 24, 1849, *loc. cit.*

[16] For valuable information on Du Pont and his interest in naval reform, I am indebted to Rear Admiral John D. Hayes, U.S.N. (Ret.), who is editing a collection of the Civil War letters of Du Pont.

Senate a number of petitions from people in New York State asking for the end of flogging and the spirit ration. In his remarks he reminded his colleagues that five years earlier an antiflogging measure had passed the House and died in the Senate. Now the same provision was in a new House bill. According to Navy Department figures, the amount of punishment on some ships during a three-month period varied from 57 to 903 lashes. And this was not all. If a hearing could be arranged, a "very intelligent sailor" was prepared to show that the punishments listed in the report were not even a third of the number actually inflicted. Cases could be found where 2,300 floggings took place in a three-month period. He cited instances where men were flogged for refusing to serve beyond their enlistment, for bad cooking, for being improperly dressed, and for drunkenness.[17]

Hale then rose to great oratorical heights in his finale.

These men are our brethren; they are not the descendants of the curly-headed African, on whose behalf it is so unpopular and offensive to speak a word of sympathy. No, sir; these are the fair-haired rosey-cheeked sons of New England and the West, who are subjected to degradation and cruelty, compared with which the servitude of the South is freedom, and the Algerine cruelty is Christian kindness. I repeat, sir, I do ask that the Senate of the United States shall not interpose, and stand up between humanity and the House, and set itself as a bulwark for the defense of this punishment.[18]

Hale's petitions were referred to the Committee on Naval Affairs whose chairman, David L. Yulee, a Democrat from Florida, had already asked their sponsor to propose a substitute for flogging.[19]

The question was reopened on February 12 when the Senate discussed the antiflogging proviso in the appropriation bill. Here, as in the House, the argument first centered around the charge that an appropriation bill was not a proper place for this type of legislation. Hale disposed of that argument by citing the precedent of the previous Congress in regard to the reports on flogging. Then came some interesting exchanges between Hale and Badger, Yulee, Niles, and Benton on the question of naval discipline.[20]

Hale offered to amend the amendment to make it repeal all laws authorizing whipping in the Navy, instead of requiring action on

---

[17] *Congressional Globe*, 30th Cong., 2d Sess., XVIII, 488–489.
[18] *Ibid.*, p. 489.   [19] *Ibid.*   [20] *Ibid.*, pp. 506–509.

the part of the Secretary. He asked that an experiment in abolition be tried. Sailors did not approve of flogging, he said, for he had known some and had heard from their own lips their opinions on the use of the lash. He felt that this question was one of the most important that could possibly come before Congress, since it was "vital to our character for humanity and civilization." The question was already before the people, and the Senate could not long defend the continued use of the lash, a "relic of barbarism," against public indignation. He predicted that it would be abolished before the year was out. "The funeral procession will soon be marshalled," he said, "and all the arguments drawn from the views of England cannot shelter it from the execrations of outraged humanity."[21]

George E. Badger, an ex-Secretary of the Navy and now a Whig senator from North Carolina, argued that the measure was the result of "mistaken philanthropy." The practice of flogging had been sanctioned by long usage, and "every officer and good seaman" opposed abolishing it. Punishment was necessary even if it was degrading, and there were abuses in every exercise of power. He believed that 99 times out of 100 an ex-Navy man preferred to reenter the Navy rather than the merchant service.[22]

Yulee believed that the proposed change was "radical" and should not be the subject of an "accidental amendment." Let the question be examined by the Committee on Naval Affairs. If it thinks that a bill is necessary, it will report one. The Navy was having no difficulty in getting men, so there was no occasion for action now. Furthermore, sailors opposed the idea. During the last session men on ships near Washington expressed their disapproval of the abolition of flogging. Worthy sailors knew that it was the only way to punish those who did not do their duty. How would Hale punish them? The spirit ration was already diminished, and Hale was proposing to abolish it altogether. Confinement robs the ship of a part of its working force. Commanders were already restricted in the use of the lash. The number of stripes inflicted was probably no more than that administered to culprits by the courts of some states. Many of the punishments were with the colt which, he said, was "not much more painful than the ferrule" administered to scholars by their masters. If Hale is opposed to this form of pun-

---

[21] *Ibid.*, pp. 506–509, 512.　　[22] *Ibid.*, pp. 506, 509.

ishment he should submit a bill embracing the whole subject and extending it to the schools, families, and the merchant service.[23]

Connecticut's Democratic Senator, John M. Niles, answered those who sought the cause for this measure by saying that those who oppose this change should give their reasons for retaining flogging. His reason for supporting the change was "that laws and regulations of the army and navy should keep pace with the progress of reform in criminal law." [24]

Thomas Hart Benton, a Missouri Democrat, was opposed to the flogging of Americans. He questioned the value of making officers of the Navy "the instruments or agents to correct the incorrigible part of mankind." It would be far better to get such men out of the Navy. Nevertheless, he was opposed to this amendment because he felt that it did not belong in an appropriation bill.[25]

When the vote finally was taken, the amendment was defeated by a vote of 17 to 32.[26] Once again the forces of abolition were defeated, but they were by no means ready to abandon the cause. Within a few weeks a new movement was afoot to bring the question before Congress again.

On the first day of March 1849 the Senate received a resolution from the legislature of Rhode Island in favor of prohibiting corporal punishment and the use of ardent spirits in the Navy. This resolution stated that American seamen preferred to work harder for less pay in the merchant service than to serve in the Navy "where they must live in constant dread of the lash." [27] Rhode Island's senators and representatives were instructed to use their influence to bring to an end the use of the lash as a means of punishment.[28]

---

[23] *Ibid.*, p. 510.
[24] *Ibid.*, pp. 510–511.
[25] *Ibid.*, p. 51.
[26] *Ibid.*, pp. 512–513. The bill was supported by 5 Whigs, 11 Democrats, and 1 senator (Hale) elected on an anti-slavery ticket. Of these 17, 14 were from northern states, 2 were from a border state (Kentucky), and 1 from a southern state (Arkansas). The opposition consisted of 12 Whigs, 19 Democrats, and 1 Unionist. It included 11 men from northern states, 19 from southern states, and 1 from a border state (Missouri). Missouri's other senator, Thomas Hart Benton, did not participate in the voting.
[27] *Senate Miscellaneous Documents*, 30th Cong., 2d Sess. (Serial 533), Doc. 63.
[28] *Ibid.*

Months passed without any great action on the part of Congress or the Secretary in regard to flogging. But the literature on the subject continued to grow. Between August and October 1849 *The United States Magazine and Democratic Review* published a four-part article on flogging in the Navy. It was later republished separately under the title *An Essay on Flogging in the Navy.* No author was given, but the publications later were identified as being the work of naval surgeon John A. Lockwood. In his essay Lockwood says: "The careful observer of the signs of the times cannot have failed to notice the strong and general feeling of opposition in the public mind to the practice of flogging in the navy. Presumed expedience is likely to yield to humanity, or in the view of some, to sentimentality, in the call for the abolition of the lash. The question, may, therefore, soon become, not whether the power to inflict corporal punishment shall be taken from the commanders of our ships of war, but, what disciplinary means shall be submitted for that authority."[29]

Lockwood proposed a graduated system of punishments embracing admonition and reprimand, simple arrest (the interruption of liberty), close arrest (confinement in irons and the loss of 25 per cent of pay), fines, reductions in rank, imprisonment (prisoners to wear special clothes and do special types of work), dismissal, and cashiering. He mentioned that punishments would be less necessary if the Navy abolished the spirit ration, increased the privilege of going ashore, and established: (a) a conduct roll with a system of demerits; (b) ships courts and courts of inquest for minor offenses; (c) a seamen's register which would rate men on their ability; (d) leave of absence pay and the encouragement of seamen to save money; (e) a new system of Navy laws and a reorganization of the service. Later in his article Lockwood pre-

---

[29] [John A. Lockwood], *An Essay on Flogging in the Navy* (New York, 1849), p. 2; "Flogging in the Navy," *United States Magazine and Democratic Review,* XXI (1849), 97–115, 225–242, 318–337, 417–432. Neeser credits Alexander Slidell Mackenzie with the authorship of these articles. In their work, *Navy Maverick: Uriah Phillips Levy* (Garden City, N.Y., 1963), pp. 185–186, Donovan Fitzpatrick and Saul Saphire credit Captain Uriah P. Levy with the authorship. But the language is identical with that in the pamphlet ascribed to Lockwood in archives of the Navy Department and presumably sent by him to the Secretary. See Neeser, I, 122; *Reports of Officers, 1850.*

sented his substitutes in the format of naval regulations which could be adopted by Congress. He also urged ministers of the Gospel to "call upon the people of their Congressional districts to memorialize Congress for the immediate abolition of corporal punishment in the Navy, as well as the spirit part of the ration." [30]

If any ministers followed Lockwood's advice, we have no record of it, but congressional action was forthcoming. Two prominent northern Whigs brought forth fresh evidence of antiflogging sentiment among the voters. At the very end of December 1849 Daniel Webster presented 13 petitions from the people of Massachusetts calling for the end of corporal punishment.[31] William Seward of New York presented a variety of petitions including one from some mercantile houses in Baltimore calling for the end of flogging in the Navy. Seward said that the man who had the power to administer the whip exercised the same control over his men "that a master exercises over his slave." And as for substitutes, he pointed out that corporal punishment was abolished in the penitentiaries of New York without loss of discipline.[32]

That same day Hale gave notice of his intention to introduce a bill abolishing flogging at an early date. In times past, he said, members of the Committee on Naval Affairs have complained that they did not have time to investigate the subject. They now had time. He proposed no alternative, leaving it to the "wisdom of the committee to devise a substitute." [33]

On December 31, Democratic Representative Job Mann of Pennsylvania presented a resolution to the House instructing the Committee on Naval Affairs to "inquire into the expediency of reporting a bill" to repeal laws authorizing flogging. His resolution was preceded by a preamble in which he declared that "public sentiment, humanity, and every principle of republicanism and justice demand that such a barbarous law should be stricken from our national statute-book." Mann's resolution touched off a debate and was set aside without action.[34]

Matters were coming fast to a decisive stage. On January 29,

---

[30] [Lockwood], p. 56.
[31] *Congressional Globe*, 31st Cong., 1st Sess., XIX, Part 1, p. 91.
[32] *Ibid.*, p. 92.
[33] *Ibid.*, p. 93.
[34] *House Journal*, 31st Cong., 1st Sess. (Serial 566), pp. 206, 208–209.

1850, Secretary William B. Preston sent a circular to a number of naval officers, ranging in rank from purser to commodore, asking for their opinions on the wisdom of abolishing flogging and grog. On the subject of flogging, the Secretary asked: "Can Corporal punishment be dispensed with consistently with the interest and efficiency of the Naval Service? If so, what punishment should be substituted? If it cannot, state your reason for the opinion, and such particulars of your experience in regard to the practice as you may deem pertinent. Can any further restriction than those which the law now imposes upon the use of this punishment be advantageously applied?"[35]

The 84 replies received by Secretary Preston give a splendid insight into the minds of the naval officers of this period. Only seven felt that flogging could be discontinued. One favored modifications in its use and a change in the type of personnel enlisted in the ranks. These things would eventually lead to the abolition of the lash. Two of the seven who opposed the use of flogging were naval surgeons.[36] Apparently no chaplains were quizzed. There is also no reply on file from Captain Uriah P. Levy. Levy's views on flogging were well known, so that it is possible that he may not have been sent the circular. This also may have been true in the case of the chaplains. The vast majority of the officers questioned wrote letters of reply which repeated the familiar arguments for retaining the lash: it was quick; its practicality had stood the test of years; it was manly; the men preferred it to other punishments; it fell upon only a small part of the crew, mostly "worthless" men and/or foreigners; most officers disliked administering the lash and did so only when absolutely necessary; and confinement was impractical because it threw extra work on the good men.[37]

Lieutenant John J. Almy had already prepared and published a pamphlet on *Naval Discipline and Corporal Punishment* which he sent to Preston with his compliments as his answer to the circular. Almy declared that in 21 years of service he had never witnessed

---

[35] Secretary of the Navy William B. Preston, Circular, Jan. 29, 1850, *Reports of Officers.*
[36] Those who favored the abolition of flogging were Captains David Conner, Robert F. Stockton, and Isaac McKeever, Lieutenants Edward B. Boutwell and William D. Porter, Surgeons Robert J. Dodd and Thomas L. Smith.
[37] *Reports of Officers, passim.*

any of the tyrannical conduct about which so many newspaper articles spoke. The Navy was made up of three classes of men, he said. The first class consisted of "good men" who went on "cruise after cruise without ever being touched by the lash." The second class were those "who require close watching and punishing occasionally," and who are kept in order through fear of the lash. The third class includes mostly foreigners and "lazy vagabonds," who have to be flogged "pretty often in the first few months of the cruise" before they settle down. The majority of the United States sailors were in favor of the lash, and two-thirds to three-quarters of them were never touched by it. He pointed out that the crew of the naval steamer *Union* drew up a memorial to the Secretary of the Navy which requested that he use his influence to prevent the abolition of flogging. A similar memorial was prepared by the crew of the frigate *North Carolina*. Those who wish to abolish flogging, said Almy, should speak to the surgeons, the pursers, and the chaplains with whom he had conversed and who "have always expressed themselves in the strongest kind of manner against the entire impracticability of abolishing flogging in the Navy."[38]

Those officers who opposed flogging were equally strong in their convictions. Commodore David Conner called the practice "the remnant of a barbarous age, contrary alike, to the spirit of our institutions and the principles of humanity — a degrading law, which ought long since, to have been expunged from our statute books."[39]

Captain Isaac McKeever believed that the laws should be changed and a distinction made between faults and crimes. Faults could be punished by fines, by confinement in irons or otherwise, by a bread and water diet during confinement, and by other ways. Crimes would be punished by the sentence of a court-martial. He felt that with the "experience of the navy, and the wisdom of Congress" a system of punishments could be worked out which would be "more congenial to the spirit of the times & the progress of civilization than the use of the lash."[40]

---

[38] A Lieutenant of the Navy [John J. Almy], *Naval Discipline and Corporal Punishment* (Boston, 1850), p. 14.

[39] Captain David Conner to Secretary Preston, Feb. 5, 1850, *Reports of Officers*, No. 10.

[40] Captain Isaac McKeever to Secretary Preston, Feb. 5, 1850, *ibid.*, No. 18.

Lieutenant William D. Porter observed that "old prejudices are
very hard to eradicate" and that apparently "custom sanctions almost any absurdity," but he favored ending flogging and the spirit
ration, and attacking the abuses relating to the payment of advance wages to recruits.[41]

Lieutenant Edward B. Boutwell felt that as soon as corporal
punishment was ended, the pay of the sailors should be increased
to attract American citizens. Foreigners and convicts should be
excluded. Offenders could be punished by reducing wages in proportion to the offenses. If a man became so bad that he forfeited
all his wages, he should be discharged from the service. He knew
that many seamen were adverse to abolishing either flogging or
grog, but he felt that the Navy would be better off without these
practices.[42]

Of those who favored abolition of corporal punishment, Captain
Robert F. Stockton's reply is particularly interesting in view of the
fact that he was soon to resign his commission and fight against
flogging as a member of the United States Senate. He believed that
good service should be rewarded by the payment of a premium at
the end of a cruise. When punishment was necessary he favored
such substitutes for the lash as "extra duty — stopping the ration
of tea, Sugar and molasses — Confinement — Solitary Confinement
on short allowance — a Badge of disgrace to be worn for a time —
and, in cases, the Tread mill." He added that "the secret of good
discipline in the service, is to be found in that spirit of Kindness
which regards the Comforts and the welfare of the Sailor, and the
Confidence which springs from a conviction in his mind, that he
has a friend in his Commander, who will stand by him while he
stands by his duty, and is true to his honor and his flag."[43]

Precise evidence is lacking, but Stockton may well have approached the subject of flogging with a deeper understanding and
a wider background than many of his colleagues. One of his uncles,
Dr. Benjamin Rush, was notable, among other things, as a crusader

---

[41] Lieutenant William D. Porter to Secretary Preston, Feb. 3, 1850, *ibid.*,
No. 64.

[42] Lieutenant Edward B. Boutwell to Secretary Preston, Jan. 31, 1850, *ibid.*,
No. 56.

[43] Captain Robert F. Stockton to Secretary Preston, Feb. 6, 1850, *ibid.*,
No. 17.

against capital punishment. Another uncle, Andrew Hunter, served as a chaplain in both the Army and the Navy. One of Hunter's sons, Richard Stockton Hunter, entered the Navy as a midshipman in 1811, the same year as Stockton. Another son, Lewis B. Hunter, served as a naval medical officer from 1828 to 1868. Dr. Hunter was one of the witnesses who testified against Captain William K. Latimer in 1841 when the latter was court-martialed for cruelty and oppression against seamen.[44]

As for Stockton himself, he received his early training under Captain John Rodgers, a strict disciplinarian, and was in close association with him throughout the War of 1812. Stockton had great respect for Rodgers and for the training he received at his hands.[45] During the 1820's he became very interested in the American Colonization Society and its work. In 1828 he took a leave of absence from the Navy and engaged in business activity in New Jersey. When he returned to the Navy in 1838 he became absorbed in the campaign to build steam warships, which eventually resulted in the construction of the *Princeton*, named for his home town.[46]

The writer has been unable to determine precisely when Stockton became interested in the cause of seamen, but in 1845 he bought one of the special seamen's libraries from the American Seamen's Friend Society and presented it to the crew of the *Congress*.[47] Chaplain Walter Colton had a high regard for Stockton, and in 1850 he published this estimate of the Captain: "He never forgets the sailor. He pities when others might reproach, forgives when others might denounce, and never abandons him even though he should abandon himself; and yet, he exacts prompt obedience." Colton believed that Stockton's discipline was based largely on "moral influences, the power of correct example and the

[44] Callahan, pp. 285, 524; Harris Elwood Starr, "Andrew Hunter," *Dictionary of American Biography*, IX (1932), 399–400; Charles O. Paullin, "Robert Field Stockton," *Dictionary of American Biography*, XVIII (1936), 48–49; *Stockton Family Papers*, Princeton University Library; *Court Martial Records*, XLI, No. 769, RG 45, NA.

[45] Paullin, "Robert Field Stockton," pp. 48–49; Robert F. Stockton to Captain John Rodgers, Jan. 9, 1815, *John Rodgers Papers*, 1st Series, II.

[46] Paullin, "Robert Field Stockton," pp. 48–49.

[47] William H. Gatzmer to A. Spaulding, Sept. 20, 1845, *Robert F. Stockton Letterbooks, 1843–47*, Princeton University Library.

pressure of circumstances."[48] Stockton was not above flogging a man if he thought it necessary, but he tried to minimize the use of the lash. Now, in 1850, he stood with the small group of officers who urged that the practice be ended.

The chorus of protesting voices and the literature urging the abolition of the lash increased. Between December 31, 1849, and June 17, 1850, the Senate received 271 petitions from citizens in Massachusetts, Pennsylvania, Maine, Maryland, New Hampshire, and New York calling for the end of corporal punishment in the Navy.[49] The proceedings of three public meetings on the subject in New York and Connecticut also were presented. During this same period the legislatures of Rhode Island and Indiana instructed their men in Congress to work for a law ending flogging.[50] The crusading spirit encouraged others to join in this effort to arouse the public and to stimulate the Congress. Captain Uriah Levy, who had long been interested in this cause, wrote articles for newspapers in Washington, New York, and Virginia.[51] He also may have been in touch with Senator Hale.[52] In New York City Dr. Usher Parsons, a former naval surgeon who had served with Perry at Lake Erie, wrote an article against flogging which appeared in the *Sunday Dispatch*.[53] And these articles stimulated the writing of other articles.

But of all the literature on flogging none matched the persuasive power of Herman Melville's *White Jacket, or The World of a Man-of-War* which appeared in 1850. Using his own service on the *United States* during 1843–44 as a basis, Melville drew upon the

---

[48] Walter Colton, *Deck and Port; or, Incidents of a Cruise in the United States Frigate Congress to California* (New York, 1860), p. 44.

[49] These were broken down as follows: Massachusetts — 124; Pennsylvania — 72; Maine — 58; Maryland — 15; New Hampshire — 3; New York — 1.

[50] *Senate Journal*, 31st Cong., 1st Sess. (Serial 548), pp. 37, 38, 44, 57, 58, 72, 94, 104, 126, 140, 142, 147, 153, 158, 160, 204, 218, 228, 340, 401.

[51] John C. Wyllie, "Uriah Phillips Levy," *Dictionary of American Biography*, XI (1933), 203–204; Abram Kanof, "Uriah Phillips Levy: The Story of a Pugnacious Commodore," *Publications of the American Jewish Historical Society*, XXXIX (1949), 47, 49; Fitzpatrick and Saphire, pp. 185–189.

[52] This has been suggested, but the present writer can find no evidence of it. There are no letters from Levy extant in the *John P. Hale Papers* in the New Hampshire Historical Society.

[53] Charles W. Parsons, *Memoir of Usher Parsons, M.D.* (Providence, 1870), p. 51; New York *Sunday Dispatch*, Feb. 17, 1850.

experiences of other men, both oral and written, to enlarge his narrative. He altered names and chronology, and gave the impression that the end product was straight autobiography.[54] A recent biographer of Melville described *White Jacket* as "a novel of purpose, in which the plot has been supplanted by a sustained attack upon naval abuses, running beneath its comedy and tragedy, its story and picture, its fact and fiction."[55] This skillful piece of propaganda contained more than 50 pages of condemnation of flogging.[56]

Melville asked his readers: "Are we not justified in immeasurably denouncing this thing? Join hands with me, then; and, in the name of that being in whose image the flogged sailor is made, let us demand of Legislators, by what right they dare to profane what God himself accounts sacred."[57]

Meanwhile more action had taken place on Capitol Hill. Thomas L. Harris, an Illinois Democrat, presented a resolution in the House on February 4, 1850, calling on the Secretary of the Navy to furnish evidence, if any, of cases where petty officers were disrated, flogged as seamen for an offense committed while a petty officer, and then rerated. This was followed by another long resolution asking for information on floggings for offenses against the law and against "the usages of the sea service," and whether the latter were recorded in the ship's log. He also wanted copies of all rules, regulations, and orders established by the Navy Department for the internal regulation of ships and the classification and punishment of offenses. Harris wondered whether such laws were the same for all vessels and whether they were observed. Nor was this all; he also wanted information on whether the crimes against the "usages of the sea service" had ever been codified, promulgated, hung up in a central part of the ship, and read to the crew once a month, as was required for other regulations. And as if the Navy Department did not have enough information to furnish already, he asked for data on any cases where sailors had been deprived of any part of

[54] Charles R. Anderson, *Melville in the South Seas* (New York, 1940), pp. 361, 364, 381, 394, 401, 418–419.

[55] *Ibid.*, p. 420.

[56] *Ibid.*, p. 425. For a discussion of *White Jacket* as fact, as romance, and as propaganda see Chaps. 13–16, pp. 349–434.

[57] Melville, p. 135.

their rations as punishment during 1849. Finally, he wanted the proportionate number of sailors who commuted their spirit ration.[58] Such an all-inclusive inquiry as this was not only vexing to the Navy Department, but also an indication that trouble was brewing.

A clearer warning came a month later when Illinois Democrat John Wentworth announced his intention to introduce a bill abolishing flogging and the spirit ration in the Navy.[59]

This storm began where it had commenced so many times before, during the discussion of the naval appropriation bill. But this time it was very late in the session when the matter came up in the Committee of the Whole House. George W. Jones, a Democrat representative from Tennessee, introduced an amendment abolishing flogging on September 21. No sooner had he done so than North Carolina's Edward Stanly, a Whig, submitted an amendment to exempt the sentences of courts-martial from this rule. Another Whig, Alexander Evans of Maryland, moved to abolish the spirit ration and pointed out that it was the cause of flogging. Opposition to the abolition of flogging came from South Carolina's Isaac Holmes, a Democrat, on the grounds that it was not germane to the bill under discussion. The proposals of Jones and Evans were denounced by Democrat Abraham Venable of North Carolina. "It is all a humbug"; he said, "and the best way to cure humbugs is to prescribe and administer a large dose of humbug. Sir, all this hyperphilanthropy is of the same origin of some other species of fanaticism which are rife amongst us." [60] Venable's idea of a large dose of humbug was to further amend the amendment so that neither wine nor ardent spirits could be used by the officers except as medicine. Venable's amendment did not please Louisiana's Isaac E. Morse, a Democrat, any more than did the other amendments. He believed that any legislation on these matters should grow out of a report by the Committee on Naval Affairs which would form "a legitimate basis for legislation." On this note the House adjourned for the day.[61]

Two days later it all began again. The amendments of Stanly,

[58] *Congressional Globe*, 31st Cong., 1st Sess., XIX, Part 1, p. 279.
[59] *Ibid.*, p. 460.   [60] *Ibid.*, XIX, Part 2, pp. 1906–07.
[61] *Ibid.*, p. 1906.

Evans, and Venable were accepted by a vote of 82 to 43. Shortly thereafter Jacob Thompson, a Democrat from Mississippi, moved to substitute for this involved statement a simple amendment abolishing flogging that was the same as Jones's proposal. The Committee of the Whole House agreed to the substitution by a vote of 88 to 42.[62]

Now the House considered the measure and passed it by a healthy majority — 131 to 29.[63] This was a relatively easy victory. Greater obstacles loomed ahead. Past experience had shown that it was possible to get a measure of this sort through the House. The real test of strength would be in the Senate. The battle began when that body took up the naval appropriation bill on September 28.

Several people were waiting for the flogging measure to come up. One of them was George E. Badger, an ex-Secretary of the Navy, who prepared an amendment throwing out the antiflogging provision. Badger was a member of the Committee on Indian Affairs, and, as chance would have it, he could not present his amendment. Mason of North Carolina offered it for him when the discussion started. He followed it by remarks on the large number of memorials against flogging that the naval committee had received, and of its endeavors to get the opinions of persons in the naval and merchant service on the subject. The committee believed it would be "utterly impracticable" to have an efficient navy without flogging. It was their intention to publish a report on their findings to bring public opinion to the same conclusion.[64]

John P. Hale began the counterattack. Holding in his hand a printed report of the floggings in the Navy which he called "The

<hr />

[62] *Ibid.*, p. 1914.

[63] *Ibid.*, p. 1922; *House Journal*, 31st Cong., 1st Sess. (Serial 566), p. 1505. This vote shows some interesting sectional characteristics. The group which voted to abolish flogging included 96 representatives from northern states, 14 from southern states (Alabama, Arkansas, Mississippi, North Carolina, Texas, and Virginia), and 21 from the border states of Tennessee, Kentucky, Maryland, and Missouri. These 131 men included 63 Whigs (including 2 Free Soil Whigs), 59 Democrats, 4 Free Soilers, 2 Republicans, 2 Independents, and 1 American party man. Of those who opposed the measure, 16 were Whigs and 13 were Democrats. This represented a voting strength of 11 from northern states, 15 from southern states, and 3 from the border states of Kentucky and Delaware. Information on party affiliations is from the *Biographical Directory of the American Congress, 1774–1927, passim.*

[64] *Congressional Globe*, 31st Cong., 1st Sess., XIX, Part 2, p. 2057.

Chronicles of the Cat-o'-nine-tails," he charged that the committee had had ample time to study it and to make plans for a substitute form of punishment. He then proceeded to examine the arguments of those who wished to retain flogging.

With regard to the argument that the lash was absolutely necessary for discipline while a ship was at sea, he pointed out the case of the receiving ship *Pennsylvania* mentioned in the report. As a receiving ship it was tied up at a wharf, yet during 1846 floggings were administered to 55 men, or a little better than one a week. The following year the same ship reported 151 floggings or three times a week. Flogging had so improved the discipline of the men, said Hale, that during 1848 it was resorted to in 239 cases! It was easy to see how effective this sort of discipline had been.[65]

He then took up the charge that only a small number of troublesome and worthless individuals were flogged. But the names of the men flogged were in the report, and "you will hardly find one recorded twice." To prove his point Hale read a list of names. It seemed as though repetition came after most of the crew had been flogged once.

Year after year, according to Hale, the Senate had defended the use of the cat and had been a stumbling block in the way of "the advances of the humanity of the age in which we live." Then, alluding to the work of that session which had resulted in the Compromise of 1850, he said that when so much had been done "to heal the 'bloody wounds' of a violated Constitution," the Senate ought not to consent "that the bleeding wounds of the lacerated backs of the white citizens of this republic shall be longer submitted to this brutalizing punishment." The naval committee planned to publish an excuse for not abolishing it. We have waited long enough, said Hale. In his judgment it would be better to lose every other section of the bill and save the flogging measure than to strike it out and save the rest.[66]

David L. Yulee, chairman of the Committee on Naval Affairs, argued that although there had been "spasmodic ebullitions both

---

[65] It should be noted, however, that since a receiving ship functioned as a collecting point, there was undoubtedly a large turnover in men during each one of the years mentioned, and especially so since these were the years of the Mexican War.

[66] *Congressional Globe*, 31st Cong., 1st Sess., XIX, Part 2, pp. 2057–58.

of eloquence and passion" on the subject of flogging, the matter had never reached the point where action was necessary until this session. The committee gathered information and was in the process of digesting it in order to arrive at a judicious decision. He had inquired of his colleague, John Davis of Massachusetts, where reliable information might be gathered as to the opinions of the commercial class on this subject. Davis referred him to the Boston Marine Society, an organization of old shipmasters. Yulee dispatched a letter of inquiry. The chairman of the board of trustees replied that the group believed that navigation and commerce would be imperiled if flogging were ended. Similar views were expressed by seamen in the Navy, by chambers of commerce, and by other reliable sources. In view of this evidence Yulee wished to avoid any hasty legislative action which would hurt the service.[67]

Hannibal Hamlin, a Democrat from Maine, added his voice to the cause of reform. He had made a reputation in the state legislature as a foe of capital punishment and had helped to abolish it in Maine. Now he fought to modernize the Navy's penal practices. To those who asked whence came this agitation for abolition, he replied that in his state the movement embraced all classes, creeds, parties, and degrees of intelligence. All regarded it as a disgrace "that any man should stand up, at this age of the world, and demand corporal punishment at this day." Some of the "oldest and most valiant officers" of the Navy, among them Commodore Charles Stewart, feel that this "relic of barbarism" should be swept away. To those who said that the present bill was not the proper place to treat the subject, he replied: "You will never find the proper bill or the proper occasion. The only way to reach that abuse is to put the remedy in some bill where we shall have some aid in carrying it through to prevent the opposition which there is against it."

The only seamen in favor of flogging, said Hamlin, were those who have been used to it since they first went to sea. It was strange indeed that they had never learned that it is not necessary to whip a man in order to make him do right. Hamlin then voiced an argument that had long been used by the naval reformers and was to be a cornerstone of future personnel policies. He said:

---

[67] *Ibid.*, pp. 2058–59.

Sir, treat your sailors like men. Refuse them the opportunities of becoming intoxicated, and you will do away with a great deal of the necessity for the cat-o'-nine-tails. Treat them as men, and as men they will behave. It is an assumed position upon the part of all who desire to retain this odious system, that the interests of the service demand it. Let the other side be heard now. We say it is not necessary. We say there are no demands, either from interest, justice, or propriety, that require the infliction of this punishment. You have had one side of it for a century almost; now let us try the other side, and see if the assumption is true. Let us see if the sailors will not behave as well without the stimulus of the lash.[68]

James A. Pearce, a Maryland Whig, denounced the "false philanthropy and sickly sentimentality" of those who would end flogging. To do so would allow officers no other discretion in punishments than hanging. Putting a man in irons only made more work for the rest of the crew. The French had tried to substitute other punishments for the lash and ended up with crueler sentences. Besides, the men in the Navy did not consider it degrading to be flogged.[69]

It was at this point that Jefferson Davis, a Mississippi Democrat, entered the discussion. As a West Pointer and a veteran of the Black Hawk and Mexican wars, he knew something about military discipline. He was not one to agitate for a reform of naval discipline, but neither was he one to underestimate the strength of the movement. This drive to end flogging was not generated from within the Navy, said Davis. "I have no doubt — and I have some time since come to this conclusion — that a feeling at the North required the abolition of flogging in the navy, and that, sooner or later, we must arrive at that result." Such being the case, one must look for substitutes. Those used in the Army will not do. Davis knew of none that would do. This dilemma led him to deduce a new approach to discipline which he announced to his colleagues. "You must, then, take the other extreme. You must go to the system of rewards. In reflecting upon this subject, I have become satisfied that, sooner or later, we must meet it. I believe that the manner by which it can be done is to increase the pay of the sailor of the navy

---

[68] Charles Eugene Hamlin, *The Life and Times of Hannibal Hamlin* (Cambridge, Mass., 1899), pp. 62–64; *Congressional Globe*, 31st Cong., 1st Sess., XIX, Part 2, p. 2059.
[69] *Ibid.*

of the United States to something materially over the pay he could get upon any marine vessel, so as to make it a punishment, and a severe punishment, to dismiss him from the navy, a dishonorable discharge preventing him from being reemployed." If such a provision were brought forward by the reformers and annexed to a bill abolishing flogging, Davis would "surrender gracefully to what I know to be the power." But in its present form, annexed to a provision for carrying the mails, he could not approve it.[70]

These were the main arguments for and against the measure. After a short exchange between Yulee and William Seward of New York about whether flogging was or was not still used in the prisons of New York, the Senate was ready to vote. Hale called for the yeas and nays. Yulee wished to amend the section before it was struck out and moved to insert a phrase covering the merchant service. This addition was accepted 25 to 13. Now the question of striking out the proviso on flogging was put to the Senate. The secretary announced the result: yeas, 24; nays, 23. The reformers had lost again.[71]

Or had they? Rhode Island's Albert C. Greene, a Whig, voted in favor of the proviso, but the secretary had not heard him. The Senate was about to consider the next amendment when Hale rose on a question of privilege and moved that the journal be corrected. This precipitated a discussion of parliamentary procedure. Also, if Greene's vote were added, now the result was a tie, and the amendment was not lost. Greene had voted against his private convictions, but in view of the instructions from the Rhode Island legislature he was anxious to have his vote recorded.

His Rhode Island colleague, John H. Clark, also a Whig, reminded the Senate of the feeling in his state on the subject and urged a proper recording to prevent injury to Greene and the falsification of the record. Finally, Mason of Virginia moved that the vote be taken over again. This time the vote was 26 to 24 against striking out the amendment. The Senate had agreed to abolish flogging! That same day, September 28, 1850, the President signed the appropriation bill, and the proviso abolishing flogging became the law of the land. In its final form the amendment read: *"Provided,* that flogging in the navy, and on board

---

[70] *Ibid.*   [71] *Ibid.*, p. 2060.

vessels of commerce, be, and the same is hereby, abolished from and after the passage of this act." [72]

The narrow margin of victory on this measure warrants a closer look at the voting statistics. On both the first and second vote there was no break in the ranks of those who opposed the abolition of flogging. Of the 24 who dissented, 13 were Whigs and 11 Democrats. This same 24 represented 2 votes from northern states,[73] 7 votes from border states,[74] and 15 votes from southern states.

An analysis of the second, or victorious, vote shows that of the 26 who voted to abolish flogging, 9 were Whigs, 14 were Democrats, 1 was an Anti-Slavery candidate (Hale), 1 was a Free Soil Democrat (Frémont), and 1 was elected on a fusion ticket of Democrats and Free Soilers (Chase). A sectional division of this group shows that 24 of the votes came from northern states, and 2 from border states.[75] Three of the Whigs and two of the Democrats who helped to bring about victory failed to vote the first time.[76] Two Democrats, including one southerner, who voted to abolish flogging the first time did not vote on the second tally.[77] We may thus conclude that the abolition of flogging was brought about largely by northern Democrats. Jefferson Davis' comment that the movement was prompted by a northern feeling seems to be borne out.

Congress adjourned the same day that flogging was abolished. The rush of the Senators to get through the necessary business seems to have curtailed extensive discussions of naval discipline, and thus worked to the advantage of the humanitarians.[78] The

---

[72] *Ibid.; U.S. Statutes at Large*, IX, Chap. 80, p. 515.

[73] William L. Dayton of New Jersey and Truman Smith of Connecticut, both Whigs.

[74] David R. Achison of Missouri, James A. Pearce and Thomas G. Pratt of Maryland, John Bell of Tennessee, Presley Spruance and John Wales of Delaware, all Whigs; and Tennessee's Hopkins L. Turney, a Democrat.

[75] Thomas Hart Benton, a Democrat from Missouri, and Joseph R. Underwood, a Kentucky Whig.

[76] The Whigs were James Cooper of Pennsylvania, Thomas Ewing of Ohio, and Albert C. Greene of Rhode Island. The Democrats were William M. Gwin of California, and James Shields of Illinois.

[77] Pierre Soule of Louisiana and James Whitcomb of Indiana.

[78] See the remarks of Senators Robert M. T. Hunter, John P. Hale, and William H. Seward in the *Congressional Globe*, 31st Cong., 1st Sess., XIX, Part 2, pp. 2059, 2060.

action of Congress was hailed by *The Sailor's Magazine* and by other publications and groups who had fought the long fight.

For John P. Hale this was a time of triumph. The crew of the U.S. frigate *Brandywine,* homeward bound after a three-year cruise, drew up a letter of thanks to Hale for his efforts in abolishing the use of the cat-o'-nine-tails. This letter, signed by the nine seamen on behalf of all, was delivered to Hale by one of the crew.[79]

Captain John C. Long of the frigate *Mississippi,* writing from the Bay of Naples, said: "For this one act of yours in favor of the navy I feel very grateful, and cordially forgive all your former attacks on our branch of the national service. But I hope you will not stop here, but follow up, and supply us with a new and enlarged code of laws for the better government of the navy as a substitute for what has been so meritoriously taken from us, and be sure never, never allow that mode of punishment to be again resorted to which has always been as painful to inflict, as for the poor Jack to receive."[80]

Captain Long also reported that he was "very much gratified" to find that he could successfully employ substitutes for punishing minor offenses if he had "the cooperation of all the officers" of the ship. A great cause of discontent among the crew was the practice of keeping them on board while the ship was in port, so he gave them shore leave, whenever possible, and with it a portion of their wages. The result was a disciplined, efficient, and contented crew.[81]

Many years after the abolition of flogging certain zealous individuals attempted to credit this reform to the efforts of a single person. Commodore Levy, Senator Hale, and Herman Melville each has his partisans. In Melville's case, credit was given by a midshipman who had served with him in the *United States.* Rear Admiral Samuel Franklin, writing in 1898 of his early years, stated that a copy of *White Jacket* was placed on the desk of every member of Congress and that this book "had more influence in abolish-

---

[79] Crew of the *Brandywine* to Senator John P. Hale, Nov. 15, 1850, *John P. Hale Papers.*

[80] Captain John C. Long to Senator John P. Hale, Jan. 23, 1851, *John P. Hale Papers.*

[81] *Ibid.*

ing corporal punishment in the Navy than anything else!"[82] But Franklin wrote this nearly half a century after the event, and his references to Melville are regarded as untrustworthy. He is the only source for the story of the distribution of *White Jacket* to the members of Congress, and while not impossible, it seems most unlikely.[83] There is no mention of the book or of its author in any of the proceedings of Congress. It also seems improbable that anyone with a flair for dramatics such as John P. Hale had would have missed the opportunity to read some of Melville's deathless denunciations into the record. And particularly so when he did refer to, and read from, a government document!

At least one naval officer was moved to write a rebuttal of Melville's book, but his effort was not published until the twentieth century.[84] In general there has been a tendency to take Admiral Franklin's statement at face value and to exaggerate the importance of *White Jacket* in ending flogging. A great deal had been said about flogging long before Melville wrote. Those who desired to investigate the matter had ample opportunities to become familiar with the arguments for and against the practice. By 1850 many people had taken sides, as evidenced by the number of memorials and the persistence of the agitation. Some persons who were as yet uncommitted may have been swayed by Melville's prose, but probably he merely solidified the convictions of the convinced, or aroused the ire of the unconvinced.

Some writers have argued that Captain Levy was the man principally responsible for the end of flogging, but their evidence has not been as strong as their claims. Levy himself only said that he was *one* of the first to protest against the use of the lash. Certainly his ideas and his example encouraged other reformers, and he *may* have worked closely with Senator Hale. I have attempted to show that many men participated in the crusade against flogging, but all of their efforts would have been in vain without leadership and support in the Congress.

---

[82] Samuel R. Franklin, *Memories of a Rear Admiral* (New York, 1898), p. 64.

[83] Anderson, pp. 429–431.

[84] Charles R. Anderson, "A Reply to Herman Melville's *White Jacket* by Rear Admiral Thomas O. Selfridge, Sr.," *American Literature*, VII (1935), 123–144.

The abolition of flogging had thrown the Navy into a state of confusion. A disciplinary practice in use before the U.S. Navy itself was born was now illegal. Many officers who were convinced that the Navy could not be run without the lash were now obliged to make the experiment. Some undoubtedly felt that the resulting disorder in the service would force Congress to reverse itself. At any rate, Secretary Graham began to receive letters from officers reporting cases of unruly seamen and asking for instructions as to substitute punishment.[85]

The Secretary himself was in doubt about proper remedies. In his annual report of November 1850 he declared that it was now the duty of Congress to revise the whole system of punishments at once. Commanders had no alternative but to put men in irons. Graham suggested that Congress take the testimony of officers and seamen concerning a proper code of discipline for the Navy.[86]

A naval board, which had been convened in Washington for another matter, had the problem of proper substitutes added to its agenda. Graham wrote to Commodore Charles Stewart, the board's president, asking for advice on several points. Stewart replied on January 1, 1851, with a suggestion that a certain amount of confinement might be used. He felt that if seamen's wages were raised, better men would be attracted to the service. Such men should then be induced to remain in the Navy by giving them good conduct discharges at the end of their enlistments. These discharges would entitle them to three months' pay if, after at least two years' service, they reenlisted within 90 days. He would also give them the right to provision in a naval asylum after 20 years of service. By the same token, unwanted individuals could be eliminated from the Navy by bad conduct discharges. Stewart believed that flogging should be restored for sentences of courts-

---

[85] *Senate Executive Documents*, 31st Cong., 2d Sess. (Serial 589), Doc. 12.

[86] *Senate Documents*, 31st Cong., 2d Sess. (Serial 587), pp. 206–208. Dr. Edward Robinson Squibb, U.S.N., published an apologia for flogging under the title "Punishments in the Navy" in the Philadelphia *North American* for Nov. 19, 1851. He argued that imprisonment was no punishment for the lazy and dissolute types who needed correction. Also, a ship's prison was "as close, damp, filthy, and unhealthy as any dungeon and as inhuman, as degrading, and as unphilanthropic as any flogging can be, without producing the desired salutary effect." See also Lawrence G. Blochman, *Doctor Squibb: The Life and Times of a Rugged Idealist* (New York, 1958), p. 47.

martial. Other methods of discipline would be reduction in ratings, badges of disgrace, a ration of bread and water, the denial of shore leave, and other minor punishments.[87] The board had prepared "the draft of a law for the establishment of summary courts martial, and a system of rewards and punishments, as the best mode of government that, in its opinion, can, under the present Circumstances, be adopted."[88] Graham sent Stewart's report to President Fillmore who, in turn, forwarded it to the Senate with the request that it receive "the immediate attention of Congress."[89] Congress, however, saw fit to delay action.

In June the Secretary issued to all officers a circular requesting answers to questions he posed on the subject of discipline. Their replies were to be in the Navy Department by October 15 of that year. Among other things Graham was interested in the effect of the abolition of flogging on the recruiting service and on the general efficiency of the Navy.[90] By fall he had a considerable body of information ready to present to Congress. In November he recommended the establishment of a Bureau of Orders and Discipline which would issue orders and keep the reports on discipline. Such an arrangement would relieve the Secretary of much routine clerical duty. He also suggested that the office of Judge Advocate of the Navy be attached to the Bureau. By such an arrangement a professionally qualified officer would administer justice. The increase in the number of courts-martial since the abolition of flogging made the establishment of such an office essential.[91]

Others also had been collecting information on the effect of the end of flogging. *The Sailor's Magazine* reported good results on board the *St. Mary's* and the *St. Lawrence*.[92]

John P. Hale was not one to expect that a change in sentiments over flogging would come suddenly. The vote abolishing it had been too close. He also was not going to let the results of many

---

[87] *Senate Executive Documents*, 31st Cong., 2d Sess. (Serial 589), Doc. 12.
[88] *Ibid.*
[89] *Ibid.*
[90] *Circulars and General Orders*, II, 188; Captain William H. Aulick to Secretary of the Navy William A. Graham, Aug. 20, 1851, "Reports of officers on effect of flogging in the Navy," *NJ-Discipline*, RG 45, NA.
[91] *House Executive Documents*, 32d Cong., 1st Sess. (Serial 635), II, Part 2, Doc. 2, p. 16.
[92] *The Sailor's Magazine*, XXIII, 276, 306.

years of effort be lost. Word had reached him of abuses in the matter of punishments. So, on December 4, 1851, just three days after the new Congress had assembled, Hale introduced a resolution instructing the Secretary of the Navy to inform the Senate of any violations of the law abolishing flogging, and, if violations existed, to state what steps had been taken to uphold the law.[93] A few days later, when his resolution came up, Hale moved to lay it on the table for the time being because he was not sure whether the abuses mentioned occurred before or after flogging was ended.[94]

If Hale's case was not quite ready, the opposition's was. On December 17 Richard Broadhead, a Democratic senator from Pennsylvania, presented a memorial signed by a large number of citizens urging the restoration of corporal punishment. No sooner had this been presented than Robert F. Stockton, the former naval officer and now a Democratic senator from New Jersey, expressed his amazement that people should request such an action. He also gave notice that he would fight such a proposal from the start.[95]

California's William Gwin, a Democrat, suggested that before the memorial was referred to the Committee on Naval Affairs it would be desirable to know whether it was intended that flogging be restored or another system of punishment be substituted. Sentiments on the subject were to be expressed when he called up the memorial in a few days.[96]

Ammunition for the forthcoming debate was assembled when Gwin presented a resolution calling on the Secretary of the Navy to furnish letters from officers of the Navy on corporal punishment, and "any code or codes of law or regulations which he may have had prepared for the better government of the Navy." Secretary Graham was well prepared to answer both requests, and the information was soon forwarded to Capitol Hill.[97]

---

[93] *Congressional Globe*, 32d Cong., 1st Sess., XXIV, Part 1, p. 30.

[94] *Ibid.*, p. 34.

[95] *Ibid.*, p. 111.

[96] *Ibid.*

[97] *Ibid.*, p. 128; Secretary of the Navy William A. Graham to Senator William R. King, Dec. 22, 1851; Secretary of the Navy William A. Graham to Senator William M. Gwin, Dec. 29, 1851, Jan. 13, 1852, *Letters to Congress*, XII, 165–166, 174, 183.

Early in the new year the debate began. Stockton, Badger, Mallory, and Hale were the principal contenders. In a stirring speech Stockton pointed out the superiority of the American sailor and the need for good men. He recalled the past glories of the Navy in the War of 1812 and said that today a sailor was treated worse than a dog. Something must be done to elevate the sailor, to appeal to his honor and his pride. One could do more with him by rewarding him for his faithfulness than by punishing him for his delinquencies. Three things were forgotten when the rules for the government of the Navy were framed: first, that an American sailor was also "an American citizen and freeman, though in service of his country"; second, that "he had yielded no legal right, not inconsistent with his obligations of duty"; third, "that naval officers are not infallible, and require as stringent regulations for their government as other citizens vested with authority." The fact that officers and some men desire to have the lash restored is evidence of the low and degraded standard by which the Navy is judged and of its failure to keep "pace with the moral improvement of the age." The sailor must be protected "from the infliction of a punishment which stands condemned by the almost universal sentiment of his fellow-citizens; a punishment which is proscribed in the best prison-government; proscribed in the school-house, and proscribed in the best government on earth — that of parental domestic affection. Yes, sir, expelled from the social circle, from the school-house, the prison-house, and the Army, it finds defenders and champions nowhere but in the Navy." For his part he would rather see the Navy abolished than flogging restored.[98]

Badger attempted to refute Stockton's argument by pointing out that the victories of the War of 1812 were won by sailors trained under the lash. All the leading commanders in the American Navy needed the lash, including Stockton himself. But Badger wanted the policy settled without hasty changes back and forth. He voted against abolishing the lash because he felt it was necessary. Now that it was abolished he wanted to wait and see if it

---

[98] *Congressional Globe*, 32d Cong., 1st Sess., XXIV, Part 1, pp. 218–222. After reading Stockton's speech, Dr. Edward Robinson Squibb, U.S.N., noted in his journal that Stockton's "side of the question is not worth much if they cannot produce better speeches and arguments than that." See *The Journal of Edward Robinson Squibb, M.D.* (no city, 1930), Part I, p. 366.

really was essential to discipline. If experience proved that it was not necessary, then he would not wish it restored.[99]

Stephen R. Mallory, a Florida Democrat who recently had defeated Yulee for the Senate seat, gave his maiden speech in favor of the restoration of the lash. His opinions were based on a familiarity of about 20 years' standing with seamen and shipping, on observations of and conversations with various ranks both in and out of the service, and on documentary evidence. To Mallory the whole thing boiled down to the question of whether we would have a Navy or not. He believed that many years of experience proved the practicality and necessity of flogging. The Navy had disintegrated since flogging was abolished. This fact was confirmed by the Secretary of the Navy, by the reports of officers, and by Mallory's own observations on board the five or six ships he visited during the past half year. Our past naval glories had been won by men trained under the discipline of the lash. While a naval officer Stockton himself had inflicted whipping on men. Mallory objected to Stockton's reference to sailors being scourged like slaves. Slaves were not scourged. If a slave or a freeman was scourged, it was because he was a criminal.

He also objected to the talk about American sailors. A large part of the Navy was composed of foreigners. The use of fraudulent "protections" was well known. Furthermore, our naturalization laws were so lax, especially in regard to residence requirements of those who followed the sea, that it was possible for a sailor to become a naturalized American citizen with no more than 30 days accumulated residence in the country. The enlisted ranks of the Navy now were composed of the worst quality of men, so why should an effective means of disciplining them be outlawed?

Mallory also attacked the way in which flogging was abolished — by a proviso in an appropriation bill passed by a narrow margin at the end of a session. The movement behind this abolition was inspired by "false philanthropy" and "sickly sentimentality," said Mallory. Why tell the sailor that the lash degrades him when he himself does not feel debased? While on this theme Mallory also made an oblique attack on the abolitionists. In the South, he said, Negro stealing was considered "about the meanest offense" on

[99] *Congressional Globe*, 32d Cong., 1st Sess., XXIV, Part 1, pp. 221–223.

earth. But in the North the theft was regarded "as the highest evidence of good morals." The North preached that southern institutions were degrading. The South preached that to steal a man's property is to violate the laws of God and man. Each side preached to the other and there was no chance of one convincing the other. Why, therefore, asked Mallory, do we try to assimilate legislation based on the same idea to the sailor? He does not consider himself debased by flogging, so why tell him he is? The old tars, "the bone and sinew" of the Navy, did not petition to end flogging. A man who enlists does so with his eyes wide open and with knowledge of the punishment for his infractions. Let a poll be taken of the sailors, and the results would show that "ninety-nine one hundredths of the bone and sinew of the Navy will say restore flogging." [100]

Hale compared the attempts to restore flogging to the floundering of a harpooned whale. He had expected such an effort, but not as serious as this one. Flogging was dead, and nothing would push back the clock. Mallory's remarks on the origin of the antiflogging measure were an attempt to combine his advocacy of the lash with an attack on the abolitionists. Hale felt that if he had to make a choice between the Navy and the lash or no Navy, he was willing to let both go down together. On his motion the measure was postponed. [101]

The subject came up briefly a week later when the petition was referred to the Committee on Naval Affairs, but to all intents and purposes flogging was dead. [102] It was now up to Congress to give serious consideration to a new code of discipline.

It was Hale's conviction that if a poll of the sailors were taken, as Mallory suggested, it would have to be by secret ballot and held away from all the officers. If such a poll were taken, he had no doubt that he would be vindicated. No such vote was ever taken; but that year Hale had additional evidence that he had not misjudged the sailor's views on flogging. When he visited the *Germantown* in Boston Harbor he was received by Commodore Nicholson and his crew, and the yards were manned in his honor.

---

[100] Speech of Stephen R. Mallory in the Senate, Jan. 14, 15, 1852, in the Appendix to *ibid.*, XXV, 108–119.
[101] *Ibid.*, XXIV, Part 1, p. 283.   [102] *Ibid.*, p. 346.

The commodore thanked him for his efforts in abolishing flogging and presented him with a medal. It was said to be one of the most gratifying moments in Hale's life.[103]

Once it was obvious that flogging would not be restored, Senator Badger made great efforts to push through a bill "to enforce discipline and promote good conduct" in the Navy. It was a preliminary measure, but it did provide for courts-martial and for various types of punishment. Badger and others were particularly anxious to get this measure through before Perry's squadron left for Japan. In view of their hazardous undertaking, as well as the general needs of the service, it was considered desirable that the officers have a definite code to follow. The measure passed the Senate without difficulty, but got bogged down in debate in the House and was laid on the table.[104] Perry sailed without benefit of a new code of regulations.

In desperation the Navy attempted to meet its needs by another move. A board of naval officers had prepared a code consisting of some 46 chapters. This code, known as the "System of Orders and Instructions," was issued by President Fillmore on February 15, 1853. Thus the outgoing Whig administration gave the Navy a code, but it was destined to be short-lived.[105]

Shortly after he took office, James C. Dobbin, the new Secretary of the Navy, requested the opinion of the Attorney General on the validity of these regulations. Attorney General Caleb Cushing reported on April 5, 1853, that the code amounted to a diminishing of the power of Congress to make rules for the government and regulation of the naval forces. The presidential order thus related to a matter not within his jurisdiction as the Executive and therefore had no legal validity.[106]

The struggle to enact a new naval code began again. While Congress procrastinated, naval commanders were forced to devise

---

[103] Daniel Hall, *Addresses Commemorative of Abraham Lincoln and John P. Hale* (Concord, N.H., 1892), p. 64; Hale's role in abolishing flogging is briefly treated in Sewell, pp. 137–139.

[104] *Congressional Globe*, 32d Cong., 1st Sess., XXIV, Part 2, pp. 389, 424, 440, 448–450, 461, 910–919, 985–990, 1015–18, 1055–57, 1137–39, 1150–54.

[105] Charles C. Andrews, ed., *Official Opinions of the Attorneys General* (Washington, D.C., 1856), VI, 10–11; James Snedeker, *A Brief History of Courts-Martial* (Annapolis, Md., 1954), p. 56.

[106] Andrews, pp. 11–19.

their own substitutes for flogging. Some of these substitutes were mentioned in a report by Senator Mallory in May 1854, in which he urged an increase in pay as a means of attracting good seamen. He said:

Our commanders are now lashing offenders by the wrists to cross beams; lashing them up in their hammocks; pumping cold water upon them; *"bucking"* and *"bagging"* them; and resorting to many other novelties unknown to the seas heretofore; but under any circumstances the prompt performance of the daily routine of duty, as a general thing, cannot be enforced. Imprisonment or confinement of the men cannot extend to many without materially impairing the ships company. An increase of the pay, and holding out extra pay, certificates of conduct, and medals for merit, will doubtless obtain a better class of seamen — and for these the bill provides.[107]

Finally, on March 2, 1855, the Navy got its code in "An Act to Provide a More Efficient Discipline for the Navy." This law provided for a system of summary courts-martial for minor offenses, for honorable discharges of seamen, for reenlistment bounties for those honorably discharged, and for leaves of absence.[108]

A summary court-martial was empowered to inflict any one of the following punishments.

First. Discharge from the service with bad-conduct discharge, but the sentence not to be carried into effect in a foreign country.

Second. Solitary confinement in irons, single or double, on bread and water, or diminished rations, provided no such confinement shall exceed thirty days.

Third. Solitary confinement in irons, single or double, not exceeding thirty days.

Fourth. Solitary confinement not exceeding thirty days.

Fifth. Confinement not exceeding two months.

Sixth. Reduction to next inferior rating.

Seventh. Deprivation of liberty on shore on foreign station.

---

[107] *Reports of the Committee of the Senate*, 33d Cong., 1st Sess. (Serial 707), Doc. 271. "Bucking" was designed to hold prisoners who were able to escape from other fetters. It consisted of placing a bar or rod crosswise beneath the hams and in front of the elbow joints, after the wrists and ankles had been placed in irons. Such an arrangement confined a man to a sitting position and greatly restricted his motions. By "bagging" Mallory probably meant "gagging," another old punishment. It was used to stop vile and profane language. Mallory was mistaken about the novelty of those punishments; they had long been known in naval circles but were rarely used in previous years. See the *Southern Literary Messenger*, XVIII (1852), 199–200.
[108] *U.S. Statutes at Large*, X, Chap. 136, p. 628.

Eighth. Extra police duties, and loss of pay, not to exceed three months, may be added to any of the above mentioned punishments.[109]

Now that the Navy had its much-needed code of discipline, it was time to restudy the entire set of rules governing that service. The naval appropriation act of March 3, 1857, directed the Secretary of the Navy to have such a code prepared and to submit it to Congress for its approval. Secretary Toucey accordingly convened a board of officers consisting of a captain, a commander, a lieutenant, the lieutenant colonel of the Marine Corps, a purser, and a surgeon, and charged them with this duty. The board applied itself to the problem, and its reports were in the hands of the Secretary by the early part of 1858.[110]

Toucey declined to lay the board's detailed proposals before Congress on the grounds that he disapproved "giving to a code of regulations, descending into all the *minutiae* of unimportant details, the force of law." The President's authority as commander-in-chief was sufficient to establish such regulations, which should be suspended, varied, or modified from time to time, as necessary, without inconvenience. Otherwise, if the President were so confined by these regulations that his "constitutional authority to command" must not conflict with them, then the rules would go far in repealing his authority.[111]

But the board also reported a code of laws in the form of regulations. This code was "not obnoxious" to Toucey because the matters covered were the proper subjects of legislation "which should not be left to executive discretion." It was not a new code but one "composed of existing laws with some amendments."[112] Toucey sent this set of rules to Congress in fulfillment of his obligations.

It was not until July 17, 1862, however, that a new "Act for the Better Government of the Navy of the United States" was passed to replace that of 1800. With respect to discipline, the points established in previous years were carried forward. Article 8 stated that all offenses committed by naval personnel which were not specified

---

[109] *Ibid.*

[110] *House Executive Documents*, 35th Cong., 1st Sess. (Serial 944), II, Part 3, Doc. 2, p. 579.

[111] *Ibid.*, 2d Sess. (Serial 1000), II, Part 4, Doc. 2, p. 12.

[112] *Ibid.*

in previous articles were to be punished according to the direction
of a court-martial; "but in no cases shall punishment by flogging
be inflicted nor shall any court-martial adjudge punishment by
flogging." Article 10 specified that no commander was to punish
enlisted personnel for a single offense or at any one time other
than as follows:

First. Reduction of any rating established by himself.

Second. Confinement with or without irons, single or double, such
confinement not to exceed ten days, unless necessary in the case of a
prisoner to be tried by court-martial.

Third. Solitary confinement on bread and water not exceeding five
days.

Fourth. Solitary confinement not exceeding seven days.

Fifth. Deprivation of liberty on shore.

Sixth. Extra duties.[113]

No other punishment was permitted except that ordered by
the sentence of a general or summary court-martial. Summary
courts-martial were allowed to disrate any rated person for in-
competency. All punishments inflicted, except reprimands, were
to be entered in the ship's log.[114]

The crucial victory in abolishing the lash in 1850 was won by
a small margin. It came about when the larger issue of the Compromise of 1850 held men's attention. The naval appropriation bill
containing the proviso abolishing flogging was passed only eight
days after the last of the Compromise bills was enacted. The spirit
of compromise was in the air. Jefferson Davis, who opposed
abolishing flogging, said as much in relation to this cause. Men
like Hale, Hamlin, and Stockton were so convinced of the right-
eousness of their cause that they were willing to risk the very
existence of the Navy to carry their point. This uncompromising
approach to the problem was similar to a growing attitude on the
part of other Americans of both the North and the South, who
would risk destroying the Union rather than compromise on the
subject of slavery.

In the case of the Navy, however, this singleness of purpose
had a much happier result. Flogging had been a keystone of naval
discipline for so long that, when it was suddenly displaced, naval
officers had to adjust to a serious new challenge. It called for the

---

[113] *U.S. Statutes at Large*, XII, Chap. 204, p. 603.   [114] *Ibid.*

best qualities of leadership in the Navy. It was a proving ground
where the inflexible or unimaginative officer showed up poorly.
And it was also a testing ground for the men in the ranks. For years
the humanitarians had declared that the law of the lash degraded
the noble tar. Just how noble, reasonable, and responsible was the
sailor? This was also the time when the good, the industrious,
and the law-abiding must prove themselves anew. Did the law-
abiding sailor act from conviction or from fear of punishment?
The five years that elapsed between the abolition of flogging and
the establishment of the system of summary courts-martial and
of the honorable discharge gave both officers and men the opportunity to reassess the real worth of the other. Congress attempted to weed out the officer ranks in 1855, and while the resulting political uproar forced it to retreat from this position
somewhat, the demands of wartime service eventually accomplished the same end. The system of honorable discharges for the
men began in 1855. Under this law the Navy was able to rid itself
of troublesome individuals and to strengthen the foundations of
a real enlisted career service.

PART FIVE

THE ALCOHOL PROBLEM

"This grog ration causes more than three-fourths of the punishments in a man-of-war; it is the subversion of discipline; it engenders disease and crime; it perpetuates drunkenness in the Navy. . . . In short this grog ration is evil, and only evil, and that continually."

Captain Andrew Hull Foote, U.S.N., 1854

THE TEMPERANCE CRUSADE IN THE NAVY

A close relationship existed between the antiflogging crusade and the movement to abolish the spirit ration in the Navy. In the eyes of the humanitarian reformers the daily ration of a half pint of whisky, or grog, produced a desire for additional intoxicants. The sailor often went to great lengths to satisfy this desire, and drunkenness was the cause of most of the flogging. Thus, if the spirit ration were eliminated and temperance promoted, better health and better discipline would result. Better conditions of service would attract a higher type of recruit, and harsh discipline would be less necessary. As time went on, the growth of a nation-wide temperance movement gave additional support to those individuals who were bent on ending the practice of issuing liquor to the crews of naval ships. Getting the government out of the liquor business thus became an appealing target for various temperance groups. As such groups grew in number, it became harder and harder for politicians to ignore their cause.

ORIGINS AND BACKGROUND

Grog originated with Admiral Edward Vernon of the British Navy during the course of his operations against the Spaniards in the Caribbean during the War of Jenkins' Ear. Vernon observed that the seamen saved up their daily rum allowances until they had enough to make themselves drunk. He believed that the wild sprees that resulted from this practice weakened the men and made them less able to withstand the perils of the tropics. Vernon's solution to this problem was his order of August 14, 1740, which directed that the daily half pint of rum be mixed with a quart of water. To make sure that no man was defrauded of his daily rum ration, he ordered the mixture served twice a day — once between ten and twelve in the morning and second time between four and six in the afternoon. Vernon's mixture became known as "grog," and it proved to be quite popular with sailors. His order, originally intended for units of the fleet in the West Indies, was accepted throughout the British Navy.[1]

This custom was well established by the time of the American Revolution, and it was carried over into the Continental Navy wherein it was fixed by the regulations which John Adams compiled from British sources. An act of Congress of March 27, 1794, provided for a daily ration of a half pint of spirits or a quart of beer.[2] The same provision was incorporated in the act of July 1, 1797.[3] The reference to beer was omitted in the act of March 3, 1801, which set up the peacetime establishment of the Navy.[4] By 1805 the annual consumption of rum in the United States Navy was 45,000 gallons.[5]

Jefferson's Secretary of the Navy, Robert Smith, believed that whisky was a cheaper and more wholesome beverage for sailors than rum. So in 1806 he ordered the purchase of 20,000 gallons of it and introduced "pure rye whiskey of 3rd or 2nd proof, and one year old" into the Navy. The whisky ration was mixed with water

---

[1] Cyril H. Hartmann, *The Angry Admiral: The Later Career of Edward Vernon, Admiral of the White* (London, 1953), pp. 45–46. According to Hartmann, the word "grog" applied to the originator of the order. It was Vernon's custom in foul weather to wear a sea cloak (and sometimes breeches) made of grogram, a type of waterproof clothing made of silk and mohair stiffened with gum. Vernon was known throughout the fleet as "Old Grog."
[2] *U.S. Statutes at Large*, I, Chap. 12, p. 351.
[3] *Ibid.*, Chap. 7, p. 524.
[4] *Ibid.*, II, Chap. 20, pp. 110–111.
[5] Secretary of the Navy Robert Smith to E. Williams, May 31, 1806, quoted in Paullin, "Naval Administration . . . 1801–1814," p. 1301.

as the rum had been, and the beverage continued to be known as "grog" or the spirit ration.[6]

Like most traditional practices in the armed services, the custom of serving grog became draped in ceremony. Twice a day (usually in the late morning and afternoon) all hands received their grog. A large wooden tub would be placed in position on the deck and filled with equal proportions of whisky and water. The tub was placed under the guard of a sentry, and an officer stood by to supervise the distribution. When all was ready, a roll of the drum called the crew to the appointed spot, where they converged behind a rope stretched a short distance from the front of the tub. As each man's name was called, he stepped over the rope, held out his cup and advanced to the tub. Here he watched the ship's corporal fill his cup with the precious liquid. Usually the grog was consumed on the spot, but in some ships the men were allowed to carry it to their mess where it was often used as a medium of exchange. Gradually it became possible for a man to receive money in lieu of his ration. In addition to this voluntary renunciation of liquor, it was a common practice to stop a man's grog for a period of time for minor offenses. In the event that a culprit was receiving money in lieu of his spirit ration there was usually no alternative but to have him flogged for his offense. For this reason many sailors kept drawing their grog ration as a kind of insurance against being flogged for an infraction at some future date.[7]

The spirit ration itself did not produce drunkenness, but it did stimulate the appetite for more. In attempting to gratify that appetite the sailor often got into trouble. Sometimes he would take advantage of a young officer and attempt to secure an additional cupful by asserting that his name had been missed when the grog was served. If caught in the act of "redoubling the tub," the thirsty sailor was flogged for his trouble. A safe way of getting a glass of brandy or some other spirits was to do some small job for an officer, such as making up his hammock. But for most men the only solution to the problem was to resort to smuggling. Whenever a

---

[6] *Ibid.*

[7] Belknap, "The Old Navy," pp. 44–45; Holbrook, pp. 58–59, 184, 250, 292–293; Ames, *A Mariner's Sketches*, pp. 197–199, 256; Gould, p. 133; Wines, I, 48; A 'Civilian' [George Jones], I, 218–220; Melville, pp. 53–54.

naval vessel was in a harbor, her officers exercised unremitting watchfulness to prevent spirits from being smuggled on board. But the ingenuity of the seamen often matched the intensity of their thirst.[8]

A common method of smuggling liquor was by use of the intestines of animals, which were known to sailors as "snakes." These "snakes" were purchased ashore, filled with alcohol, wrapped around the legs, and concealed by bell-bottomed trousers. When the sailor returned to his ship, an officer searched him by running his hands down the length of the body. A properly wrapped "snake" would not be detected during this touch inspection.[9]

A naval watering party once used these "snakes" or "skins" to conceal liquor smuggled on board in casks of water which bore identification marks recognizable to those involved in the scheme.[10]

Herman Melville tells of a sailor on the *United States* who had "skins" of liquor delivered to, and moored on, the anchor chain just underneath the surface. During the night the sailor would slip over the side, pick up these containers, and return to the ship.[11] But most men resorted to tricks that required less physical stamina but no less imagination.

On one occasion sailors employed in loading stores at a naval yard managed to whitewash a barrel of whisky so that it resembled the barrels filled with tar. They then rolled it onto the deck without difficulty and that night indulged in a drunken spree.[12]

A chaplain reported a case involving men who were engaged in whitewashing a hospital wall with a mixture of Spanish white, olive oil, and whisky. These men would wait until the oil had collected on the top of their tub, and the Spanish white had settled at the bottom. Then, by means of a quill they would drink the

---

[8] Belknap, "The Old Navy," pp. 44–46; Wines, I, 152–153, 173–175; A 'Civilian' [George Jones], I, 219–220.

[9] Rockwell, II, 413.

[10] Charles R. Anderson, ed., *Journal of a Cruise to the Pacific Ocean, 1842–1844, in the Frigate United States, with Notes on Herman Melville* (Durham, N.C., 1937), pp. 127–128.

[11] Melville, pp. 168–169.

[12] Rockwell, II, 412.

whisky in the middle layer of the tub. Suffice to say that their ingenuity was often equal to the task that confronted them, but they were not alone in their plotting and scheming.[13]

When a ship dropped anchor in a harbor, small boats loaded with tradesmen and their wares swarmed around her sides waiting for permission to come on board. These "bumboat men," knowing that a sailor would pay almost any price for spirits, put their imaginative talents to work to create containers that would pass inspection by the ship's officers. Containers shaped like sardine boxes, tins shaped like hams, cigar boxes lined with parchment, and numerous other devices were used in an attempt to insure the safe delivery of spirits. A five-gallon container of whisky was once found packed in the center of a barrel of potatoes. A naval chaplain recorded an instance where bladder skins filled with liquor had been dropped into an earthenware jug filled with milk. Once the taste for liquor had been stimulated in these men there was bound to be smuggling and drunkenness, and as long as there was drunkenness there was a great deal of corporal punishment.[14] It was therefore with good reason that Chaplain Rockwell referred to intemperance as "the mother of abominations" and the source of most of the sailor's troubles.[15]

Intemperance was also to a great extent the result of the notion of the time that strenuous work could not be performed without the stimulus of alcohol. It was customary to serve liquor to many types of workers, including teachers and ministers, as a part of or a supplement to their compensation. Many a young man got his first taste of liquor as an apprentice. When an apprentice reached the age of 21, it was customary for his master to give him a "freedom treat" at which cold meats and various types of liquor were dispensed. The young apprentice would invite all his friends to participate in the festivities, and the occasion provided a splendid excuse for all concerned to get drunk.[16]

---

[13] *Ibid.*, p. 413.

[14] A Fore-Top-Man [Henry J. Mercier], pp. 166–167; Rockwell, II, 413; Belknap, "The Old Navy," pp. 47–48; Wines, I, 173; Melville, pp. 166–175.

[15] Rockwell, II, 411.

[16] *National Intelligencer*, Washington, D.C., Jan. 16, 1830; Edward Channing, *A History of the United States* (New York, 1933), V, 172–174; Alice F. Tyler, *Freedom's Ferment: Phases of American Social History to 1860* (Minneapolis, 1944), pp. 308–316.

It was entirely in keeping with the ideas of the time that the government served grog to its sailors and to the workmen of the naval yards. Given a taste for alcohol which was whetted by food preserved with a large amount of salt, a dangerous, hard, and sometimes lonely life with infrequent shore leave, and the general attitude of the age, it is not surprising that drunkenness was common. With the obstacles that it had to overcome, it is surprising that the temperance movement ever made any headway at all in the old Navy.

TEMPERANCE EFFORTS

A pioneer in the cause of temperance in the armed forces, as well as of temperance generally, was Dr. Benjamin Rush. As early as 1772 he published a work condemning the use of strong drink.[17] His first acquaintance with naval life came in July 1775, when he served as a surgeon to the Pennsylvania gunboat fleet.[18] Two years later he wrote his "Directions for Preserving the Health of Soldiers, Addressed to the Officers of the United States," which appeared in the *Pennsylvania Packet*. Later, when Rush became Physician General to the Military Hospitals of the United States, the Board of War ordered him to republish his directions in pamphlet form.[19]

The years following the Revolution found Rush zealously engaged in the cause of temperance. His *Enquiry into the Effects of Spirituous Liquors on the Human Body and Mind* was published in 1784 and widely distributed. It was reprinted many times for half a century.[20] Rush's interest in this cause led the Philadelphia College of Physicians to go on record for temperance in 1787. They also appointed him the chairman of a committee to draft a memorial for presentation to the state legislature requesting the enactment of a law to diminish the consumption of liquor.[21] Rush helped to prepare the way for a national temperance movement through his correspondence with prominent men and his promotion of a petition to Congress in 1790 from physi-

<hr>

[17] Nathan G. Goodman, *Benjamin Rush, Physician and Citizen, 1746–1813* (Philadelphia, 1934), p. 274.
[18] *Ibid.*, p. 48.   [20] Goodman, p. 275.
[19] Cutbush, Appendix.   [21] *Ibid.*, p. 276.

cians at Philadelphia, which sought to restrict the traffic in liquor.[22]

When Rush's friend and former student, Dr. Edward Cutbush, published his *Observations on the Means of Preserving the Health of Soldiers and Sailors* in 1808, he reprinted his teacher's Revolutionary War pamphlet in an appendix. Cutbush had seen service with the Pennsylvania militia during the Whiskey Rebellion and was later the surgeon general of the Pennsylvania line. At the time his *Observations* appeared he had more than ten years of experience as a surgeon in the U.S. Navy. This work is believed to be "the first book written by a medical officer of the Navy," and it reflects the author's familiarity with the works of prominent medical men of Europe.[23] In this work Cutbush declared "that almost unlimited severity" should be used by commanders to prevent "indiscriminate commerce with women and intemperance." Yet he also wrote one of the earliest criticisms of the practice of flogging in the United States Navy.[24]

The medical men were not the only ones who recognized the pernicious influence of alcohol on the Navy. Captain Thomas Truxtun complained to the Navy Department in 1801 that the daily ration of a half pint of rum per man was too much. Men and boys who did not drink would sell or trade it to those who did, and it required great attention to keep many of the crew from being in a constant state of intoxication. Truxtun reacted by forbidding the boys to draw rum. For the others, he made the withholding of the rum ration "a principal punishment for crimes & Misdeameanors" committed on board his ship. In this way he not only maintained order by humane means but also saved money on rum.[25]

The captain also kept his eyes on his officers and let them know what he expected of them. As early as 1797 he told a lieutenant that the "destestable vice of drunkenness" rendered every officer a

[22] Merle Curti, *The Growth of American Thought* (2d ed.; New York, 1951), p. 202.

[23] F. L. Pleadwell, "Edward Cutbush, M.D., the nestor of the Medical Corps of the Navy," *Annals of Medical History*, V (1923), 367.

[24] Cutbush, pp. 19–20.

[25] Captain Thomas Truxtun to Samuel Smith, Acting Secretary of the Navy, May 9, 1801, *Quasi-War*, VII, 223, 231.

nuisance and made him "unworthy and unfit for Service particularly for any important Service." But he also added that: "I do not mean to insinuate that a Convivial fellow is a drunkard, who may become Chearful [*sic*] in Company, the distinction is too great to make it necessary for me to draw any line on that Subject." [26]

Concern about the officers extended to the Navy Department itself. Secretary of the Navy Paul Hamilton was disturbed by the sight of some drunken midshipmen at the Washington Navy Yard. Writing to the commandant of the yard about the incident, he warned that "the eye of the Department" was upon the midshipmen and if they continued such practices they would be dismissed. [27]

Drunkenness was also a problem at the Marine Barracks in Washington. Lieutenant Colonel Franklin Wharton, the Commandant of the Marines, issued an order on April 28, 1805, forbidding the introduction of rum directly or indirectly to Marines within the barracks at Washington. The use of rum by the Marines was "productive of serious Consequences, by bringing on them Public Disgrace." Any man caught receiving supplies from civilians, except in the presence of a noncommissioned officer, was subject to immediate punishment.

When the rum ration was increased by an official order, Wharton moved to counteract any bad effects that might result from it. He stated: "As the late Increase of Rum to the Rations, has greatly tended to the Increase of Intoxication, among the Troops of the Garrison, it is Ordered, That in future one half of the Rum allowance per day be issued in the Morning, the other half reserved for Dinner, which is to be placed under the charge of the Sergeant having for the day charge of the Mess Rooms, this is to be mixed in three waters & to be issued in equal proportion to each and every man belonging to the general Mess — to which it has only reference." [28]

There is also some evidence that there were other attempts to eliminate the causes of intemperance some time before the rest of the nation became temperance conscious. Efforts were made to

---

[26] Truxtun to Lieutenant Simon Gross, Aug. 30, 1797, *ibid.*, I, 15.

[27] Paullin, "Naval Administration . . . 1801–1814," p. 1306.

[28] Frank E. Evans, "The Corps a Hundred Years Ago," *Marine Corps Gazette*, I (1916), 52; McClellan, I, Chap. 16, p. 37.

abolish the spirit ration by substituting porter and beer, but these attempts failed because the contents of the casks soured, fermented, and burst in the tropics. The quantities necessary for a crew could not be procured in all ports where other supplies were available, and a great deal of space was required for shipboard storage. In addition, many seamen refused to accept this substitute for their rations. In ships where the substitution did take place it was found that drunkenness was still a problem. To many observers it was apparent that the substitution experiment had failed, and the project was abandoned.[29]

In the nation at large the temperance movement had a very slow growth. From time to time the subject of drunkenness and/or its causes appeared in letters or in newspapers. The sight of drunken individuals, whether civilian or military, undoubtedly disturbed people from time to time, and some temperance movements began before the War of 1812, but it was not until some years after the war that the movement gained strength. The temperance crusade mirrored the increased concern of the humanitarians for the welfare of mankind and was closely related to the evangelical movement.[30]

The early groups who sought to improve the lot of the sailor were well aware of his addiction to liquor. The personnel of the American Seamen's Friend Society were no less aware of the problem of drunkenness, for *The Sailor's Magazine* of November 1828 declared that the magazine should not neglect the cause of temperance — a cause that was absorbing the interest of other religious publications. The article also stated that the besetting

---

[29] Commodore Charles Stewart to Secretary of the Navy William B. Preston, March 11, 1850, *Reports of Officers*, No. 1; *Congressional Globe*, 32d Cong., 1st Sess., XXI, 112. In 1803 the War Department conducted an experiment among the Army troops at New Orleans whereby malt liquor was substituted for the spirit ration. The next year malt liquor and light wines replaced the normal spirit ration (1 gill of rum, brandy, or whisky) at such posts or during such seasons of the year when the President considered it necessary for the health of the troops. But difficulties soon arose as both wine and beer were hard to come by. Wine had to be imported, and there were too few brewmasters to manufacture beer locally. So, the unpopular experiment was abandoned. See Erna Risch, *Quartermaster Support of the Army: A History of the Corps, 1775–1939* (Washington, D.C., Government Printing Office, 1962), p. 118.

[30] Curti, pp. 202–203; Tyler, pp. 312–322.

sin of the sailor was his addiction to grog and whisky.[31] From the very beginning virtually every issue of *The Sailor's Magazine* carried some reference to the progress of the temperance movement in the merchant service and in the Navy.

In his book, *Sketches of Naval Life*, published in 1829, Chaplain George Jones stated that there were many men on his ship who would have been ornaments to society but for drink. He felt that the Navy was a good place for such dissolute men, as the "severe discipline" might restore their character. Although they were served grog regularly, they were less exposed to the temptations of liquor than they would be on shore. He believed that any experiment in abolishing grog must be conducted with caution, for there was "nothing that would sooner stir up a mutiny in the ship, than a refusal to serve out grog." In view of this fact he would never recommend this "fatal experiment" in the United States Navy. The situation could be improved, however, if the daily ration of grog was cut by a third or a half. The practice of some officers of giving extra grog or other spirits to the men in return for small favors should also be ended. Since such rewards were dispensed at the end of the day, while the last grog ration was still working in a man's system, Jones believed that it contributed to much of the drunkenness on board.

But, as far as Jones was concerned, the real attack on drunkenness should take place on shore. "Yes, let [the] government lay a strong hand on distilleries; they are a nuisance, a blot, the source of horrible pollutions, and ought to be an abomination in the land. If I were a minister, I should preach, and if a legislator, I should vote against them; if I were monarch in the country, the first exercise of my authority would be to put them down. Why are they tolerated? ten thousand breaking hearts in the country reiterate, why are they tolerated? Here let your societies direct their efforts, and something may be done." Jones believed that intemperance was "a curse greater than even slavery itself." [32]

It is not possible to establish what influence, if any, Chaplain Jones's book had on the subject of reforms in the Navy, but books of travel were popular fare in this period, and this work went

---

[31] *The Sailor's Magazine*, I, 69.
[32] A 'Civilian' [George Jones], I, 65, 217–222.

through three editions between 1829 and 1834. At any rate, action on the subject of temperance soon came from Congress and the American Seamen's Friend Society.

Early in 1829 Dr. Lewis Condict, a congressman from New Jersey, introduced a resolution in the House of Representatives on the subject of the spirit ration in the Army. His resolution requested information on the beneficial effects of the daily ration of spirits in the Army and asked whether that ration was not injurious to health, morals, and discipline. A year passed before Condict had his answer in the form of a letter from George Gibson, Commissary General of Subsistence, to Peter B. Porter, the Secretary of War. Gibson said that he knew of neither beneficial effects nor great evils resulting from the daily ration. He claimed that drunkenness in the Army was the result of civilians supplying liquor clandestinely to the soldiers.[33]

In the meantime, in the January 1829 issue of *The Sailor's Magazine,* the editor commented on the inquiry before Congress and suggested that a general inquiry ought to be conducted by the surgeons "respecting the fitness of the rations to promote the health and moral strength of soldiers and sailors." He added that probably the best method was to allow each sailor who did not draw his grog so many cents per month in addition to the cost of his spirit ration.[34] This idea was again mentioned in the February issue of the magazine.[35]

The suggestion may have fallen upon receptive ears, for later in the same month the House of Representatives passed a resolution calling upon the Secretary of the Navy to institute such an inquiry. On February 25, 1829, Secretary of the Navy John Branch asked three prominent naval surgeons for their individual opinions on several questions relating to the spirit ration. Branch wanted their views as to whether the ration was "necessary or expedient" for midshipmen, as well as their opinions on its effect on their

---

[33] *House Documents,* 21st Cong., 1st Sess. (Serial 195), I, Doc. 22. Condict's political affiliation at this time is not a matter of record. In 1811–17 he was an Anti-Federalist, and in 1840 he was a presidential elector on the Whig ticket. See *Biographical Directory of the American Congress,* p. 837.
[34] *The Sailor's Magazine,* I, 156.
[35] *Ibid.,* p. 179.

morals and health and upon "the discipline and character of the Navy."[36]

The surgeons apparently spent some time in considering and in drafting their replies, for Branch did not receive all of them until September. All three men stated that the spirit ration was unnecessary and harmful to morals and health. Dr. Lewis Heerman called it "subversive in the end of rational discipline." Dr. William P. C. Barton added that a more wholesome ration could be established for midshipmen. He questioned the wisdom of leaving the disuse of spirits to the discretion of the commander of a ship. "If evil exists under the present circumstances and usages, the corrective, to be efficient must be universal," said Barton. "In a word, I believe an Act of Congress is called for, and would be important in its principle and beneficial in its operation."[37] Dr. Thomas Harris wrote that he had been questioned about midshipmen, but he hoped he might be pardoned for "suggesting that the inquiry might be advantageously extended to an examination of its effects on the boys and young men who compose the crews of our national vessels." "The baneful practice of serving out grog to this class of persons, and thus making them habitual drinkers, is, perhaps, the chief cause of the general intemperance among sailors." He pointed out that the law made no distinction between the old sailor and the young boy, and that giving the full ration of spirits to boys who were unaccustomed to it made them intoxicated to some degree. By the end of a three-year enlistment this practice created a craving for liquor in the youths. Harris suggested that tea or coffee might be substituted, but he admitted that many old sailors would not submit to the abolition of the spirit ration.[38]

Secretary Branch expressed his concurrence in the views of the surgeons and forwarded their replies to the House in January 1830. He recommended that a liberal sum be paid to seamen who commuted the spirit ration and that this sum could be used to purchase small stores.[39]

While all this was in progress, *The Sailor's Magazine* printed an

---

[36] *American State Papers: Naval Affairs*, III (1860), 469.
[37] *Ibid.*, pp. 469, 475.
[38] *Ibid.*, p. 477.
[39] John Branch to the Speaker of the House of Representatives, Jan. 13, 1830, *Letters to Congress*, VI.

item in which a chaplain alleged that experienced officers in the Navy were of the opinion that the whisky allowance should be cut in half. The editor hoped that the matter would soon interest congressmen.[40]

On December 28, 1829, Condict introduced a resolution to allow soldiers and seamen to be paid the value of the liquor ration in lieu of the grog. By mid-January the House had received a letter from Major General Alexander Macomb and two from Commissary Gibson on this subject, which had been forwarded by John H. Eaton, the Secretary of War. General Macomb favored the discontinuance of the spirit ration and suggested the substitution of rice and molasses, the payment of a dollar per month bounty, and the issuance of total abstinence certificates at the end of the term of enlistment. Commissary Gibson sent a copy of his earlier reply and another letter in which he reported that the bounty plan had been tried in 1820 under Secretary of War Calhoun and had proved ineffective.[41]

The matter was referred to the Committee on Military Affairs, and the members of that body, believing that the naval aspect of the question was outside their jurisdiction, reported the measure favorably so far as the Army was concerned.[42]

On February 25, 1830, Condict introduced three resolutions. One was to inquire into the advisability of paying seamen and Marines double the value of a discontinued whisky ration at the end of their voyage. Another involved the payment of a bounty in money and/or clothing for total abstinence and good behavior. The third aimed to hold out inducements and incentives for total abstinence to the younger officers.[43]

Condict's resolutions precipitated a debate which offers a good insight into the minds of the legislators concerning this problem. Michael Hoffman, a New York Democrat and chairman of the House naval committee, said that he would rejoice in the discontinuance of ardent spirits in the Navy, but he felt that the matter ought "to be left to the discretion of individuals." It was inexpedient to make our sailors "cold water drinkers," he said, for it would

[40] *The Sailor's Magazine*, II, 92.
[41] *House Documents*, 21st Cong., 1st Sess. (Serial 195), I, Doc. 22.
[42] *Ibid.*
[43] *Register of Debates*, 21st Cong., 1st Sess., VI, Part 1, p. 584.

reduce their efficiency and impair their courage, generosity, and bravery. But if some practical scheme could be devised, he would support it.[44]

Representative Charles A. Wickliffe, a Democrat from Kentucky, objected to the measures on the grounds of what a future historian would think of their times. "That historian would say, to such an extent had this vice been carried, that ladies formed themselves into societies for the promotion of temperance, and for the suppression of the vice of drunkenness." He hoped that "to such a description of the state of our society, erroneous in point of fact, Congress would not give its false sanction by legislating on this subject," especially when no practical benefit could come from the adoption of the resolution.[45]

The chairman of the House Committee on Military Affairs, William Drayton, a Union Democrat of South Carolina, felt that liquor served some useful purpose and ought not to be interdicted. He placed no reliance on legislation as a remedy for the abuse of liquor. Such a law would cause discontent, he felt. Furthermore, he was opposed to "sudden and violent innovations." Reformation must come from the sailor himself. He favored such actions as appealing to the sailor's moral sense, increasing his comforts and pay, and thereby decreasing the temptations to which he was exposed. Drayton shared his colleagues' dislike of the spirit and language of the memorials frequently received from temperance societies. He said that he himself had dealt only with Army and Navy physicians and military officers, but that he would listen to visionaries if they had any practical suggestions. It was the duty of the House to see that they brought about what the resolutions hoped to effect. It would be an opportunity to make an experiment which would do no harm and which might do some good.[46]

John Reed, a Massachusetts "Whig," spoke in favor of the resolutions and declared that temperance societies had contributed much to the improvement of society.[47]

Another Massachusetts representative, Joseph Richardson, who was a Unitarian minister, urged that the resolutions be adopted, as they would not deprive anyone of his ration but would be an

[44] *Ibid.*   [46] *Ibid.*, pp. 584–585.
[45] *Ibid.*   [47] *Ibid.*, p. 587.

inducement to abstain. He declared that "if there be one vice which, more than any other, threatens the liberty and prosperity of this country, it is the vice of intemperance."[48]

Tristram Burges, a Rhode Island "Whig" and a former medical student, favored the resolutions because he believed that the liquor ration trained drunkards.[49]

William W. Ellsworth, a "Whig" from Connecticut, called attention to the letters of the Secretary of the Navy on the subject. He hoped that the House would give the matter serious attention, for there was no resolution before Congress at that time "of greater magnitude and urgency." He argued that the Navy ration legalized drunkenness. Young boys who were sailors and midshipmen were thrown in with veteran drinkers and corrupted by perpetually being compelled to consume 23 gallons of spirits a year. A Navy lieutenant had informed him that approximately eight-tenths of the flogging on board ships was made necessary as a result of intemperance. If the smuggling activities of civilians made it impossible to restrain intemperance in the Army, they could not affect a ship at sea. Ellsworth "did not believe that there would be much difficulty in inducing habits of temperance if the Government would set seriously and perseveringly about it."[50]

Two days after Condict introduced his resolutions, Thomas Chilton, "Whig" representative from Kentucky, attempted to amend them. His resolution requested the Committee on Naval Affairs to inquire "whether the public interest and the cause of morality would be most effectively promoted, by emphatically prohibiting the use of ardent, vinous, and other fermented liquors in the Navy of the United States, by the officers and seamen belonging thereto, or by permitting a continuation of the practice of issuing them as rations in said service." If the committee thought that the Navy should have its spirit ration, then a similar inquiry should be made into the expediency of providing some means for discontinuing the use of fermented liquors among members of Congress and among all others who held offices of "trust, honor or profit" under

---

[48] *Ibid.* Richardson's party affiliation is not a matter of record. See *Biographical Directory of the American Congress*, p. 1460.

[49] *Register of Debates*, 21st Cong., 1st Sess., VI, Part 1, p. 588.

[50] *Ibid.*, pp. 588–589.

the authority of the American people. For his part, he was determined to ascertain whether his colleagues were as willing to curtail their own allowances of intoxicants as they were to limit that
of others.[51]

Chilton proudly hailed these days of "Retrenchment and Reform," and he noted that great progress had been made in both
areas. He was surprised to discover men who were "so vastly inconsistent, and yet so externally sensitive, and ferociously virtuous." These "American system gentlemen" favored the tariff and
the encouragement of domestic industries, but were now advocating a doctrine that was contrary to their own previously expressed
beliefs. He declared that whisky was a staple of the western country and the farmer's means of converting surplus grain into a mar-
ketable commodity. This market depended on the continued
demand for whisky, and no legislative act could prevent its consumption. "Sir," he declared, "I am no friend of intemperance,
either on land or at sea; but I think it infinitely better to abandon
the votary of intemperance to his fate, than to abridge the natural
liberties of man."[52]

Chilton's words apparently did not move his colleagues, and his
amendment failed to pass. An attempt to lay the original resolutions on the table failed by a vote of 57 to 108. The House then
agreed to Condict's resolution.[53]

---

[51] *Ibid.*, p. 589.
[52] *Ibid.*
[53] *Ibid.*, pp. 589–590. The group that voted to lay the original resolutions
on the table included 22 from northern states, 20 from southern states, and 15
from border states (Kentucky, Maryland, Missouri, and Tennessee). This
group of 57 included 8 men with military backgrounds who had served in the
War of 1812 or the Creek War, 1 former clerk in the Navy Department, 1 ex-
midshipman, 1 minister, and 3 doctors. Of the 108 who voted against laying
the measure aside, 79 were from the northern states, 18 from the southern
states, and 11 from border states (Delaware, Kentucky, Maryland and Tennessee). This number also included 24 men with military experience, all but
2 of whom served in the War of 1812 or the Creek War. It also included 5
doctors and 4 others who had received some medical training, 3 ministers, 1
son of a Revolutionary War naval chaplain, and 1 former prison superintendent. There were also 2 hotel keepers, but one of these was also a militia
officer, and he is counted in the military group above. Thus, a little less than
one-third against it (39 out of 108) had a type of specialized background
which probably gave them a better insight into the problem of intemperance
in a military organization.

About this time the Reverend Joshua Leavitt, the agent of the Seamen's Friend Society, went to Washington to present a me-morial to the Secretary of the Navy, John Branch. This memorial, which had been signed by Smith Thompson and a large member-ship of the Society, asked for an increase in the number of naval chaplains; that they be paid an amount equal to what they would receive on shore; that their duties be made more specific; and that the Secretary of the Navy hold out every inducement to sailors to renounce their liquor voluntarily.[54]

Leavitt was cordially received in all circles. Secretary Branch promised to give the memorial his attention. Leavitt also had the opportunity to explain the plans and objects of the Society to President Jackson. Of this interview Leavitt wrote: "He seemed much interested, highly approved of such objects, spoke freely of the importance of morality among seamen, was sensible of the evils resulting from their boarding houses . . . expressed his desire to have the use of grog given up in the navy, and his satis-faction at some facts which were detailed on this subject."[55]

When Leavitt turned his attention to Congress, he found that "Dr. Condict of New Jersey, a staunch temperance man" had al-ready introduced the subject. Several other members were "quite interested in the subject." Democratic Senator Robert Y. Hayne, the chairman of the Senate naval committee and "an enlightened friend" of that branch of service, was in favor of increasing the number and quality of the chaplains. "He also promised to examine the subject of the liquor rations, and to lay before the committee some statements on that subject, which were furnished in writing." The chairman of the House Committee on Military Affairs, to whom Condict's resolutions had been referred, also was given documents containing factual information and the names of "offi-cers, sea captains, and shipowners" in various parts of the country who could authenticate the cases listed and give any additional information that might be necessary.[56]

On the following Sunday Leavitt attended "Mr. Post's church" in Washington where he heard a sermon on the country's obliga-tions to seamen. This was particularly interesting in view of the

---

[54] *The Sailor's Magazine*, II, 223.   [56] *Ibid.*
[55] *Ibid.*

fact that President Jackson, several members of Congress, and Commodore Rodgers were among the congregation.[57]

Later a member of the Board of Navy Commissioners pointed out to Leavitt that the idea of sailors voluntarily giving up their grog was not a new one. He said that during his last cruise on the *Constitution* several of his men renounced their grog, and he hoped that the trend would become universal.[58]

When he visited the Marine Barracks, Leavitt was informed that several of the Marines subscribed to *The Sailor's Magazine*. The chaplain who held services for the officers, Marines, and mechanics of the naval yard also was interested in the welfare of seamen.[59]

This visit to Washington made Leavitt thank God for the gains that had been made and take courage for the struggles that lay ahead. Soon afterward Leavitt's attention was drawn to a statement by Navy Chaplain Edward McLaughlin that the whole tone of the Navy could be improved if competent chaplains were appointed, if regular religious services were held, and if flogging and grog were abolished.[60]

The passage of time showed more and more evidence of a temperance tendency. The columns of *The Sailor's Magazine* carried news of such progress in various ships of the Navy. In January 1831 it expressed the hope that something would be done about the liquor ration before the present short session of Congress ended. It added hopefully that the staunch "friends of the navy and army, such as Messrs. Hayne, Webster, Drayton, Miller, Condict, and others, will not let the matter rest, until something is done by which these arms of our national defense will be delivered from the debasing influence of strong drink." [61]

In the spring of 1831 Jackson's cabinet faced a crisis when the

---

[57] *Ibid.* The Reverend Reuben Post was pastor of the First Presbyterian Church at South Capitol and B Streets. See Wilhelmus B. Bryan, *A History of the National Capitol* (2 vols.; New York, 1916), II, 185.

[58] *The Sailor's Magazine*, II, 224. This was Captain Daniel T. Patterson, who returned from a cruise in the *Constitution* in 1828, after which he became a Navy Commissioner. This appointment was supposedly due to the fact that he was a "warm friend and supporter of Jackson." See Allan Westcott, "Daniel Todd Patterson," *Dictionary of American Biography*, XIV (1934), 302.

[59] *The Sailor's Magazine*, II, 224.

[60] *Ibid.*, III, 116.   [61] *Ibid.*, 149.

wives of the cabinet officers, led by Mrs. Vice-President Calhoun, refused social recognition to Secretary of War John Eaton's wife. Jackson's staunch defense of Mrs. Eaton caused a serious rift within his party and led to the resignation of his first cabinet.

By summer Jackson had a new cabinet that included Levi Woodbury of New Hampshire as Secretary of the Navy. Soon after Woodbury assumed office on May 23 it became apparent to the friends of temperance that their cause was gaining ground. In a circular dated June 15, 1831, Woodbury decreed: "All persons in the naval service entitled to rations, who shall voluntarily relinquish the use of that part of them composed of spirits, shall be paid therefor at the rate of six cents per ration, it being the estimated value of that part, as approved by this Department, September 17th, 1817." Payments for such stoppage were to be charged to the appropriation for provisions.[62]

In praising Woodbury's action *The Sailor's Magazine* stated that such a general order had long been necessary because not all naval officers were aware of the fact that there was legal authority for commutation payments. It looked forward to the day when all men would renounce their grog of their own accord. Such voluntary reformation was more honorable than compulsion.[63]

The Washington *Gazette* declared that Woodbury's first official act "deserved the thanks of every friend of Temperance." A letter to the editor of the Washington *Globe* stated: "It is a source of commendation with the friends of the administration, to see in its measures a powerful auxiliary aid to the temperance societies."[64]

Praise also came from within the Navy. Commodore Charles Morris wrote unofficially from the Charlestown Navy Yard that he believed the order would produce "great and lasting benefits to discipline of the Navy and to the comfort, health and character, of the Seamen."[65]

But an individual who signed himself "A man-of-war's man" wrote a letter to the Providence *Patriot* in which he declared that

---

[62] *Ibid.*, 361.   [63] *Ibid.*

[64] Undated clippings from Levi Woodbury's scrapbook marked "Clippings on Naval Affairs, June 1831-June 1832 . . . ," pp. 9–10, *Gist Blair Papers*, Library of Congress.

[65] Commodore Charles Morris to Secretary of the Navy Levi Woodbury, July 11, 1831, *Levi Woodbury Papers*, X, Library of Congress.

Woodbury's order was "unnecessary and silly." This letter stimulated replies which indicated that, insofar as printed opinions were
concerned, the man-of-war's man belonged to a minority.[66]

An article on "The American Navy," which appeared in the Norfolk *Beacon and Daily Advertiser* under the name "A 'Spark' of
Liberty," commended Woodbury and declared that Branch had
favored the entire abolition of the spirit ration. Woodbury's revival of an earlier order promised "practical utility for the present,
and may ultimately produce great general good." "How far the use
of ardent spirits can be prevented, it is difficult to say — experience
will decide; but there is no doubt that *temperance* should be *enforced.*"[67]

Encouraging reports of the voluntary renunciation of grog
came from units of the fleet. From the Mediterranean, Commodore
James Biddle wrote that not a single man of the frigate *John Adams*
drew his grog and that of the 1,107 men in his squadron, only 819
drew their allowance. Captain John C. Long wrote from the Pacific
that only nine men of the crew of the *Dolphin* drew their liquor
ration. *The Sailor's Magazine* carried a notice that Secretary Woodbury stated that the crew of one naval vessel was being shipped
"with direct reference to an experiment on the principle of total
abstinence."[68]

Schoolmaster Enoch C. Wines touched on the problem of intemperance in 1832 when he described the character of seamen on the
Constellation. He believed that the discontinuance of ardent
spirits, the establishment of ship libraries, and a regular moral and
religious instruction would produce happy results for both the men
and the Navy. "The disuse of intoxicating liquors alone would be
a revolution more cheering in itself, and most propitious in its
tendency. This is beginning to be felt to be the truth by the officers
of the Navy themselves. For their exertions to induce the crew of
the Constellation to discontinue the use of them, Captain Wads-

---

[66] Levi Woodbury scrapbook marked "Clippings on Naval Affairs, June
1831–June 1832 . . . ," *Gist Blair Papers, passim.* See clipping of an undated
1831 letter signed "An Older Man-of-War's Man" to the editor of a Boston
[?] newspaper in reply to the statements of "A man-of-war's man."

[67] Clipping from an unidentified newspaper dated June 27, 1831, in Levi
Woodbury scrapbook marked "Clippings on Naval Affairs, June 1831-June
1832 . . . ," *Gist Blair Papers,* Library of Congress.

[68] *The Sailor's Magazine,* V, 293.

worth and Mr. Paulding are worthy of all praise; and the success they met with, was beyond any thing before known in the service. About two-thirds of the crew stopped their grog, and received money instead of it." [69]

An improvement in the habits of seamen with respect to temperance was noted by Secretary Woodbury in his annual report for 1832. Corporal punishment also was less necessary. [70]

Other elements of the maritime community likewise manifested an interest in the cause of temperance. In 1833 the Marine Temperance Society was founded as an auxiliary to the New York Port Society. A year later similar societies were founded in Boston, Oswego, and Le Havre. The New York society boasted some 800 members including 70 shipmasters. [71]

Early in 1834 the Merchants Insurance Company of Boston offered a 5 per cent discount on the premiums of all vessels insured if the owners or masters would swear that no spirits had been furnished or used by the officers or the crew either in port or at sea. [72]

In the meantime a general temperance movement was making great strides in the nation. Much of this growth was due to the spread of revivalistic religion and to the growing public interest in humanitarian reforms. The broadening of the electorate through the extension of manhood suffrage helped to emphasize the country's need for sober, intelligent voters. Temperance leaders stressed the connection between drunkenness and pauperism, and the hard times caused by the Embargo, the Panic of 1819, or more local economic distress helped to drive home their arguments. By 1829 there were a thousand local temperance societies in America with a membership of one hundred thousand persons. Within two years this was doubled, and 19 state societies were formed as well. By 1834 there were five thousand local societies with a total membership of a million persons. [73]

The movement was strongest in New York, Pennsylvania, and

---

[69] Wines, II, 113. The reference is to Captain Alexander S. Wadsworth and to Lieutenant Hiram Paulding. Hiram Paulding was a cousin of Secretary of the Navy James K. Paulding.

[70] *House Documents,* 22d Cong., 2d Sess. (Serial 233), I, Doc. 2.

[71] *The Sailor's Magazine,* VI (1833–34), 289.

[72] *Ibid.,* p. 192.   [73] Tyler, pp. 316–326.

New England. The Old Northwest also was strong for temperance, and in the South the societies had their greatest membership in Virginia and Georgia.[74]

Temperance crusaders were responsible for the establishment of total abstinence railroads and temperance publications, hotels, houses, and dinners. There was also a temperance essay contest, and Duff Green of Washington, D.C., published the winning essays. With the movement making so much headway it was only a matter of time before larger organizations would be attempted. In May 1833 delegates from 21 state societies met in Philadelphia and formed the United States Temperance Union.[75]

Temperance societies also were active in the nation's capital. In May 1830 a group composed chiefly of printers met at the general Post Office and formed the Franklin Temperance Society. In January 1832 a meeting was called at the Capitol for the purpose of promoting the cause of temperance. Men and women attended the meeting in such numbers that all the seats were taken, and others stood in the lobbies and in the galleries. Lewis Condict called the meeting together, and the Secretary of War was invited to be its chairman. The group was addressed by the Chaplain of the House of Representatives, and prayers by the Chaplain of the Senate concluded the meeting. The resolutions and speeches heard at this meeting were printed in pamphlet form and distributed to the public. At a later date the Temperance Society of Washington issued a 12-page "national Circular" on temperance addressed to the head of every family in the United States. News of various local temperance groups was printed in the Washington *National Intelligencer*, and a number of letters to the editor lamented the amount of intemperance in the country. In 1834, in keeping with the organization of state societies elsewhere in the nation, the various societies in Washington united to form the Temperance Union of Washington.[76]

The emphasis on the need for sober voters had its counterpart in the attempts to organize legislative temperance societies in

---

[74] *Ibid.*

[75] Sister Clare Francis Stanton, "The National Intelligencer and Humanitarianism, 1830–1840" (unpublished M.A. thesis, The Catholic University of America, Washington, D.C.), pp. 12–13.

[76] *Ibid.*, pp. 9–13.

several states. This was presumably done more for prestige purposes than for the influencing of legislation. In February 1833 a
Congressional Temperance Society was formed by Felix Grundy
of Tennessee, Lewis Cass of Michigan, and Theodore Frelinghuy-
sen of New Jersey. Its object was to discourage the use of liquor
by example and moral influence.[77] Thus in both their home states
and at the seat of government senators, representatives, and other
public officers were exposed to a great deal of temperance sentiment.

Until about 1840 the temperance propaganda had as its objective the education of the public on the evils of spirituous liquors.
It also attempted to engender a feeling among the people that not
only the use but the manufacture and sale of intoxicants was
morally wrong.[78]

A plea for governmental action toward the goal of total abstinence in the Navy was heard from Representative Henry L. Pinck-
ney of South Carolina when he addressed a meeting of the Congressional Temperance Society in the spring of 1834. After rejoicing
over the discontinuance of the liquor ration in the Army, he asked
why the same reform should not be extended to the Navy. He
understood that such a plan was being considered, and he believed
the officers and men of the Navy would approve the action.[79]

Such a plan was indeed being considered. Campbell P. White, a
Jackson Democrat of New York and chairman of the House naval
committee, sent Woodbury the resolutions of that body calling for
a change in the regulations in regard to spirits. In a letter of May
2, 1834, Woodbury replied that he was in favor of the abolition of
the spirit ration and had already written a report on the subject for
the President. He referred to his earlier order on the commutation
policy and stated that the ration was given a high monetary value
in order to encourage voluntary renunciation. With regard to the
progress made in the Army he said: "Finding the component parts
of the navy ration, unlike those of the army, fixed by law, it was not
in my power to diminish or abolish it; but I invited the attention of

---

[77] Tyler, p. 326.
[78] *Ibid.*, p. 338.
[79] *The Sailor's Magazine*, VI, 243. The War Department abolished the
whisky ration in the Army in 1830 and gave money in lieu of it. Two years
later sugar and coffee were substituted for the money.

Congress to a revision of the subject, and have hoped that some salutary changes would, at an early day, be provided for." [80]

Woodbury claimed that his earlier order brought about a great improvement in health, morals, and temperance. If Congress would change the law as he requested, he believed the Navy would benefit. He added: "The character and habits of seamen are so peculiar, that a gradual, rather than sudden change is supposed to be most acceptable, and that, under the authority proposed in the report, a total abolition of the use of spirits can, ere long, be introduced, if not with the entire consent and approbation of all concerned, yet without any danger of creating dissatisfaction or injury in the public service." [81]

In August *The Sailor's Magazine* informed its readers that the bill was still being prepared. The bill apparently died in committee for no further news of it appeared. [82]

In the meantime there was evidence of increasing activity among temperance groups. The New York *Observer* reported that insurance underwriters had appropriated funds to finance the free distribution of temperance publications among sailors. It also reported that more than 1,200 temperance vessels had sailed from U.S. ports. [83]

Edward Richardson, a merchant captain and the president of the Marine Temperance Society, reported in 1837 that the 2,170 members of that society included 140 shipmasters, 120 mates, and 1,100 seamen. Some boarding house keepers had been induced to discontinue the use of ardent spirits, but much still needed to be done. Richardson promised that if the present landlords refused to cooperate in the reforms, then the reformation would be brought about by others. "It is not to be endured by a Christian community, in this age of light, that this state of things should continue much longer." [84]

In December 1837 the Rhode Island State Temperance Society resolved to petition Congress to end the spirit ration in the Navy.

---

[80] *House Documents*, 23d Cong., 1st Sess. (Serial 259), VI, Doc. 486.
[81] *Ibid.*
[82] *The Sailor's Magazine*, VI, 376.
[83] The New York *Observer* quoted in *The Sailor's Magazine*, VIII, 260–261.
[84] *The Sailor's Magazine*, IX (1836–37), 287.

A circular was sent to other state societies inviting cooperation on this measure.[85]

The appeal did not go unheeded. The year 1838 was only two days old when Congress received the first of several memorials. Senator William C. Rives, a Democrat from Virginia, presented the memorial from the District of Columbia Temperance Society. In March the Pennsylvania State Temperance Society's memorial was presented by Samuel McKean, a Democratic senator from that state. This memorial stressed the "serious objections in the minds of parents" to their sons' serving in the Navy while the spirit ration was still in effect. Such legalized drinking also operated against the temperance movement in the merchant service. The latter point was emphasized again in April in the memorial from the state society in Rhode Island. The petitioners argued that under the present circumstances temperate sailors chose to enlist on board temperance merchant ships, thus leaving the naval service as a haven for drunkards and foreigners. A convention held in Claremont, New Hampshire, on the subject of the importation of foreign alcohol and the use of spirits in the Navy led to the presentation of another memorial to Congress in June.[86]

The month of February 1839 brought a long and detailed memorial signed by 362 persons including a number of men prominent in New England maritime concerns. It referred to the efforts of individuals and societies for sailors and declared that no attempt to improve the lot of the seamen would be successful as long as the spirit ration remained. It mentioned the efforts of merchants on behalf of sailors and called attention to the diminishing insurance premiums on temperance ships. The spirit ration had been abolished in both the English and American armies, and to a large extent in the U.S. merchant service as well. Since the merchant service constituted a reserve force for the Navy, the exposure of temperate merchant sailors to the Navy's spirit ration would undo a great deal of good. Men in the naval service were shipped for longer periods of time and were exposed to stricter discipline and to fewer indul-

---

[85] *Ibid.*, X (1837–38), 131–132.

[86] *Congressional Globe*, 25th Cong., 2d Sess., VI, 70, 256; *Senate Documents*, 25th Cong., 2d Sess. (Serial 317), IV, Doc. 326; *House Executive Documents*, 25th Cong., 2d Sess. (Serial 329), IX, Doc. 321; *ibid.* (Serial 331), XI, Doc. 436.

gences. The whisky ration constituted their main enjoyment. The new system of training apprentice seamen required every ship to carry a certain number of boys. Under present conditions these boys were in danger of being ruined by bad example and of the public service being damaged. The government paid strict attention to the task of keeping the West Point cadets from forming intemperate habits. Why not apply similar rules to the training of men for the Navy?

Appended to this petition was a letter from Captain John Downes, U.S.N., to the Reverend Edward T. Taylor of Boston, a well-known crusader for temperance among seamen. Downes expressed his approval of the memorial and added: "I feel well assured that our ships would be more efficient, our seamen better contented, and much less punishment necessary, were the spirit part of the ration taken from the navy." [87]

Additional information on the need for drastic changes in the floating world came in 1839 with publication at Boston of William McNally's *Evils and Abuses in the Naval and Merchant Service, Exposed; with Proposals for Their Remedy and Redress*. McNally, an ex-Navy gunner, wrote that the Navy's spirit ration "directly favors intemperance," by creating an appetite for strong drink. Drunkenness led to corporal punishment, "which has been so much censured by the citizens of our country, as being degrading and incompatible with the principles of our free institutions and government. . . ." He said that the half pint of spirits per day affected him when he first entered the Navy, and he had every reason to believe that it affected others the same way. If this was true, then "to stop the spirits on board our vessels of war becomes a private, public and christian duty." [88]

A year later a memorial signed by 45 inhabitants of Addison and Steuben counties, New York, was presented to Congress. The memorialists asked for the passage of a law which would prohibit the furnishing of intoxicating drinks to members of the Army or Navy or to Indians under federal control. They sought to prohibit the sale of such beverages at or near any naval or military installation or ground under U.S. jurisdiction, including the city of Washing-

---

[87] *Senate Documents*, 25th Cong., 2d Sess (Serial 340), III, Doc. 223.
[88] McNally, pp. 35–41.

ton, D.C. This petition also called for an increased duty on imported spirits and the use of every constitutional means "to discourage the manufacture of such drinks in these United States."[89] Similar petitions were received from other New Yorkers in Chautauqua and Onondaga counties, and from the village of Greenbush in Rensselaer County.[90] Such pressure on Congress was probably due to the efforts of the influential New York State Temperance Society which organized extensive protests against intemperance and the traffic in liquor.[91] These petitions, like those mentioned previously, were apparently allowed to die in the Committee on Naval Affairs.[92]

A private letter of a naval officer bearing on this subject was printed in *The Sailor's Magazine* in June 1840. He wrote of the evils of the spirit ration and expressed the hope that, in addition to the efforts to publish "right views" on the nature of intoxicants, a sympathy for the sailor be awakened. As for the objections of certain naval officers that no seamen could be obtained if grog were eliminated, he pointed out that when the temperance crusade began, farmers believed that they could not hire laborers for their harvests without supplying them with liquor, but all these objections vanished when the experiment was tried. In view of the large number of boys joining the Navy as apprentices it was important that the older hands set a good example.[93]

The National Temperance Convention which met at Saratoga, New York, in 1841 passed a resolution praising the War Department for stopping the spirit ration in the Army and urged a similar reform in the Navy. Such a regulation would save "high minded and gentlemanly officers" of the Navy from the mortification of serving liquor and would allow them to set "a salutary temperance example before every foreign nation" that they visited.[94]

Praising the War Department for the reforms in the Army was a case of emphasizing the positive side of things. In 1820, during

[89] *House Executive Documents*, 26th Cong., 1st Sess. (Serial 365), III, Doc. 63.
[90] *Congressional Globe*, 26th Cong., 1st Sess., VII, 284, 295.
[91] J. H. French, *Historical and Statistical Gazeteer of New York State* (Syracuse, 1860), p. 147.
[92] *Congressional Globe*, 26th Cong., 1st Sess., VII, 295.
[93] *The Sailor's Magazine*, XII, 307–309.
[94] *Ibid.*, XIV, 80.

Secretary of War Calhoun's administration, Commissary General Gibson instituted a program of voluntary relinquishment of the spirit ration in return for its value in money. The program met with little response and was abandoned. Secretary of War Eaton tried the experiment again in 1830. Two years later sugar and coffee were issued in place of the commutation money. In 1838 Congress authorized the issuing of sugar and coffee in lieu of the whisky ration. Meanwhile, orders issued in 1830 and 1832, and incorporated in subsequent Army regulations, forbade civilian sutlers on military posts to sell spirituous liquors to the troops. But other civilians, not bound by such regulations, provided the soldiers with liquor and drunkenness continued to be a problem in the Army.[95]

In some parts of the Navy, however, there were further encouraging signs of temperance. Letters from individuals participating in the Exploring Expedition to the Pacific under Lieutenant Charles Wilkes told of some progress toward temperance in that command. In printing excerpts from these letters *The Sailor's Magazine* helped to pass on encouraging news.[96]

At the Charlestown Navy Yard the men of the receiving ship *Columbus* organized a temperance society, elected officers, and enrolled some 200 members. Much of the credit for this movement was due to the commander of the *Columbus*, Captain Joseph Smith. Another friend of temperance was Captain Foxhall A. Parker of the *Columbia*, who permitted representatives of the *Columbus* and the Charlestown temperance societies to hold meetings on board his frigate. *The Boston Journal* reported that $2,500 had been paid to the men of the *Columbus* for spirits relinquished over a three-year period. Three hundred men of the frigate *Ohio* signed the total abstinence pledge. After printing this news *The Sailor's Magazine* ventured a hope that "very soon, our noble tars may with one voice say to Congress, *we will have no more of your grog.*"[97]

Fresh evidence of the conditions in the Navy was supplied to the reading public in 1842 with the publication of Chaplain Charles

[95] Prucha, *Broadax and Bayonet*, 50n; *Army Life on the Western Frontier*, 110n, 111n; Risch, p. 203.
[96] *The Sailor's Magazine*, XIII, 331.   [97] *Ibid.*, XIV, 221, 281.

Rockwell's *Sketches of Foreign Travel and Life at Sea*. He lamented the shameful drunken conduct of our sailors in foreign ports and reported that the balance of punishments on shipboard for drunkenness and other crimes was seven to one against whisky drinkers. Many others who were never drunk were made irritable, silly, disobedient, or reckless by the Navy spirit ration. Because men on the sick list did not draw their grog, many men neglected to report themselves when sick. Many forfeited their lives for this neglect. Commodore Daniel T. Patterson of the *Delaware* told him that the 23 men of that ship who died of cholera could have been saved if they had reported themselves to the surgeon. Chaplain Rockwell called upon all persons to exert themselves to end intemperance. Congress gave the men of the Navy a spirit ration to furnish a market for the surplus grain of the West. "Representatives in Congress are not ashamed to argue in favor of this evil, because their constituents are whiskey makers." Referring to a case of a sailor who was hanged for killing a shipmate while drunk, Rockwell said that at the time of the execution he thought "that could this man, sunken as he was, but be placed within the halls of Congress, where those who make our laws could see and hear him, it would do more than any human eloquence to lead them, as one man, to rise up and refuse longer to furnish the poor sailor with this liquid fire." Nevertheless, he felt that flogging was necessary to restrain the crew.[98]

The question of the spirit ration came up again in the Senate in August 1842 during the discussion of a bill to regulate the pay and emoluments of pursers in the Navy. Under the system then in effect the purser was paid from funds collected through the sale of such articles as tea, coffee, and sugar to the seamen. In effect, the sailor was taxed to pay the purser. The bill under consideration was an attempt to make the Navy more attractive by increasing the comforts of sailors. The aforementioned articles would be supplied by the government, and the Treasury would pay the pursers. A part of the plan also called for decreasing the spirit ration. On this point Levi Woodbury, now a senator from New Hampshire, observed that he was in favor of the objects of the bill, but he felt that the

---

[98] Rockwell, II, 412–417, 409.

spirit ration should be abolished entirely and not merely decreased.[99]

Woodbury's remark was prompted by a suggestion of the Secretary of the Navy. Secretary Upshur wrote to Willie P. Mangum, the
chairman of the Senate Committee on Naval Affairs, asking him
"to introduce and endeavor to pass" an enclosed bill relating to the
naval ration. Upshur's plan was to cut the spirit ration in half and
to introduce tea, coffee, and sugar in lieu of it. "This would be
highly acceptable to the seamen and would contribute much to the
discipline and good order of the service." He also sought the power
to increase the value of the ration according to circumstances and
within prescribed limits.[100]

Upshur got his way. The bill passed on August 29, 1842, reduced
the daily ration of spirits to one gill per man. An ounce of tea,
coffee, or cocoa, and two ounces of sugar were added. There was
also to be a weekly allowance of half a pound of pickles or cran-
berries, half a pint of molasses, and half a pint of vinegar. Payments
to those who relinquished the spirit ration were placed on a
sounder legal basis. Finally, no commissioned officer, midshipman,
or enlisted man under the age of 21 years was permitted to draw
the ration of grog.[101]

This law might prevent the young apprentices from acquiring
a taste for alcohol for a time, but it would not save them from a
great deal of bad example. Nevertheless, it was a further implementation of Woodbury's circular of 11 years earlier.

The very origin of grog was an attempt to combat the drunkenness which resulted from an overindulgence in rum. It was an
effort to improve the health and discipline of the crews. Early in
the history of the American Navy experiments were made to determine the best beverage for use on board naval vessels. Secretary

---

[99] *Congressional Globe*, 27th Cong., 2d Sess., XI, 865.

[100] Secretary of the Navy Abel P. Upshur to Senator Willie P. Mangum,
April 8, 1842, *Letters to Congress*, VIII, 413–414. Upshur also intended that
the bill give the Secretary of the Navy the power to vary the food ration
according to the service performed. As the law then stood, the same rations
had to be supplied to every ship regardless of where stationed in the world.
The result was a great deal of waste and unnecessary expense. Upshur favored
letting the ships buy fresh provisions in the ports that they touched.

[101] *U.S. Statutes at Large*, V, Chap. 267, pp. 546–547.

Smith's introduction of whisky was based on the argument that it was cheaper and more wholesome than rum for use in the grog ration. Military and naval officers felt that the government's spirit ration was not the cause of drunkenness in the ranks but that it was due to the intoxicants sold to the men by civilian liquor dealers. To the best of their ability they attempted to control the introduction of alcoholic beverages into military and naval installations. But they had no control over the men on liberty. The only way to stop drunkenness, if it could be stopped at all, was to have some measure of control over the civilian sources of supply. Obviously the naval and military leaders themselves could not openly attack or attempt to control a legitimate business enterprise, but a national temperance movement could.

As the cause of temperance grew in importance, it was only a matter of time before the government's connection with the dispensing of liquor came under scrutiny. A doctor turned congressman instigated a series of inquiries. When questioned about the necessity for liquor rations in the Navy, the Secretary turned the matter over to a panel of naval surgeons. The doctors agreed that the spirit ration was harmful to morals and health and called upon Congress to take action. This request for the abolition of grog was repeated many times over in memorials and petitions from various temperance groups in the country. Such petitions were referred to the House and Senate Committees on Naval Affairs where they were promptly forgotten.

Since the components of the Navy's rations were set by law, there was little that a Secretary could do to support the cause of temperance, if he were so inclined. There is evidence that Secretary Branch was moving toward the abolition of grog before his forced resignation from the cabinet put an end to such plans. Secretary Woodbury was an exponent of the "proceed with caution" school of naval reform. Under the circumstances the best he could do was to encourage temperance in the Navy by clarifying and publicizing the rules governing the payment of money to those men who chose not to consume the spirit part of their ration. Thereafter it was up to the individual sailor on every ship to make his own choice. Officers who were advocates of temperance did what they could to encourage the renunciation of grog, but there was no evidence of any coercion. In fact, it was the custom of some captains to stop a man's grog as punishment for minor offenses. If a sailor did not draw grog, his captain often felt that he had no alternative but to flog the man. As a result of these practices some seamen who might be inclined toward temperance kept drawing their grog as a form of insurance against being flogged! Given this state of affairs, it was sometimes difficult to win converts to temperance on any long-range basis. At the same time, the need to abolish flogging was underscored.

When the cause of temperance had so much support from large segments of the population, as well as from medical men, clergymen, Navy men, congressmen, and senators, why did not Congress abolish the spirit ration? The answer lies in the attitudes of various other members of the Congress, particularly those who belonged to the naval committees of the House and Senate. The abolition of grog was opposed on the grounds that it would decrease the consumption of American whisky, the manufacture of which helped to absorb the grain surplus of the farmer; that is was against tradition; that it was needed as a punishment; and that it was essential to health, medical opinion to the contrary notwithstanding. But most of all it was opposed because it was felt that it constituted an unwarranted interference with individual liberty. Members of the committee felt that a man should be free to drink or not as he chose. Even *The Sailor's Magazine* admitted that voluntary reformation was more honorable than compulsion.

The trouble with the argument on natural rights was that it put its exponents in a difficult position when the subject of naval apprentices came up. Everyone agreed that youth should not be corrupted. Therefore even those who were opposed to the abolition of grog felt that it should be kept from those under 21 years of age. No member of Congress was in a position to object to the argument that if parents should encourage their sons to enter the Navy, then those sons should be placed in a wholesome environment. It was this state of affairs which made it possible for the temperance reformers to get an act of Congress passed in 1842 which decreased the amount of spirits issued, which forbade its use by minors, and which regularized the practice of paying money in lieu of the ration.

Almost all of those who wrote or petitioned about abuses in the Navy recognized the cause and effect relationship between liquor and punishment. If temperance in the Navy could be achieved only by gradual steps, then sailors should be given additional encouragement to renounce their grog ration voluntarily. Men who kept their grog as an insurance against a flogging would no longer need that excuse if flogging were abolished. Therefore, a successful attack on flogging might well result in additional gains for the cause of temperance. And so, as we have seen earlier, the battle against the lash became more intense and victory finally came in 1850. By that time those who struggled to end the grog ration still had a long hard fight ahead of them.

THE END OF GROG

By 1842 the word temperance was a misnomer for many of the crusaders against alcohol. More and more they were committed to the idea of total abstinence. Driven by emotionalism and moral fervor, some of the temperance reformers advocated programs that were coercive, and which were dangerous to individual liberties. Such inflexibility, such thoroughness, and such immediatism served to divide and to weaken the temperance cause in the country as a whole.

The naval aspect of the temperance crusade fared much better. Encouraged by the gains made in 1842, the antigrog agitators continued to work in slow but persistent fashion for an act of Congress to end the spirit ration. Meanwhile, the work of popularizing the cause of total abstinence went forward on a man by man and ship by ship basis.

The *Boston* completed a cruise around the world in 1843 during which only 72 of her crew of 203 drew their grog ration. The rest accepted six cents a day in lieu thereof. While in Honolulu the officers of the *Boston* presented a cash contribution to the chaplain of the American Seamen's Friend Society to aid the cause of temperance. Captain John C. Long, the ship's commander, presented a Bethel flag.[1]

---

[1] *The Sailor's Magazine*, XVI, 34–35.

Through the efforts of Lieutenant Andrew H. Foote, the *Cumberland* became a temperance frigate in 1843. Foote's interest in the seamen's cause dated from his call to religion during a cruise in 1827. His father, Senator Samuel A. Foote, a Whig from Connecticut, helped him to secure copies of *The Sailor's Magazine* for distribution to his men while they cruised in the Pacific Ocean. Both Andrew Foote and his first wife, Caroline, became life members of the American Seamen's Friend Society. His dedication to the Society's goals was such that the editor of *The Sailor's Magazine* later wrote: "Our cause has no better friend than Andrew H. Foote." During 1841–43, while in command of the Philadelphia Naval Asylum, Foote had a great deal of trouble with the drunken old seamen. At length he decided to take the temperance pledge himself. His example and his "unceasing persuasion" convinced the old sailors that they should also take the pledge. In a petition to the Secretary of the Navy the pensioners gave Foote credit for making every man in the Naval Asylum a sober, grog-refusing human being.[2] Not long after this Lieutenant Foote received an assignment to the flagship *Cumberland*.

While the *Cumberland* was being prepared for sea, some sailors managed to sample a barrel of whisky. During the drunken spree that followed, some of the men insulted and attacked one of the officers. When order was restored the guilty individuals were flogged. Foote took this occasion to form a temperance society, and his first members were his fellow officers. His efforts were encouraged by Commodore Joseph Smith, and soon the idea spread to the enlisted men. At length all but one sailor commuted his grog for money, and before long that rugged individual was transferred. *The Sailor's Magazine* reported that "coca water" was used instead of grog on the ship. The *Cumberland* soon gained a reputation for being not only a total abstinence ship, but also a ship with excellent discipline.[3]

When the officers of the frigate *Brandywine* pledged themselves

---

[2] Allan Westcott, "Andrew Hull Foote," *Dictionary of American Biography*, VI, 499; *The Sailor's Magazine*, III, 98; VIII, 262; XVI, 371; XXXIV, 218; James Mason Hoppin, *Life of Andrew Hull Foote, Rear Admiral United States Navy* (New York, 1874), pp. 56–59.

[3] *Ibid.*

to temperance, it was said that the name of the ship should be changed, since neither brandy nor wine were consumed on board.[4]

A temperance address on board the frigate *Ohio* led to the formation of a temperance society with a membership of 154 men.[5]

The crew of the frigate *United States* drew up a temperance pledge which was adopted by some of the officers and men of the Pacific Squadron. Members of this North Pacific Total Abstinence Society No. 1 pledged themselves not to drink wine or any other intoxicating beverage unless it was recommended by a physician.[6]

A similar pledge was circulated by Commodore Thomas Ap Catesby Jones among the officers and men of his squadron under somewhat dramatic circumstances. When drunkenness resulted in the flogging of several men of the *Yorktown*, Jones chose the occasion to read to the assembled ships' companies a long discourse on the evils of drink which he had written himself. Among other things, Jones said that shore liberty was not given to the men because drunkenness was always the result. "It has been said that a man-of-war is a states prison, if that be the case, Rum is the jailer; destroy that and the shipped man can be as free as the Commissioned Officer."[7] William Myers, a seaman present at this occasion, noted in his diary that Jones's speech denoted a "deranged state of mind. . . ." A week later Myers wrote that he "heard that 3 first signers of the Temperance Pledg [*sic*] Comore [*sic*] Jones, Capt. Armstrong & Capt. Stribling were drunk last night."[8]

Later, Jones drew up a memorial to Congress requesting that ardent spirits be banished from the Navy, except those used by the medical department. He sent a copy of this memorial to *The Sailor's Magazine* which the editors published. It was designed for the signatures of all grades of officers as well as those of seamen, landsmen, marines, and boys. Jones announced that he would submit such a petition to Congress even if he could get no more than six signers.[9]

It would be a mistake, of course, to assume that all of the conversions to temperance reported by *The Sailor's Magazine* repre-

---

[4] *The Sailor's Magazine*, XXXIV, 362–363.   [5] *Ibid.*, XVI, 148.
[6] *Ibid.*, p. 218.   [7] Bradley, pp. 164–165.
[8] Unpublished diary of William Myers, quoted in Bradley, p. 165.
[9] *The Sailor's Magazine*, XVI, 218–219. The writer has found no evidence that this petition was ever presented to Congress.

sented any permanent change in the habits of the seamen. The reformers themselves were well aware of the fact that a number of men would become backsliders. The statistics previously cited for the various ships represented the results of a three-year experiment at best. Sometimes the figures represented the gains of a considerably shorter period. By and large the Navy chaplains seemed to have a realistic approach to their charges. Chaplain Rockwell considered lying one of the vices of seamen, and he says:

They are, for example, very fond of playing tricks on seamen's preachers on shore; and I have heard a seaman amuse his shipmates by telling them how, when he was in Boston, he went and joined Father Taylor's Temperance Society, and the next day had a good drunken spree to wash it down. One of the first tricks they try to play on a chaplain when he comes on board, is, falsely to pretend they do not drink, or are religiously inclined, with a view to secure some favor from him, that thus they may ridicule him with their messmates. If a chaplain is not warned of this fact, and fails to keep a bright outlook for such tricks, he may find his influence as nothing with the crew, merely because they think he is wanting in shrewdness and sagacity. If, on the other hand, they find him ready for them, and he sends them off, as they say, with a flea in their ear, they soon learn to let him alone, and will treat him with uniform respect.[10]

Rockwell firmly believed that the spirit ration was unnecessary. He cited a case where, on their own accord, the men gave up their grog for two months in order to raise money to buy a sword for a favorite officer. When the money was collected they went back to their old habits again.[11] Nevertheless, with due allowance made for backsliders and those caught up in the enthusiasm of the moment, the evidence indicates that there was a slow but steady growth of the temperance idea in the Navy.

In May 1844, when the House of Representatives was at work on the naval appropriation bill for the coming year, Daniel P. King, a Massachusetts Whig, introduced an amendment to prohibit the spirit ration and to supply money in its place. The House approved the amendment by a vote of 75 to 49. Immediately after this vote John P. Hale, a New Hampshire Democrat, introduced an amendment to abolish flogging which also passed, by a vote of 53 to 39.[12]

---

[10] Rockwell, II, 396–397.   [11] *Ibid.*, p. 415.
[12] *Congressional Globe*, 28th Cong., 1st Sess., XIII, Part 1, p. 618.

When the appropriation bill went to the Senate, Richard H. Bayard, a Delaware Whig, moved to strike out these amendments. In the discussion that followed, Benjamin Tappan, an Ohio Democrat, stated that he was opposed to both the spirit ration and to flogging. Robert J. Walker, a Democrat of Mississippi, added that the spirit ration was an unnecessary nuisance that did more harm than good. George McDuffy, a Democrat of South Carolina, said that if the giving of spirits "on great and exciting occasions" was forbidden, then they might as well abolish the Navy. Nevertheless, he was opposed to keeping the spirit part of the ration. John J. Crittenden, a Kentucky Whig, thought that the spirit ration was necessary due to the exposed nature of the sailor's life. Ambrose H. Sevier, a Democrat of Arkansas, was opposed to taking away the sailor's grog. Bayard pointed out that the act of 1842 regulated the ration and protected the apprentices. He added that: "There was no officer who did not favor this particular nature of reform — that is, of permitting a choice to the sailors of taking spirits or not, at will." [13]

When the vote was taken the amendment was stricken out by a vote of 26 to 14. The measure to abolish flogging was also rejected. Three days later Congress adjourned.[14]

Upon the completion of the cruise of the temperance frigate *Cumberland* in 1844, her crew sent a petition to Congress urging the abolition of the whisky ration. According to Lieutenant Foote, the men did this "of their own accord — no coercion, no force was used. The subject was placed before them — they chose, they acted for themselves; and by it have not only astonished people abroad,

---

[13] *Ibid.*, pp. 681–682.

[14] *Ibid.*, p. 682. Among those who supported King's amendment to end grog were Thomas Hart Benton of Missouri and Rufus Choate of Massachusetts. The senatorial group favoring abolition included 5 Whigs, 7 Democrats, 1 senator elected on a Law and Order ticket (John B. Francis of Rhode Island), and 1 elected on a combination Whig-Democrat ticket (William Woodbridge of Michigan). Of this number, 10 were from northern states, 2 from southern, and 2 from border states. Both senators from Michigan and New Hampshire supported the move to end the spirit ration. The majority who rejected the amendment included 13 Whigs and 13 Democrats. The sectional breakdown of this vote was 6 from northern states, 12 from southern, and 8 from border states. Both votes of Alabama, Delaware, Georgia, Illinois, Kentucky, Louisiana, Maryland, North Carolina, Pennsylvania, and South Carolina were cast against the measure. Of the 26 in favor of keeping the spirit ration, 8 had at least some military background.

but the papers at home are resounding with their praise. . . ."
Their memorial was also signed by Commodore Joseph Smith,
commander of the Mediterranean Squadron, and by the officers of
the flagship *Cumberland*. It was presented to the House Committee on Naval Affairs by George P. Marsh, a Whig representative
from Vermont, in January 1845.[15]

In reviewing the arguments against the memorials, the committee reported that the Navy Department did not recommend a
change in the regulations regarding the spirit ration or the com-
pensating payment, and that many naval officers were opposed to
the innovation. It was feared by some that to discontinue the allowance would cause discontent, lead to illicit indulgence in
liquor, violations of discipline, and increased difficulties in recruiting men, and would cause experienced men to enter foreign service. They pointed out that public opinion was bringing about a
reformation in the use of intoxicants, and any attempts by the
government to hasten the process by stringent measures would
increase the evil. These objections had weight, said the committee,
but in spite of that fact "public opinion in the country demands,
and that public opinion in the navy itself sanctions the change proposed." Advantages in health, discipline, efficiency, the saving of
space, the removal of temptation from apprentices and young men,
"and, above all, the moral bearing of the question, are more sufficient to counterbalance the arguments in favor of continuing the
allowance. . . ." The committee, accordingly, reported a bill for
the discontinuance of the spirit ration.[16]

"We are glad to find our naval officers moving in this matter at
this time," said *The Sailor's Magazine*, "and doubt not that a large
majority of them would gladly see it abolished." It would be far
better to give the sailor a pay raise of six cents a day than to pay
this money to the distillers, said the editor.[17]

Another symptom of the spread of temperance in the Navy was
found in the pages of the *United States Nautical Magazine* published in June 1845. Lieutenant T. Augustus Craven, U.S.N., its
editor, announced himself as an advocate of temperance in his

---

[15] Hoppin, p. 59; *House Reports*, 28th Cong., 2d Sess. (Serial 468), Report
No. 73.
[16] *Ibid.*   [17] *The Sailor's Magazine*, XVII, 209.

review of a blank verse poem by William O. Bourne entitled "The Sale of a Distillery."[18]

Everything seemed to point to the fact that it was a very auspicious time for bringing an end to the spirit ration. The total abstinence agitation waxed strong in various parts of the nation. In the city of Washington the movement had a tremendous growth between 1841 and 1846. Freeman's Vigilant Total Abstinence Society was organized in October 1841, and its weekly meetings were reported in the *National Intelligencer*. At one meeting in 1842 Representative Thomas F. Marshall of Kentucky addressed an audience of 1500 members of this society. In December 1842 the Navy Yard Total Abstinence Society was formed. Similar societies of tradesmen, firemen, and mechanics were formed at the same time. Many members of the medical profession threw their efforts and influence into the cause. A group of young men in Washington formed the Cold Water Association, which was devoted to temperance and to literary improvement. Later Junior Temperance Societies were formed for youths. On January 25, 1844, members of the House of Representatives met at the Capitol and organized the Congressional Total Abstinence Society. In November of the same year a new society known as the United Brothers of Temperance was organized in the Washington Navy Yard. Within less than two years this group had grown to five associations and four junior associations.

During the presidential election of 1844 there was some decline in interest in the abstinence movement, but after the voting it was revived. Temperance speeches marked part of the observance of the Fourth of July in Washington in 1845. These orations were heard by the Secretaries of State, War, and Navy, and by the Mayor of Washington.[19]

Why then, in view of all this interest in temperance and in total abstinence, did Congress fail to take action in the matter of the naval grog ration? The remarks in Congress previously cited show that many senators felt that temperance should be an entirely vol-

---

[18] *United States Nautical Magazine*, I (1845), 261.

[19] Sister Catherine Crowe, "The National Intelligencer and Humanitarianism, 1841–1850" (unpublished M.A. thesis, The Catholic University of America, Washington, D.C.), pp. 5–13.

untary action. The correspondence between two champions of temperance, Captain Joseph Smith and Lieutenant Andrew H. Foote, gives an additional insight into the problems of dealing with Congress.

Past association had made Captain Smith and Lieutenant Foote warm friends. After their cruise in the *Cumberland*, Smith was assigned to duty in Washington and Foote was transferred to the Boston Navy Yard. This separation did not diminish their interest in, or efforts toward securing the abolition of the spirit ration. Smith was in an excellent position to keep abreast of things in Congress, and he kept Foote informed. In his letter of January 30, 1846, Smith reported as follows: "I conversed with many persons on the feasibility of carrying through Congress our project of abolishing the spirit-ration. I do not believe the committees in both houses would report in its favor; and if they should, I do not believe that this Congress will ratify the measure. There is a strong opposition to it, and a good many wires would be pulled to check it." [20] A month later he wrote of his further conversations on the subject: "I have talked with Mr. Choate about the matter. He told me Mr. Calhoun voted against the reform and that he could not carry it. We have some officers high in rank who will oppose it; nevertheless, I think it will come round by-and-by." [21]

While various reformers waited for that distant by-and-by, their efforts to convince men to renounce their grog continued. The Secretary of the Navy fixed the rate of commutation at two cents a day.[22] The men of the *Cumberland* and other ships drew their grog money on this basis. In November 1843 Secretary Henshaw recommended to Congress that no spirit ration be allowed to men who enlisted in the future, and that the right to commute the ration for money be continued for those already in service. He argued that if grog were abolished, flogging and disease would decrease and the whole moral and physical condition of the men would be improved as well as their character.[23] Henshaw had few opportunities to elaborate on these points. The Senate refused to confirm

---

[20] Hoppin, p. 61.
[21] *Ibid.* Rufus Choate was an ex-Whig senator from Massachusetts. Senator John C. Calhoun was a Democrat of South Carolina.
[22] *U.S. Statutes at Large*, V, Chap. 267, pp. 546–547.
[23] *Senate Documents*, 28th Cong., 1st Sess. (Serial 431), I, Doc. 1, p. 480.

his appointment as Secretary to the Navy and he left this post in February 1844.

In January 1847 John A. Rockwell, a Whig representative from Connecticut, and a life member of the American Seamen's Friend Society, introduced an amendment to the naval appropriation bill abolishing the spirit ration and providing for the payment of six cents a day in lieu thereof. Speaking in favor of this measure, Rockwell pointed out the results of the experiment on the *Cumberland*, and quoted Captain Smith and Captain Charles Wilkes on the desirability of ending the grog ration.[24]

Rockwell's amendment was stricken out, but in March 1847 the rate of commutation was increased to three cents a day, which was to be paid monthly. The ratio was further increased to four cents a day in August 1848, but this still fell short of the declared value of six cents a day for the ration commuted.[25]

John A. Rockwell's interest in temperance in the Navy did not end with the rejection of his amendment. Instead, it deepened. As chairman of the naval committee of the House he had already collected facts on the subject and had presented them to Congress. In this work he was aided by Captain Smith, Captain Wilkes, and Lieutenant Foote. Thereafter during several sessions of Congress he fought in vain for the end of the spirit ration. Later, when the subject of flogging come to the fore, he pointed out that liquor was the cause of most of the flogging. But nothing was achieved. Rockwell's contemporaries were unable to explain the continued failure. No doubt the same wires which Captain Smith had alluded to earlier were still being pulled to check the measure. The author has not been able to uncover evidence of specific persons who were responsible for pigeonholing the measures. Such actions seem to have been common during the whole period of this reform movement. In Rockwell's day, some persons believed that the Medical Bureau at Washington was behind the delay, but no evidence has been found to substantiate these views.[26]

In spite of these discouragements the reformers continued to work for the abolition of the grog ration. Foote forwarded to Rockwell the views of Lieutenant Commandant Charles H. Davis,

[24] *The Sailor's Magazine*, IX, 231; XIX, 273–276.
[25] *U.S. Statutes at Large*, IX, Chap. 48, p. 169; Chap. 121, p. 271.
[26] See the remarks in *The Sailor's Magazine*, XXXIV, 363.

Commander John Pope, Commander John C. Long, and other officers who were friends of temperance. Foote told Rockwell that he was aware of the fact that many naval officers opposed the abolition of the ration, but that the officers of the *Cumberland* and others in the merchant service had been of like mind until the experiment was given a fair test. To those who declared that the abolition of grog was a coercive act, Foote replied that it did not forbid the sailor to drink, it merely ceased to present alcohol on the same basis as bread and meat. His views on the practice of paying the men who did not draw their grog were as follows:

> I can not regard the commutation at even $1.80 per month, leaving it optional with the crew, as calculated to have the desired effect. This would leave it still an open, unsettled, exciting question, enabling a few old seamen, most of them foreigners, to influence many of the younger and inexperienced men to use this portion of their ration against their better judgment. In this case, also, the expense to the government, and inconvenience to the ship of filling the spirit-room without knowing what portion would be required, is another objection. On the other hand, strike the whiskey unqualifiedly [*sic*] from the ration-table; pay the men $1 per month in lieu thereof, and it will prove acceptable to the men, economical to the government, and in all respects beneficial to the service.[27]

When a naval appropriation bill was under consideration in the House on February 1, 1849, Rockwell presented an amendment which provided: "That neither ardent spirits nor liquor of any kind whatever shall be introduced or kept aboard any national vessel, or other vessel in the service of the United States except as a part of the medical stores." [28]

Whig Representative Thomas B. King of Georgia suggested that this latter part of Rockwell's amendment be stricken out, and the original proposal be amended by a provision authorizing the Secretary of the Navy "to limit the use of ardent spirits in the navy as far as he may deem it expedient to promote the efficiency of the service." The commutation payment was to remain as before. The House then agreed to Rockwell's proposal as amended, but five days later it defeated this amendment by a vote of 71 to 63.[29]

---

[27] Hoppin, pp. 62–63.
[28] *Congressional Globe*, 30th Cong., 2d Sess., XVIII, 427.
[29] *Ibid.*, p. 468. No roll call of votes was printed in the *Congressional Globe* or in the *House Journal*.

Before the month was out the Committee on Naval Affairs reported to the House on 21 petitions from citizens of New York state requesting the exclusion of intoxicating liquors from all naval vessels except for medicinal purposes. Other petitions calling for the abolition of flogging were also presented to the committee. On the motion of Ohio's Robert Schenck, the chairman, the petitions were laid on the table and the committee was relieved from the further consideration of them.[30]

Meanwhile in the Senate, John P. Hale, an ex-Democratic representative and now an Anti-Slavery senator from New Hampshire, had spoken in vain for two days in favor of an amendment abolishing flogging in the Navy. He prefaced his first day's speech by presenting a group of resolutions, petitions, and proceedings from various groups of citizens in Syracuse, Troy, Buffalo, Rochester, and other places in New York state, calling for the abolition of flogging and the spirit ration.[31]

On March 1, the Senate received a similar resolution from the legislature of Rhode Island. That state also instructed her senators and representative to exert themselves to bring about the end of flogging and grog.[32]

The next day Hale offered an amendment authorizing the Secretary of the Navy to forbid the use of spirits, and to substitute money for it whenever he deemed it expedient. Hale pointed out that this amendment did not abolish the ration but allowed the Secretary of the Navy to act according to his own discretion. Senator John M. Berrien, a Georgia Whig, objected to this transfer of the Senate's responsibility to the Secretary of the Navy. "If this thing ought to be abolished let us do it; if not, let us submit to it. But do not let us shrink from our responsibility, and transfer it to an Executive officer," he said. Whig Senator John Davis of Massachusetts argued that the present law was better than the one proposed. When the vote was taken Hale's amendment failed to pass.[33]

For more than nine months thereafter nothing further was heard

---

[30] *Ibid.*, p. 615.

[31] *Congressional Globe*, 30th Cong., 2d Sess., XVIII, 488–489.

[32] *Senate Miscellaneous Documents*, 30th Cong., 2d Sess. (Serial 533), Doc. 63.

[33] *Congressional Globe*, 30th Cong., 2d Sess., XVIII, 654. No roll call vote was printed in either the *Congressional Globe* or the *House Journal*.

on the subject on the floors of Congress. In the March 1849 number of *The Sailor's Magazine*, the editor wrote that they had an article in type congratulating the friends of seamen on the abolition of flogging and grog in the Navy. "But we were too fast; *Congress will do no such thing*." [34] The November and December issues of the magazine carried letters of Commodore Robert F. Stockton and Commodore Charles Stewart urging a change in the naval regulations governing flogging and grog. [35]

About this same time there appeared a pamphlet entitled *Practical Reflections upon the Grog Ration of the U.S. Navy*, by William M. Wood, M.D., Surgeon of the U.S. Navy. Wood took exception to the remarks made on the floor of Congress by those who opposed the abolition of the grog ration. To those who argued that the sailor should be given his grog he said: "Upon this principle our national ships were once legitimated brothels, and in foreign ports, commanding officers, who claimed to be respectable men when at home, thought they did no more than right by filling their vessels with prostitutes and facilitating open, general and disgusting licentiousness. Thanks to the moral sense of the community, we have reached a step above this degradation, and there is hope that 'Jack' may yet be elevated above the necessity for grog." [36]

Wood argued that the ration made the men irritable, promoted insecurity, was physically harmful to them, and was directly or indirectly responsible for the diseases that placed "chronic invalids" in hospitals for care at government expense. The ration was also inconvenient and uneconomical. The three thousand gallons of whisky in the spirit room of a frigate also constitute a fire hazard, especially when the room had to be opened several times a day. In regard to the relationship between drunkenness and floggings he observed that: "It is the most heartless tyranny for the government to enact punishments for the drunkard, its laws and usages have thus been educating. Such inconsistency and such tyranny become the most unjustifiable cruelty if, as scientific writers now assert, intemperance is an uncontrollable physical and moral dis-

---

[34] *The Sailor's Magazine*, XXI, 205.
[35] *Ibid.*, XXII (1849–50), 92, 119.
[36] William M. Wood, "Practical Reflections upon the Grog Ration," in *Shoulder to the Wheel of Progress* (Buffalo, 1853), pp. 138–139.

ease, requiring medical treatment rather than physical punishment."[37]

He stressed the need for good example by officers in the matter
of the use of liquor. As for the grog ration, its abolition would not
only save money and space, but also would greatly elevate the tone
of the service. At present, American men who desire to maintain
some degree of family and self-respect refuse to enter a service
whose usages make necessary the relinquishment of such respect.
As long as these usages continue, said Wood, "we shall never have
a Navy worthy of the Republic. Our principle should be, not to
bring our Navy up to the standard of other Navies; but, as we have
done in other things, up to the standard of the nation"; and Congress should begin the work of ending the grog ration.[38]

The subject was reopened in Congress on December 31, 1849,
when Daniel Webster presented the Senate with 15 petitions from
citizens of Massachusetts and 1 from citizens of Baltimore, Maryland, calling for the abolition of the spirit ration. "I think the time
has come, and fully come, when a law should be passed in con-
formity with the prayer of these petitions," said Webster in referring them to the Committee on Naval Affairs. William H. Seward
of New York expressed agreement with Webster's sentiments when
he presented a variety of petitions from shipping and mercantile
firms of Baltimore. One of these petitions, signed by 237 persons,
called for the end of the grog ration. Other petitions sought to end
the practice of flogging, and Webster, Seward, and Hale all expressed sentiments against the practice.[39]

Late in January 1850 William Ballard Preston, the Secretary of
the Navy, sent a letter to the officers of the Navy requesting their
opinions on the abolition of, and a substitute for, corporal punishment and the spirit ration. Of the 84 officers who submitted
opinions, 12 believed that the spirit ration could be abolished.
Three were in favor of abolishing both flogging and grog. But
many of the letters bore out the statement of Captain Charles Morris that: "The desire to banish intemperance from the navy is nearly
universal among officers, they differ only as to the best means of
accomplishing it." In this connection, it is interesting to note that

---

[37] *Ibid.*, p. 152.   [38] *Ibid.*, pp. 161–162.
[39] *Congressional Globe*, 31st Cong., 1st Sess., XIX, Part 1, pp. 91–93.

such a staunch friend of temperance as Captain Joseph Smith would eliminate the grog ration but would keep the flogging. He argued that the grog ration brought low types into the Navy, and these men were the ones who received most of the whippings. But eliminate grog, give the seamen monthly payments for their suspended ration and you would attract a higher type of recruit. He also pointed out that better men could be obtained if the Navy raised the pay of its seamen.[40]

Captain Charles Skinner believed that the matter of commuting the liquor ration should be left to the individual. A pay increase was the best substitute for grog in the opinion of Captain Robert F. Stockton, a foe of flogging and of drunkenness. With higher pay as an incentive, good men could be induced to enter the Navy on the condition that they would not be allowed to draw the spirit ration. In the case of older seamen, they would still draw their grog, but "moral suasion" would be used to induce them to relinquish their liquor. In both cases temperate habits could be cultivated without sacrificing the principle of voluntary renunciation.[41]

With many an old Navy officer the general feeling was that the ration was too small to cause drunkenness. But if you abolished it smuggling and drunkenness would increase.

Commander Robert B. Cunningham wrote that he was informed that the first reduction of the spirit ration in the U.S. Navy led a number of men with long service to transfer to the English service, where their comforts received more consideration.[42]

While Secretary Preston was still receiving answers to his letter, Thomas L. Harris, Democrat of Illinois, read the House a resolution directing the Secretary of the Navy to report any instances of the flogging of disrated naval petty officers. The last paragraph of this resolution requested the Secretary to inform the House "the proportionate number of sailors in the United States service, who

---

[40] Captain Charles Morris to Secretary of the Navy William B. Preston, Feb. 6, 1850, *Reports of Officers*, No. 2; Captain Joseph Smith to Preston, Feb. 6, 1850, *ibid.*, No. 15.

[41] Captain Charles Skinner to Secretary of the Navy William B. Preston, Feb. 6, 1850, *Reports of Officers*, No. 13; Captain Robert F. Stockton to Preston, Feb. 6, 1850, *ibid.*, No. 17.

[42] Commander Robert B. Cunningham to Secretary of the Navy William B. Preston, Feb. 6, 1850, *ibid.*, No. 41.

have chosen the commutation money in lieu of grog, under the law of August 3d, 1848"; and the number under preceding rules.[43]

Representative John Wentworth, a Democrat of Illinois, gave notice on March 5, 1850 that he would introduce a bill abolishing flogging and the spirit ration.[44]

In the meantime, the friends of temperance in Rhode Island had not been idle. During the January session of the General Assembly a resolution was passed which denounced the spirit ration as "the foundation of intemperance" which made the use of the lash necessary. Rhode Island's senators were "instructed" and her representatives "requested" to use their influence to end the use of the spirit ration and the lash in the Navy. This resolution was presented to the Senate on March 18, 1850, and was referred to the Committee on Naval Affairs where it died.[45]

Once again many months went by before the subject was again broached in Congress. And once again it was while the naval appropriations bill for the coming year was being discussed that the reforms were put forward. On September 23, 1850, Representative George W. Jones, a Tennessee Democrat, offered an amendment abolishing flogging in the Navy. On a motion of Alexander Evans, a Maryland Whig, this amendment was further amended by a provision abolishing grog and allowing the sailors five cents a day in lieu of it. Abraham Venable, a North Carolina Democrat, then offered to amend these amendments further by inserting a proviso that "neither wine nor ardent spirits shall be used by the officers on board ship, whilst in actual service, except as medicine."[46]

With this proviso as his opening wedge, Venable then proceeded to denounce the aforementioned reforms. "Now, sir, the spirit ration as well as flogging have been known in all navies for centuries; and as I do not suppose that we are much better or wiser than those who have gone before us, I must be permitted to say, with all respect, that I consider this whole attempt at reform as more flummery and humbuggery." Since both Jones and Evans

---

[43] *Congressional Globe*, 31st Cong., 1st Sess., XIX, Part 1, p. 279.

[44] *Ibid.*, p. 460.

[45] *Senate Miscellaneous Documents*, 31st Cong., 1st Sess. (Serial 563), I, Doc. 74.

[46] *Congressional Globe*, 31st Cong., 1st Sess., XIX, Part 2, p. 1914.

seemed satisfied that there would be sober sailors in the future, said Venable, it was no more than just that they should have sober officers. As for himself, he never heard of a sailor who could get drunk on five cents worth of whisky. "It is all humbug; and the best way to cure humbugs is to prescribe and administer a large dose of humbug. Sir, all this hyperphilanthrophy is of the same origin of some other species of fanaticism which are rife amongst us."[47]

Venable's amendment was opposed by Isaac E. Morse, a Louisiana Democrat, on the ground that one wrong was no cure for another. Furthermore, he was opposed "to this mode of legislation on matters which ought to be left untouched by Congress, because they could not be meddled with so as to produce any beneficial results." If the proposed changes were for the good of the Navy, he said, then there should be a resolution referring the matter to the Committee on Naval Affairs. A report on these subjects by the committee would then form "a legitimate basis for legislation." He felt that it would be unwise to abolish flogging, and that the abolition of grog "would be quite as subversive to discipline as the abolition of flogging."[48]

When the House resumed its discussion of Venable's amendment to the amendment, it was adopted by a vote of 82 to 43.[49] Then Evans presented a motion to give the ship's surgeon the right to administer the spirits to the officers. Evans noted that the British Parliament had concluded that the U.S. merchant and whaling service was superior to the British largely because ardent spirits had been discontinued in ours. Insurance rates were lower on vessels that did not carry liquor. Furthermore, the Supreme Court of New York had declared that the carrying of liquor for use on ships so insured was a violation of the policy. As a result, many of the dissipated sailors of the merchant service were now entering the Navy where they could get their grog. He said that he did not wish to stop the spirit ration by an arbitrary legislative act, but he thought that it ought to accompany the end of flogging. He thought that the substitution of three to five cents per day in lieu of the grog would be generally acceptable to the sailors. He was willing that they receive five cents.[50]

[47] *Ibid.*
[49] *Ibid.* No roll call vote available.
[48] *Ibid.*
[50] *Ibid.*

Shortly after this discourse Jacob Thompson, a Democrat of Mississippi, offered to substitute for the composite amendment of Jones, Evans, and Venable his own amendment providing only for the abolition of flogging. He announced that he was in favor of the grog ration, and he refused to modify his amendment to include its abolition. Evans made another attempt to restore the prohibition against spirits but failed. The House approved Thompson's substitute amendment by a vote of 88 to 42. Five days later it was the law of the land.[51] At long last flogging was ended!

To the editor of *The Sailors' Magazine* the abolition of flogging and the continued issuance of grog was a plain case of striking at the effect and not at the cause. Nevertheless, he hailed the measure and congratulated seamen and the friends of seamen on the work accomplished. He ventured to predict that better men — men "more accessible to the means of social and moral improvement" would now be willing to enter the Navy. He also predicted that naval officers in general would join other citizens "in respectfully and earnestly petitioning Congress to abolish the Grog Ration." [52]

Two months later the magazine expressed its disappointment that a recommendation for the abolition of the spirit ration was not brought up during a recent discussion regarding substitutes for flogging.[53]

In the meantime, many hard-won victories for temperance in the Navy were threatened when the commutation program ran into difficulty. The naval appropriation bill passed in March 1851 contained a provision that no one but officers and their attendants could commute their spirit ration, and that only those persons attached to and doing duty on a vessel, or at a naval yard were entitled to a ration.[54] The Secretary of the Navy requested the repeal of this act stating that it had been "improvidently recommended and passed." The repeal was brought about in the appropriations act of 1852.[55]

The Sailor's Magazine continued its agitation for congressional

[51] *Ibid.*
[52] *The Sailor's Magazine*, XXIII, 83.
[53] *Ibid.*, pp. 145–146.
[54] *U.S. Statutes at Large*, X, Chap. 34, p. 621.
[55] *Senate Executive Documents*, 32d Cong., 1st Sess. (Serial 612), II, Doc. 1, p. 16; *U.S. Statutes at Large*, X, Chap. 109, p. 100.

action on the matter of the grog ration. Mention has been made of the fact that it was hoped that the officers of the Navy would petition for such an action. Many of them were known to feel that the abolition of the spirit ration was necessary to elevate the service, but whether enough names could be secured to give the petition weight and prestige was a matter of doubt. "But whether the officers in the Navy move in this appeal or not, let the friends of seamen on land and sea, send up such an appeal as shall command the respectful hearing, and the efficient action of our national legislators."[56]

Once again the action of the Rhode Islanders was a source of encouragement to the friends of temperance. In January 1852 the General Assembly passed a resolution requesting their senators and representatives "to use all proper means to continue the act abolishing flogging in the navy a law of the United States, and to procure, in addition thereto, an act abolishing spirit rations in all naval ships and navy-yards in the United States."[57] Before the month was out this resolution was in the hands of both the Senate and the House of Representatives, but no action was taken on it.

A few days earlier, on January 22, the Senate agreed to a resolution presented by Charles Sumner, a Massachusetts Whig, directing the Committee on Naval Affairs to inquire into the expediency of abolishing the spirit ration and of increasing the monthly pay of the enlisted men.[58]

The same measure was introduced to the House on February 2, 1852 by Robert Goodenow, a Whig representative from Maine, in a vain attempt to get the unanimous consent of that body to the resolution.[59]

In February 1853 Joseph Cable, an Ohio Democrat, failed in an attempt to get an amendment into the naval appropriation bill which forbade the purchase or use of wine, brandy, or any intoxicating drinks by any one employed in the Navy. A violation of this prohibition would result in dismissal.[60]

---

[56] *The Sailor's Magazine*, XXIV, 498.
[57] *Senate Miscellaneous Documents*, 32d Cong., 1st Sess. (Serial 629), Doc. 24; *House Miscellaneous Documents*, 32d Cong., 1st Sess. (Serial 652), Doc. 11.
[58] *Congressional Globe*, 32nd Cong., 1st Sess., XIV, Part 1, p. 346.
[59] *Ibid.*, p. 443.
[60] *Congressional Globe*, 32d Cong., 2d Sess., XXVI, 893.

Again on March 3, 1853, Charles Sumner submitted an amendment to the naval appropriation bill abolishing the grog ration and giving the men six cents a day for it. The proposed amendment failed by a vote of 14 to 28.[61]

The same year saw the republication of a series of essays by William M. Wood, M.D., a surgeon of the U.S. Navy, under the title *Shoulder to the Wheel of Progress*. This compilation included Wood's pamphlet on the grog ration, and his reflections upon it were still as pertinent as they had been a few years earlier.

But the movement seems to have lacked the necessary driving force to push the abolition measure through. Probably it was because so many of the reformers were now distracted by the slavery issue, and were more concerned about the operation of the Fugitive Slave Law than the plight of the drunken sailor.

A resolute few continued to strive for the cause of total abstinence. Captain Foote, speaking as one who had more sea experience than any other officer of his grade, wrote to a member of Congress to urge the abolition of the grog ration. After citing the temperance records of the *Cumberland* and the *Perry*, he declared that officers who were opposed to the abolition had never witnessed the effect of the experiment. Foote was confident that a fair trial would remove all doubts.[62]

Two years later, in April 1854, Foote addressed the anniversary meeting of the Pennsylvania Seamen's Friend Society and urged that the grog ration be ended. He reviewed some of the great improvements in the condition of the men of the Navy since his own entry into service more than a quarter of a century before. It had long been demonstrated that ardent spirits were not only unnecessary for health, but were positively injurious. "Yet the government, or more properly speaking Congress, for the government had no control in the matter, still refuse to abolish the whiskey ration." He informed his audience that it was believed that a majority of the sailors themselves favored the abolition as did a large number of the "best officers" of the Navy. On two occasions the House of Representatives passed a measure abolishing the ration, but the Senate defeated the proposals. The merchant service abolished the whisky ration with beneficial results. "Why then should Congress

---

[61] *Ibid.*, p. 1072. No roll call vote available.
[62] *The Sailor's Magazine*, XXIV, 620.

suffer this foe to the sailor's welfare, longer to remain in the Navy." [63]

This state of affairs was well known to the men of *The Sailor's Magazine*. Those who read the magazine or heard the society's speakers were urged to speak out until Congress corrected the situation. The editor declared that he had fought for the abolition of spirits for 12 years, and that "God willing I will continue to fight it till the hideous hydra shall be finally and forever destroyed." [64]

Encouraging news came in May 1854 when the legislature of Maine passed a resolution asking its senators and representatives to use their efforts to bring about the abolition of the spirit ration. [65]

In the Navy Lieutenant David D. Porter, of the U.S. storeship *Supply*, made an arrangement whereby the men who shipped for the Far East agreed that no grog would be served on the cruise. [66]

In May 1858 Secretary of the Navy Isaac Toucey issued a general order forbidding commanding officers to give letters of entitlement to final examinations to midshipmen addicted to drunkenness. [67]

In December of the same year, Toucey submitted a proposed code of regulations for the government of the Navy along with his annual report. A section of that code that dealt with the duties of commanders of vessels stated that such commanders should "endeavor to induce the men to relinquish the spirit part of the ration, provided they will relinquish it for not less than three months, or for the remainder of the cruise; and may withhold it from all persons guilty of drunkenness." [68] Other sections of the code stated that individuals having less than three months to serve of their enlistment could relinquish their grog for their unexpired time. This code also declared that no money was to be paid to persons in debt to the United States "except for stopped spirits or rations." [69] This

[63] *Ibid.*, XXVI (1853–54), 321–327.

[64] *Ibid.*, p. 327.

[65] *Senate Miscellaneous Documents*, 33d Cong., 1st Sess. (Serial 705), Doc. 59.

[66] *The Sailor's Magazine*, XXVII, 338.

[67] General Order, May 17, 1858, *IG-General Orders*, Box 2, RG 45, NA.

[68] "A Code of Regulations for the Government of the Navy," Chap. 9, Sec. 3, Art. 16, in *House Executive Documents*, 35th Cong., 2d Sess. (Serial 1000), II, Part 4, p. 88.

[69] *Ibid.*, Chap. 21, Art. 24, p. 136.

code, with its grant of powers to commanders, could have stopped a great deal of the intemperance in the Navy. It was never enacted, but it marks a step forward toward eventual abolition.

A national convention of chaplains, ministers of mariners' churches, and other individuals interested in the welfare of seamen met in New York City in November 1859. At their request, Commodore Foote drew up a lengthy memorial to Congress calling for the end of grog, which the convention adopted unanimously.[70]

More time passed without congressional action. In a speech before the Senate in April 1860, Lafayette S. Foster, a Connecticut Republican, presented 19 memorials signed by nearly 700 persons including high ranking naval officers, as well as those of lesser grade, petty officers, and seamen, all urging the abolition of the spirit ration.[71] But still no action was taken.

By 1861 the cause of temperance had lost much of its appeal to the rank and file of the nation, but among maritime groups it was still an important issue. When the Marine Temperance Society of New York held its 28th anniversary meeting in May 1861, it boasted a membership of 37,343 persons. Some 886 of this number had been recruited within the past year. There was still a hard core of determined leaders within this organization.[72]

By this time nearly everybody was concerned about the outbreak of the Civil War. Fort Sumter fell on April 14, 1861. Five days later President Lincoln called for 75,000 volunteers and gave the Navy the task of blockading the ports of the Confederate states.

When John P. Hale took the floor of the Senate on July 11, he introduced a number of bills on such subjects as the authorization of an additional naval force, the regulation of the employment of volunteers in the Navy, and for the better organization of the Marine Corps. But the first bill introduced was the one to alter and regulate the Navy ration. In view of Hale's earlier activities, it is interesting to note that this bill concerned itself with the entire ration of the sailor and contained no provision for the abolition of the grog. The sailor would still get his gill of spirits, but a half pint of wine could be substituted for it if necessary. No one under 21

[70] *The Sailor's Magazine*, XXXIV, 364.
[71] *Ibid.*, XXXII, 275; *Congressional Globe*, 36th Cong., 1st Sess., XXIX, Part 2, p. 1546.
[72] *The Sailor's Magazine*, XXXIII (1860–61), 270.

years was to draw the spirit ration. Persons who were prohibited from drawing the ration, or who had relinquished it were to be paid four cents a day. Toucey's old plan authorizing the commanding officer to suspend the spirit ration for drunkenness was incorporated into this bill. The Senate Committee on Naval Affairs approved the measure and it became a law on July 18, 1861.[73]

On that same day Hale, as the chairman of the Committee on Naval Affairs, requested that the bill reported from the committee calling for the appointment of an Assistant Secretary of the Navy be taken up. The act authorizing that office became a law on July 31, 1861, and the first incumbent, Gustavus Vasa Fox, was to play an important part in the final struggle against grog.[74]

With the country in the midst of a civil war, and the energies of the Navy Department directed toward the needs of the blockade and to the coast and river campaigns, the Union was fortunate in having a man of the caliber of Gideon Welles as Secretary of the Navy. Unlike many of his predecessors, Welles came to this cabinet post with some experience in naval matters. For three years he had served as the chief of the Bureau of Provisions and Clothing. That plus his residence in Connecticut made him acceptable to the maritime interests in New England. Of special interest to this study is the fact that he was also a former college classmate, fellow townsman, and close friend of Captain Andrew Hull Foote. Welles tackled the problems of naval administration with great energy and soon transformed the Navy Department into a highly efficient organization.[75]

Welles's new Assistant Secretary, Gustavus Vasa Fox, also came to his new post with a background in naval matters. For 18 years he had served as an officer in the Navy, resigning in 1856 as a lieutenant. From that time until April 1861 he worked as a mill superintendent in Lowell, Massachusetts, where he gained additional experience in the handling of men and the problem of supplies. Fox was energetic, tactful, aggressive, persuasive, and he enjoyed his work. He knew the problems of the Navy and he was unafraid

---

[73] *Congressional Globe*, 37th Cong., 1st Sess., XXXI, 62, 78, 208; *U.S. Statutes at Large*, XII, Chap. 7, pp. 264–265.

[74] *Ibid.*, Chap. 27, pp. 282–283.

[75] Paullin, ". . . Naval Administration . . . 1861–1911," *U.S.N.I.P.*, XXXVIII, 1311–13.

to make his decisions. He was also acquainted with most of the officers of the Navy. Nor was this all. He was a close friend of Republican Senator James W. Grimes of Iowa, a member of the naval committee. The chairman of the committee, John P. Hale, who had long been a critic of the abuses in the Navy, now had some ambitions to be Secretary of the Navy, but his pretensions were never taken seriously. Welles had little use for Senator Hale. This and other factors contributed to make relations between the Secretary and the Senator coldly official.[76]

In view of this state of affairs the Assistant Secretary's friendship with Senator Grimes took on a new importance. Grimes's close relationship with the Navy Department was apparently well known to his colleagues. On the floor of the Senate one of them referred to Grimes as one "who speaks *ex cathedra* with regard to all matters belonging to the navy. . . ."[77]

While the naval appropriation bill was being prepared Grimes sent Fox a copy of it for his consideration. Fox returned the bill with his comments, and in a covering letter of May 28, 1862 he said: "I beg of you for the enduring good of the service, which you have so much at heart, to add a proviso abolishing the spirit ration and forbidding any distilled liquors being placed on board any vessel belonging to, or chartered by the U. States, excepting of course, that in the Medical Dept. All insubordination, all misery, every deviltry on board ships can be traced to rum. Give the sailor double the value, or more, and he will be content."[78]

Grimes did not disappoint his friend. On June 13, 1862 he introduced an amendment to the appropriation bill calling for the end of the spirit ration after September 1, 1862, and for the payment of five cents a day in commutation money. He declared that he wished to end the government issue of two dips of grog a day, and to pay the men approximately $1.50 a month instead. He added:

I desire to say that I have offered it in accordance with the wishes of almost every officer with whom I have been brought in contact. I have a letter of one of them here before me, urging me by all means possible to

---

[76] Robert M. Thompson and Richard Wainwright, eds., *Confidential Correspondence of Gustavus Vasa Fox, Assistant Secretary of the Navy, 1861–1865* (2 vols.; New York, 1919), II, xv; Richard S. West, Jr., *Gideon Welles, Lincoln's Navy Department* (Indianapolis, Ind., 1943), p. 116.

[77] *Congressional Globe*, 37th Cong., 2d Sess., XXXII, Part 2, p. 1423.

[78] Thompson and Wainwright, II, 304.

do what I can to abolish the spirit ration, and have a provision made forbidding any distilled liquors being placed on board any vessel belonging to or chartered by the United States, except for the use of the medical department. In conversation with the Navy Department I am informed that hardly any difficulty has grown up during this war on board a single one of our vessels, that has not been traced directly to the fact that spirituous liquors were allowed on board the ship. By abolishing the whiskey ration we shall take away one of the strongest reasons why parents are unwilling that their minor sons should enlist in the naval service of the United States.[79]

Senator James A. McDougall, Democrat of California, denounced the amendment as "a piece of illegitimate legislation" and "one belonging to the present popular system of humbuggery." But when these verbal fireworks were over the Senate adopted the amendment.[80]

While the matter was still before the Congress, Flag Officer Andrew H. Foote, convalescing from injuries received during his operations with Grant in the West, wrote to the editor of the *Journal of the American Temperance Union* asking him to convey his thanks to Senator Grimes for introducing his resolution. "It will even add to his reputation as the true friend of the navy," wrote Foote. Grimes wrote to the editor that he had no doubt that his measure would pass the House.[81]

The House of Representatives, however, disagreed with several items in the bill including the provision relating to grog. A conference committee was arranged consisting of Hale and Grimes of the Senate and Thaddeus Stevens, of Pennsylvania, and Charles B. Sedgwick, of New York, of the House. The composition of the committee was a bit of good fortune for Grimes, who considered Sedgwick a friend of the Navy. On July 9, Hale reported from the committee that the House had receded from its opposition to the abolition of grog. The measure became law with the signature of President Lincoln on July 14. In its final form the provision abolishing grog read as follows:

And be it further enacted, That from and after this first day of September, eighteen hundred and sixty-two the spirit ration in the Navy of the United States shall forever cease, and thereafter no distilled spirituous

[79] *Congressional Globe*, 37th Cong., 2d Sess., XXXII, Part 3, pp. 2707–08.
[80] *Ibid.*, p. 2708. No vote was recorded on this measure.
[81] *The Sailor's Magazine*, XXXIV, 364.

liquors shall be admitted on board vessels-of-war, except as medical stores, and upon the order and under the control of the medical officers of such vessels, and to be used only for medical purposes. From and after the said first day of September next, there shall be allowed and paid to each person in the Navy now entitled to the spirit ration, five cents per day in commutation and lieu thereof, which shall be in addition to their present pay.[82]

Three days after Lincoln signed this measure Gideon Welles issued a general order to the personnel of the Navy advising them of the law, directing that this provision "be rigidly enforced," and ordering all persons in the service to report violations.[83] Thus died the spirit ration in the Navy.

There is one instance on record where the enlisted men of a naval ship drew up a petition to have the law repealed. Rear Admiral Samuel F. Du Pont returned it on the grounds that it was couched in improper terms and that it did not go through the proper channels. He advised them that if they petitioned respectfully it would be his duty to forward their request.[84] But the spirit ration question was dead.

To commemorate the passing of an era Pay Director Caspar Schenck of the *Portsmouth* wrote a ballad entitled "Farewell to Grog" which was sung in the wardroom of that ship on August 31, 1862. The following two stanzas may be sufficient to convey the essence of the ballad.

> Oh! messmates, pass the bottle round,
>   Our time is short, remember
> For our grog must stop, our spirits drop,
>   On the first day of September.
>
> .   .   .   .   .   .
>
> Jack's happy days will soon be past,
>   To return again, no, never
> For they've raised his pay five cents a day
>   And stopped his grog forever.[85]

---

[82] *Congressional Globe*, 37th Cong., 2d Sess., XXXII, Part 3, pp. 2709, 3056–58; Part 4, pp. 3080, 3109, 3182, 3215, 3237, 3261, 3266, 3363; *U.S. Statutes at Large*, XII, Chap. 164, p. 565. There is no record of the vote on the adoption of this amendment.

[83] *Official Records of the Union and Confederate Navies in the War of the Rebellion*, Series 1, VII, 584.

[84] *Ibid.*, Series 1, XIII (1901), 275–276.

[85] Constance Lathrop, "Grog: Its Origin and Use in the United States Navy," *U.S.N.I.P.*, LXI (1935), 380.

As might be expected, the editor of *The Sailor's Magazine* rejoiced over the abolition of grog, as did many other reformers. After many years of false hopes the final abolition was rather anticlimatic. There was no time for many congratulations. The reformers and their fellow countrymen were already absorbed in the new cause of preserving the Union in which the Navy, temperate or not, was playing a vital role. In a way, the abolition of grog at this time was something of a reward to Foote, whose services at Forts Henry and Donelson, and Island No. 10 had won so much praise. In the sametradition ofhisuncle Isaac Hull, Foote had won victories which brought encouragement to his countrymen at a time when they were hearing many reports of defeats on land.

The movement to abolish the spirit ration in the Navy had its roots in the nationwide crusade for temperance. The various humanitarian reformers who were particularly interested in the maritime aspects of this crusade repeated the arguments over and over again that the Navy's manpower troubles were due to the spirit ration and to flogging. The former created a craving for liquor and made the Navy a haven for the dregs of society, for alcoholics, and for foreigners. This craving for liquor resulted in smuggling and in other activities dangerous to the health and welfare of the seamen. The drunkenness that usually resulted from drinking smuggled liquor was the cause of most of the floggings in the Navy. Therefore, said the reformers, if you abolish the spirit ration and encourage temperance, you will attract a better type of man to the service. Disciplinary problems will arise less frequently, and there will be less reason for floggings. The health of the men and the tone of the service will be greatly improved. To support their arguments, they cited the experiments conducted in the merchant marine with temperance ships, which had resulted in better crews, and in lower rates for marine insurance.

This movement was backed by various temperance groups which included politicians, naval officers and men, representatives of the maritime interests, and religious leaders. Their cause was assisted from time to time by both secular and religious newspapers and periodicals. Strong and persistent support came from the American Seamen's Friend Society through its monthly publication *The Sailor's Magazine*.

The forces of temperance won an important victory in 1842, when Congress, on the suggestion of Secretary Upshur, passed a law which cut the spirit ration in half, and forbade it entirely to persons under 21 years.

Encouraged by this success, the reformers continued to exert themselves to spread the idea that the Navy could function efficiently without grog. Publicity was given to the crews of various naval vessels who tried the experiment of a cruise in a temperance ship. Such experiments seem to have been rather successful, at least for short periods of time. Officers such as Foote and Smith pointed out that such experiments were carried on without any coercion. The lack of any record of protest from the ranks, in an age when protests against other abuses were publicized, seems to confirm this. The reformers hoped that such experiments would eventually induce Congress to end the grog ration.

In spite of the fact that there was a great deal of interest in the cause of temperance on the part of the members of Congress, many were unwilling to go so far as to ban the spirit ration altogether. They believed that every man should decide for himself whether or not he would drink. They believed that a temperate use of liquor by the sailors was desirable, but they did not wish to completely prohibit the use of spirits. The former aided the cause of religion, good citizenship, and prudent living; the latter infringed upon human liberty. This was not a party issue. Democrats and Whigs were about equally divided on the merits of ending the grog ration, and a few Republican leaders finally accomplished that end. The issue did, however, tend to be a sectional one. Most of the petitions calling for the end of grog came from the North, and particularly from New England. Also, the fact that such northern leaders as Webster, Seward, Sumner, and Hale, who were prominent in the fight against slavery, lent their names to the antigrog agitation served to link the two causes in the minds of some southern members of Congress. They regarded both crusades as symptoms of a dangerous lunacy.

It has also been suggested that naval medical officers used their influence against the abolition of grog, presumably on the grounds that the temperance enthusiasm might extend to a ban on alcohol in medical supplies. But it is also true that some naval doctors supported the cause of abolition. In any case, petition after petition calling for the end of grog died in the Senate naval committee.

In addition to the obstructionist policies of the Senate committee, the antigrog cause was weakened by the gradual decline of the temperance fervor in the country. This cooling was due in part to the transition of many reform societies from temperance to total abstinence groups, with a resulting loss in membership. It was also due to the fact that other causes, and particularly that of anti-slaveryism, grew in importance and consumed more and more of the time and energy of the humanitarian reformers.

Despite the loss of much of the broad base of support for their cause, a small but resolute number of the antigrog group persisted in their agitation. This group included several naval officers, of whom Andrew H. Foote and Joseph Smith were the most important. The temperance and total abstinence spirit continued to be important in the Navy long after it had declined elsewhere in the country. The antigrog humanitarians regarded the abolition of flogging and the retention of the spirit ration as a plain case of striking at the result rather than at the cause. Their chance finally came when the nation was involved in the Civil War. The passage of time saw a thinning in the ranks of their powerful opponents through death, retirement, and the secession of the southern states. Men who had been junior officers in other periods of agitation now held important positions in the Navy. The Secretary of the Navy, his new Assistant, and several of his officers all saw eye to eye on the need for reform. Also in favor of the change were two powerful leaders of the Senate, including the chairman of the Committee on Naval Affairs. Through this combination of circumstances, as well as the fact that most of the Congress was distracted by the many problems of the war, the men who favored the abolition of grog finally won their cause.

PART
SIX

EPILOGUE

"Mark this period then as the auspicious time on which the nation can look back with pride and pleasure, as the day of its regeneration and the first dawning of a liberal policy, whereon to found our future hopes for its distinguished character, discipline and chivalry."

The National Gazette, 1830.

CONCLUSION

Public concern for the welfare of the sailor had its roots in the renewal of interest in the dignity of man that was a heritage of the Enlightenment. The counterattack of organized religion on the secular outlook of men of the Enlightenment had the effect of drawing public attention to the spiritual and physical needs of all classes of society. When Great Britain engaged in warfare against Revolutionary France, religion became a bulwark of patriotism for Englishmen. A small group of religious-minded Englishmen became concerned about the fact that sailors, by virtue of their employment, were removed from the usual sources of religious life. These Englishmen attempted to fill the religious vacuum in the sailor's life by supplying him with tracts and Bibles. No systematic distribution took place before 1814, but about 1808 a revival of interest in religion took place on board some vessels of the Royal Navy. This revival encouraged at least two officers to leave the Navy and enter the ministry. One of these men, George C. Smith, devoted the remainder of his life to the religious and physical welfare of sailors and their dependents, and was instrumental in founding a number of seamen's societies in England, Scotland, and Ireland, of which the most important was the London-based British and Foreign Seamen's Friend Society.

In the United States national attention was focused on the plight of American sailors by the harassment and captivity that they endured at the hands of the pirates of North Africa, and from the naval forces of England and France. The United States government resorted to diplomacy and warfare to eliminate these hazards to our men and our commerce.

By the time the plight of our sailors had ceased to be a matter requiring diplomatic attention or an armed response, it had become increasingly important to Americans caught up in the religious revivalism that swept the country in the years following the War of 1812. Public interest in bringing the gospel and religious services to seamen led to the formation of marine, Bethel, and port societies in various cities. Members of these societies soon recognized that their resources were inadequate to accomplish their self-imposed task, and in 1826 they formed a national organization, the American Seamen's Friend Society, with headquarters in New York City. Through its affiliated organizations, and the support of clergymen, prominent citizens, merchant and naval officers and men, and of religious newspapers, the American Seamen's Friend Society was able to reach a wide audience with its proposals for reforms. It also gave its encouragement to the formation of women's groups dedicated to raising funds, distributing tracts, and making clothing for the benefit of sailors. There is a direct connection between the society and some of the most important leaders of the agitation for reform in the Navy.

Bringing religion into the sailor's life, and keeping him from falling back into old habits which undermined it, involved efforts to control the man's environment on a broad scale. To look after the religious needs of seamen far from home the society sent out, or helped to support, ministers stationed at various ports throughout the world. Such men conducted religious services for sailors either on board the visiting vessel or in mariners' churches on shore. A few of these cooperative arrangements were worked out with the British and Foreign Seamen's Friend Society.

In the United States, members of the society were not content to simply preach and distribute tracts, or to conduct religious services on shipboard or in seamen's churches. The society and its affiliated organizations established seamen's banks, employment registry offices, libraries and reading rooms, schools to give practical training to seamen and their dependents, and clean and safe boarding houses where a sailor could stay at a reasonable price.

Members of the society had a special interest in the men of the United States Navy. They petitioned Congress for an increase in the number, quality, and compensation of naval chaplains. They urged that divine services be performed regularly, as Navy regulations prescribed. They argued for reforms in the naval establishment that would improve both the quality of the men and the efficiency of the service. They singled out for particular attention the customs of giving men intoxicating liquors as a part of their daily ration, and the inflicting of corporal punishment. Their efforts to protect the sailor on shore also directed their attention to various abuses in connection with the enlistment and discharge of sailors.

Those working for the seamen's cause included ministers and naval chaplains, doctors, some members of Congress, a few Secretaries of the Navy, representatives of the maritime community, and various groups of citizens, mainly in the northern states. Some sailors also supported the cause through the publication of letters, a few books and pamphlets, petitions and memorials, and by their contributions to various religious and reform conscious organizations.

The humanitarian reformers both in and out of the Navy got their opportunity as the result of the chronic lack of seamen to man the warships in service. As a result of this deficiency the Navy had to rely more and more on foreigners, and this became a matter of increasing concern to naval officers, to various Secretaries, to members of the maritime community, and gradually to the populace as a whole. Unlike the later Native American political movement in the country, the concern of the naval reformers over the foreigners was not connected with religion. It was more a matter of national pride and of wondering how reliable such types might be in the event of war. They therefore addressed themselves to the problem of what could be done to attract young American-born males to the naval service of their country. Whatever was to be done had to take cognizance of the fact that the tradition of voluntary service was still strong, and that the memories of an era of impressment were still vivid.

The Navy Department tried various devices with limited success. Throughout the period of groping, the humanitarian reformers argued that no self-respecting young man would be attracted to a naval career as long as he was debased by liquor and flogged like a criminal. The Navy should concentrate on building a program that recognized the dignity of man, that would be fostered by regular religious services, and that would provide for promotion through merit.

The whole argument became more animated and more vital when the Navy decided on a plan to enlist young boys with their parents' consent to serve as naval apprentices until they reached the age of 21. Then, having learned the trade of the sailor, it was hoped that they would decide to remain in the Navy.

The apprentice program had a triple appeal. It took young boys out of overcrowded cities, thus removing a temptation to crime and mischief; it lessened the drain on the resources of organizations which cared for the poor; and it met the Navy's manpower needs. But if getting the boys away from the evil influences of the city was the rationalization for putting them into the Navy, then it followed that the Navy itself should provide a more wholesome atmosphere. Chaplains and other humanitarians pointed out that the Navy was no proper environment for a young boy. Therefore, the agitation for the apprentice program stimulated and encouraged reform in other areas. Parents, religious leaders, and humanitarians felt quite correctly that the Navy should put its own house in order before appealing to the youth of the nation to enlist.

The sailor's ration of spirits was a natural target for such groups. No matter how individual members of Congress, chaplains, naval officers, or citizens felt about other reforms and about the temperance question generally, there was universal agreement that young boys should not draw the whisky ration. Thus an important opening wedge in the cause of personnel reform was won quite easily.

With this as a starting point, it was easy to argue about the need to improve the sailor's environment in other ways. Between the time that the young apprentices came on board and the day when they would constitute the backbone of the fleet, they were exposed to all the harsh and corrupting influences of the old system. How could you insulate these boys from evil? It was for precisely these considerations that men who normally were not overly concerned about humanitarian reforms had to think along some of the same lines as the most ardent of the reformers. There were disagreements on the relative merits of the grog ration and the cat-o'-nine tails, but nearly everybody wanted to see the Navy manned by healthy, reliable, native American seamen.

The task of improving the lot of the man in the ranks was made more difficult partly because the reforms were brought forward at a time when most of the Secretaries were trying to assert their authority over the officers without losing their support. Some also attempted to encourage the younger, more forward-looking officers without antagonizing their seniors. It was a difficult path to tread, and few Secretaries could do it well for very long, especially at a time when virtually the entire naval establishment was in need of a thorough overhauling. Amid so many tensions, it was hard to build any *esprit de corps* or to transmit any traditions to the young.

With so many tasks calling for attention it was difficult to know what to do first. The Secretary and the members of Congress were exposed to conflicting advice. There seems to have been some fear on the part of tradition-minded officers and some members of Congress that before all the humanitarian, technological, and political reformers were through, there would be no naval force left.

Throughout the period of this study it was customary for both the Secretaries and the members of Congress to rely on the judgment of naval officers on matters pertaining to that service. Even when abuses showed that all was not well, and when a large portion of the public had ceased to see an aura of glory surrounding that service, the opinions of experienced naval officers and the force of tradition continued to outweigh many a memorial. It was only when naval officers of proven ability joined in the cries for reform that the measures received more serious consideration.

These concepts and opinions were a part of the mental make-up of those in Congress who were to decide on any changes in naval regulations. When the majority of Navy officers felt that there was no substitute for flogging, it was difficult for many congressmen to think otherwise. Those who were familiar with the experiments in prisons could see through the officers' arguments. Others who were aware of the fact that the Army had experimented with the abolition of flogging may have had reason to doubt.

While improvement societies, memorials, tracts, experiments, and the appeals of distinguished advocates of reform all played a part, in the last analysis almost everything hinged on convincing the Senate Committee on Naval Affairs that the proposed reform was necessary. Members of this committee often tended to follow the course of least resistance and to let memorials and other reform proposals die in committee. Where agitation was strong enough to force reports or debates, the disapproving arguments usually hinged on a statement that distinguished officers of the Navy said this cannot be done without hurting that service. Reform-minded officers destroyed the notion that all officers thought as one, and they helped to dislodge measures from the committee.

Flogging finally was abolished in a somewhat accidental fashion. There is some reason for believing that the abolition was approved by some with the idea that within a short time the measure would be repealed as a result of the deterioration of discipline. Once the experiment was tried and had been proved a failure, that would be the end of the antiflogging agitation. But the proflogging faction underestimated their opposition. When Congress received mixed reports on the results of the experiment, an attempt to restore the lash was abruptly stopped. The man who won that battle was Robert F. Stockton, the naval officer turned senator. Stephen Mallory and other members of the Senate Committee on Naval Affairs, who hoped to restore flogging, were checkmated by Stockton's stirring appeal to the Senate.

The spirit ration was abolished long after the temperance agitation in the nation had passed its peak. Final abolition was due to the happy meeting of minds between Secretary Welles, Assistant Secretary Fox, Captain Foote, and Senator Grimes of the Senate naval committee, with the assistance of Senator Hale, who also was a member of the committee. At least one friend of naval reform was a member of the conference committee which met with delegates from the House to hold out for the amendment which abolished grog.

Both the antiflogging and the antigrog crusades retained an importance in a period that saw an increasing concern over the spread of Negro slavery, because some of the southerners in Congress chose to link those causes with that of the abolitionists. This gave the cause of naval reform an implied position within the hierarchy of reform movements. Many of the arguments about the plight of the slave served to emphasize the sad condition of the sailor. Both flogging and grog were abolished at a time when most men were concerned with the larger issues of slavery and of preserving the Union. Flogging was abolished shortly after the adoption of the Compromise of 1850. The measure to end grog was passed on the day after the battle of Antietam, which ended the Confederate invasion of Maryland.

Between 1828 and 1862 the policies of the United States Navy in regard to its enlisted men were drastically changed, and the foundations were laid for a career enlisted service. Opportunities also were held out for the talented and ambitious to rise to the commissioned ranks. These changes were the naval equivalent of the rise of the common man.

One of the best summaries of the social changes that took place in the Navy during this period was that written by Chaplain Charles S. Stewart. Appointed in 1828, he was among the first of a group of vigorous young chaplains who worked to reform the Navy. In June 1862, while completing his last cruise, he wrote a letter to the *New York Observer* in which he reviewed the gains that had been made.

Thirty years ago profane and abusive language, by officers on duty on the quarter-deck and other parts of the ship, if not general, was so common as to attract little notice or concern. It was thought and avowed by many that the necessary work in the navigation and management of the ship could not be gained from the sailor without them; that he was so degraded that curses and hard language only could drive him to the right performance of his duty. In the last two ships in which I have served, within the ten years past, I do not recollect to have heard an oath; and scarce a reproachful epithet, from an officer in charge of the deck, or from his subordinates. At the period first named, the "cat" and the "colt" were the arbiters of discipline, and exercised, without stint, almost every day; now, for ten years past, both have been abolished as instruments of punishment, by act of Congress, and notwithstanding, as a general thing, all work is performed as effectively and more cheerfully than ever before. The reform, in respect to profane language in the social intercourse with the officers on board, is as marked and decisive as on the deck.

Thirty years ago the use of strong drink on board ship by the officers, at various hours of the day, was not uncommon, if not customary; and wines and liquors constituted a regular part of the mess stores. In the ships in which I have last served water has been the only general beverage. Wine is seldom taken, even at dinner, and then only at individual and private cost — chiefly in hospitality to a visitor. Once, for an officer to be seen evidently under the influence of intoxicating drink, especially if such was not habitually the case, was thought lightly of; now it would be highly disreputable, and justly regarded, in a single instance, as a reproach.

Thirty years ago a professedly religious officer was seldom met or heard of. Even where piety of heart may have existed, little, if any, demonstration of it was made. Church membership in an officer was a novelty, and a thing unheard of in a fore-mast hand. In the last two cruises I have made, one half of the ward-room mess, in both cases, have been professedly religious men; and for the last few years it has not been unusual to find ten, fifteen, twenty, and even a greater number of consistent and zealous church members, in the crew of a single ship.[1]

In the years ahead various American leaders would be confronted with the problem of trying to build and hold a peacetime naval force. Aspects of the life of both the officer and the enlisted man would be studied to see how the military life could be made more appealing. Making the naval service a proud, honorable, and meaningful alternative to civilian life would remain a challenging goal. But by 1862, with the various changes in the regulations governing the treatment of the enlisted man, some long steps forward had been taken.

---

[1] *The Sailor's Magazine*, XXXIV, 356–357.

BIBLIOGRAPHY

MANUSCRIPTS

Bancroft-Bliss Papers, Library of Congress (hereafter LC).
Gist Blair Papers (Levi Woodbury Scrapbooks), LC.
David Conner Papers, LC.
John M. Clayton Papers, LC.
Caleb Cushing Papers, LC.
Richard Henry Dana Papers, Massachusetts Historical Society.
Mahlon Dickerson Papers, New Jersey Historical Society.
James C. Dobbin Manuscripts, Duke University Library.
Dreer Naval Collection, Historical Society of Pennsylvania.
Andrew Hull Foote Papers, LC.
Louis M. Goldsborough Papers, LC.
Gratz Autograph Collection, Historical Society of Pennsylvania.
John P. Hale Papers, New Hampshire Historical Society.
Harwood Family Papers, LC.
Roswell Hoes Papers, LC.
Internal Rules and Regulations of the Ship Franklin, LC.
Andrew Jackson Papers, LC.
Thomas Jefferson Papers, LC.
William Jones Papers, Historical Society of Pennsylvania.
Uriah P. Levy Papers, LC.
James Madison Papers, LC.
Willie P. Mangum Papers, LC.
William L. Marcy Papers, LC.
Matthew F. Maury Papers, LC.
James Monroe Papers, LC.
Naval Manuscripts, New York Historical Society.
Personal Papers Miscellaneous, LC.
Franklin Pierce Papers, LC.
James K. Polk Papers, LC.
John Rodgers Papers, LC.

Short Family Papers, LC.
Stockton Family Papers, Princeton University Library.
Robert F. Stockton Letterbooks, 1843–47, Princeton University Library.
Samuel Southard Letterbook, New York Public Library.
Samuel Southard Manuscripts, LC.
Samuel Southard Manuscripts, New York Public Library.
Samuel Southard Papers, Princeton University Library.
Tucker-Coleman Collection (Abel P. Upshur Letters), Colonial Williamsburg.
U.S. Navy Miscellaneous, LC.
U.S. Navy Papers, 1820–60, New York Public Library.
Martin Van Buren Papers, LC.
Henry A. Wise Papers, LC.
Levi Woodbury Papers, LC.
Winterthur Collection (Samuel F. Du Pont Papers), Eleutherian Mills Historical Library, Wilmington, Delaware.

ARCHIVES

U.S. Navy Department Archives, Record Group 45, National Archives
 Captains Letters, 1827–1828.
 Circulars and General Orders.
 Corporal Punishment and the Spirit Ration, Reports of Officers, 1850.
 Court Martial Records.
 General Letter Book, 1821–28.
 Letters to Congress.
 Letters to Officers, Ships of War, 1826–30.
 Miscellaneous Letters, 1827–28.
 Officers Letters, 1823–24, 1827–28.
 Subject File: *IC – Circulars*
   IG – General Orders
   IR – Regulations
   NJ – Discipline
   NR – Naval Personnel: Recruiting and Enlistments.
Legislative Records, Record Group 233, National Archives.

OFFICIAL PUBLICATIONS

U.S. Congress
 American State Papers: Naval Affairs. 4 vols. Washington, D.C.: Gales and Seaton, 1834–61.
 Annals of Congress, 1798–1824.
 Annual Reports of the Secretary of the Navy, 1824–62.
 Congressional Globe, 1833–62.
 House Documents.
 House Journals, 1820–62.
 House Reports.

Register of Debates in Congress, 1824–37.
Reports of the Committee of the Senate.
Senate Documents.
Senate Journals, 1820–62.
U.S. Statutes at Large, 1798–1862.
U.S. Navy Department
    Naval Documents Related to the Quasi-War Between the United States and France. 7 vols. Washington, D.C.: Government Printing Office, 1935–38.
    Naval Documents Related to the United States Wars with the Barbary Powers. 6 vols. Washington, D.C.: Government Printing Office, 1939–44.
    The Navy Register, 1828–60.
    Official Records of the Union and Confederate Navies in the War of the Rebellion. Ed. by Richard Rush *et al.* 1st Series. 30 vols. Washington, D.C.: Government Printing Office, 1894–1914.
    Rules of the Navy Department, Regulating the Civil Administration of the Navy of the United States. Washington, D.C.: F. P. Blair, 1832.
U.S. War Department
    The War of the Rebellion: A Compilation of the Official Records of the Union and Confederate Armies. Ed. by R. N. Scott *et al.* 130 vols. Washington, D.C.: Government Printing Office, 1880–1901.

NEWSPAPERS AND PERIODICALS

Army and Navy Chronicle.
Boston Daily Advertiser, February 5, 1892.
The Boston Herald, February 5, 1892.
Concord Evening Monitor, February 6, 1892.
The Daily Chronicle (Philadelphia), April–June 1828.
The Hebrew Standard (New York), January 27, 1911.
The Mariner's Church Sailor's Magazine (London), 1833–34.
The Mariners' Magazine.
The National Gazette (Philadelphia), December 1827–June 1828.
National Intelligencer (Washington, D.C.), January 1830, April–July 1838.
The Naval Magazine.
The New Sailor's Magazine and Naval Chronicle (London), 1828, 1831–32.
New York Evening Post, June 27, 1831.
New York Herald, March–June 1847.
Sunday Dispatch (New York), January–September 1850.
New York Times, February 5, 1892.
New York Tribune, March–June 1847.
Niles Register, 1811–49.
The North American (Philadelphia), November 19, 1851.

The Sailor's Magazine, 1828–63, 1878.
The Sailor's Magazine and Naval Miscellany (London), 1823–25.
The Southern Review, 1828–30.
United States Nautical Magazine.

BOOKS AND PAMPHLETS

A Citizen. *The Navy.* No city: no publisher, 184–.
A "Civilian" [George Jones]. *Sketches of Naval Life, with Notices of Men, Manners and Scenery, on the Shores of the Mediterranean, in a Series of Letters from the Brandywine and Constitution Frigates.* 2 vols. New Haven, Conn.: Hezekiah Howe, 1829.
Adams, Charles Francis, ed. *Memoirs of John Quincy Adams, Comprising Portions of His Diary from 1795 to 1848.* Vol. IV. Philadelphia: J. B. Lippincott and Co., 1875.
Adams, Henry. *A History of the United States of America.* 9 vols. New York: Charles Scribner's Sons, 1909.
Aderman, Ralph M., ed. *The Letters of James Kirke Paulding.* Madison: The University of Wisconsin Press, 1962.
Aegyptus, Tiphys. *The Navy's Friend, or Reminiscences of the Navy; Containing Memoirs of a Cruise, in the U.S. Schooner Enterprise.* Baltimore: printed for the author, 1843.
A Few Sea Officers of both the Line and Staff. *Suggestions upon Naval Reform.* No city: no publisher, 1850.
A Fore-Top-Man [Henry J. Mercier]. *Life in a Man of War. Scenes in "Old Ironsides" During Her Cruise in the Pacific.* Boston: Houghton Mifflin Co., 1927.
A Gentleman of New York. *Remarks on the Home Squadron, and Naval School.* New York: J. P. Wright, 1840.
A Lieutenant of the Navy [John J. Almy]. *Naval Discipline and Corporal Punishment.* Boston: Charles C. P. Moody, 1850.
Allen, Gardner W., ed. *Commodore Hull; Papers of Isaac Hull, Commodore United States Navy.* Boston: The Boston Athenaeum, 1929.
———. *A Naval History of the American Revolution.* 2 vols. Boston: Houghton Mifflin Co., 1913.
———. *Our Naval War with France.* Boston: Houghton Mifflin Co., 1909.
[Ames, Nathaniel]. *A Mariner's Sketches.* Providence: Cory, Marshall and Hammond, 1830.
———. *Nautical Reminiscences.* Providence: W. Marshall and Co., 1832.
Ammen, Daniel. *The Old Navy and the New.* Philadelphia: J. B. Lippincott Co., 1891.
Anderson, Charles R., ed. *Journal of a Cruise to the Pacific Ocean, 1842–1844, in the Frigate United States, with Notes on Herman Melville.* Durham, N.C.: Duke University Press, 1937.

————. *Melville in the South Seas.* New York: Columbia University Press, 1940.

Andrews, Charles C., ed. *Official Opinions of the Attorneys General.* Vol. VI. Washington, D.C.: published by Robert Farnham, 1856.

An Observer [John Murphy]. *An Inquiry into the Necessity and General Principles of Reorganization in the United States Navy, with an Examination of the True Sources of Subordination.* Baltimore: John Murphy, 1842.

Anonymous. *Biographical Sketch and Services of Commodore Charles Stewart of the Navy of the United States.* Philadelphia: J. Harding, 1838.

Anonymous. *The Cruise of the Somers: Illustrative of the Despotism of the Quarter Deck; and the Unmanly Conduct of Commander Mackenzie.* 3d ed. New York: J. Winchester, 1844.

Appleton's Cyclopaedia of American Biography, eds. James G. Wilson and John Fiske. 7 vols. New York: D. Appleton Co., 1888–1900.

Aptheker, Herbert. *To Be Free, Studies in American Negro History.* New York: International Publishers, 1948.

Barney, Mary, ed. *A Biographical Memoir of the Late Commodore Joshua Barney: From Autobiographical Notes and Journal in Possession of His Family, and Other Authentic Sources.* Boston: Gray and Bowen, 1832.

Barrows, Edward M. *The Great Commodore: The Exploits of Matthew Calbraith Perry.* Indianapolis, Ind.: The Bobbs-Merrill Co., 1935.

Bassett, John Spencer, ed. *Correspondence of Andrew Jackson.* Vol. IV. Washington, D.C.: Carnegie Institution of Washington, 1929.

Baxter, James P. *The Introduction of the Ironclad Warship.* Cambridge, Mass.: Harvard University Press, 1933.

[Bayard, Samuel John]. *A Sketch of the Life of Com. Robert F. Stockton.* New York: Derby & Jackson, 1856.

Beale, Howard K., ed. *Diary of Gideon Welles.* 3 vols. New York: W. W. Norton & Co., 1960.

Beard, James F., ed. *The Letters and Journals of James Fenimore Cooper.* 4 vols. Cambridge, Mass.: Harvard University Press, 1960–65.

Bell, Frederick J. *Room to Swing a Cat.* New York: Longmans, Green and Co., 1938.

Bemis, Samuel F., ed. *The American Secretaries of State and Their Diplomacy.* Vol. III. New York: Alfred Knopf, 1927.

Blau, Joseph L., ed. *Social Theories of Jacksonian Democracy.* New York: The Liberal Arts Press, 1954.

Blochman, Lawrence G. *Doctor Squibb: The Life and Times of a Rugged Idealist.* New York: Simon and Schuster, 1958.

Bohner, Charles H. *John Pendleton Kennedy: Gentleman from Baltimore.* Baltimore: The Johns Hopkins Press, 1961.

Boston Port and Seamen's Aid Society. *Life of Father Taylor, the Sailor Preacher.* Boston: The Boston Port and Seamen's Aid Society, 1904.

Brant, Irving. *James Madison: Secretary of State, 1800–1809.* Indianapolis, Ind.: The Bobbs-Merrill Co., Inc., 1953.

——. *James Madison: The Presidency, 1809–1812.* Indianapolis, Ind.: The Bobbs-Merrill Co., Inc., 1956.

——. *James Madison: The Commander in Chief, 1812–1836.* Indianapolis, Ind.: The Bobbs-Merrill Co., Inc., 1961.

Brown, Roger H. *The Republic in Peril: 1812.* New York: Columbia University Press, 1964.

Bruce, William C. *John Randolph of Roanoke.* 2 vols. New York: G. P. Putnam's Sons, 1922.

Bryan, Wilhelmus B. *A History of the National Capitol.* 2 vols. New York: The Macmillan Co., 1914–16.

Burr, Henry L. *Education in the Early Navy.* Philadelphia: The Author, 1939.

Callahan, Edward W., ed. *List of Officers of the Navy of the United States and of the Marine Corps, from 1775 to 1900.* New York: L. R. Hamersly and Co., 1901.

Carroll, John A., and Mary Wells Ashworth. *George Washington: First in Peace.* New York: Charles Scribner's Sons, 1957.

Channing, Edward. *A History of the United States.* Vol. V. New York: The Macmillan Co., 1933.

Claver, Scott. *Under the Lash: A History of Corporal Punishment in the British Armed Forces.* London: Torchstream Books, 1954.

Cobb, Lyman. *The Evil Tendencies of Corporal Punishment as a Means of Moral Discipline in Families and Schools, Examined and Discussed.* New York: Mark H. Newman and Co., 1847.

Cole, Charles C., Jr. *The Social Ideas of the Northern Evangelists, 1826–1860.* New York: Columbia University Press, 1954.

Colton, Walter. *Deck and Port; or, Incidents of a Cruise in the United States Frigate Congress to California.* New York: A. S. Barnes and Burr, 1860.

——. *Ship and Shore, in Madeira, Lisbon, and the Mediterranean.* New York: A. S. Barnes and Co., 1851.

——. *The Sea and the Sailor.* New York: A. S. Barnes and Co., 1856.

Cooper, James F., ed. *Correspondence of James Fenimore-Cooper.* 2 vols. New Haven, Conn.: Yale University Press, 1922.

Curti, Merle. *The Growth of American Thought.* 2d ed. New York: Harper and Brothers Publishers, 1951.

Cutbush, Edward. *Observations on the Means of Preserving the Health of Soldiers and Sailors; and on the Duties of the Medical Department of the Army and Navy: With Remarks on Hospitals and Their Internal Arrangement.* Philadelphia: Fry and Kammerer Printers, 1808.

Dana, Richard Henry. *Two Years Before the Mast.* New York: T. Y. Crowell Co., 1907.

Dearborn, H. A. S. *The Life of William Bainbridge, Esq., of the United States Navy,* ed. James Barnes. Princeton, N.J.: Princeton University Press, 1931.

De Roos, Lieutenant Frederick Fitzgerald. *Personal Narrative of Travels in the United States and Canada in 1826*. London: William Harrison Ainsworth, 1827.

Dictionary of National Biography. Eds. Sir Leslie Stephen and Sir Sidney Lee. Vols. VII, XVIII. London: Oxford University Press, 1960.

Drury, Clifford M., chief comp. *United States Navy Chaplains, 1778–1945*. Vol. I. Washington, D.C.: Government Printing Office, 1949.

Durand, James R. *James Durand, an Able Seaman of 1812*, ed. George S. Brooks. New Haven, Conn.: Yale University Press, 1926.

Durkin, Joseph T., S.J. *Stephen R. Mallory: Confederate Navy Chief*. Chapel Hill, N.C.: The University of North Carolina Press, 1954.

Dutton, Charles J. *Oliver Hazard Perry*. New York: Longmans, Green and Co., 1935.

Dwight, Henry Otis. *The Centennial History of the American Bible Society*. New York: The Macmillan Co., 1916.

Farnam, Henry W. *Chapters in the History of Social Legislation in the United States to 1860*. Washington, D.C.: Carnegie Institution of Washington, 1938.

Farragut, Loyall. *The Life of David Glasgow Farragut, First Admiral of the United States Navy, Embodying His Journal and Letters*. New York: D. Appleton and Co., 1879.

Ferguson, Eugene S. *Truxtun of the Constellation*. Baltimore: The Johns Hopkins Press, 1956.

Fitzpatrick, Donovan, and Saul Saphire. *Navy Maverick: Uriah Phillips Levy*. Garden City, N.Y.: Doubleday & Co., Inc., 1963.

Foster, Charles I. *An Errand of Mercy: The Evangelical United Front, 1790–1837*. Chapel Hill, N.C.: The University of North Carolina Press, 1960.

Franklin, Samuel R. *Memories of a Rear Admiral*. New York: Harper and Brothers, 1898.

French, J. H. *Historical and Statistical Gazeteer of New York State*. Syracuse: R. Pearsall Smith, 1860.

Ganoe, William Addleman. *The History of the United States Army*. New York: D. Appleton and Co., 1924.

Garrison, James Holley. *Behold Me Once More. The Confessions of James Holley Garrison, Brother of William Lloyd Garrison*, ed. Walter McIntosh Merrill. Boston: Houghton Mifflin Co., 1954.

Gill, Conrad. *The Naval Mutinies of 1797*. Manchester: Manchester University Press, 1913.

Gilman, William H. *Melville's Early Life and Redburn*. New York: New York University Press, 1951.

Goldsborough, Charles W. *The United States Naval Chronicle*. Vol. I. Washington, D.C.: James Wilson, 1824.

Goodman, Nathan G. *Benjamin Rush, Physician and Citizen, 1746–1813*. Philadelphia: University of Pennsylvania Press, 1934.

Gould, Roland F. *The Life of Gould, an Ex-Man-of-War's Man, with Incidents on Sea and Shore, Including the Three-Year's Cruise of the*

Line of Battle Ship Ohio, on the Mediterranean Station, Under the Veteran Commodore Hull. Claremont, N.H.: Printed by Claremont Manufacturing Co., 1867.

Grant, Bruce. *Captain of Old Ironsides: The Life and Fighting Times of Isaac Hull and the U.S. Frigate Constitution.* Chicago: Pellegrini and Cudahy, 1947.

Green, Ashbel. *Memoirs of the Rev. Joseph Eastburn, Stated Preacher in the Mariner's Church, Philadelphia.* Philadelphia: G. W. Mentz, 1828.

Griffin, Clifford S. *Their Brothers' Keepers: Moral Stewardship in the United States, 1800–1865.* New Brunswick, N.J.: Rutgers University Press, 1960.

Griffis, William Eliot. *Matthew Calbraith Perry: A Typical Naval Officer.* Boston: Cupples and Hurd, 1887.

Grossman, James. *James Fenimore Cooper.* New York: William Sloane Associates, 1949.

Hall, Claude H. *Abel Parker Upshur: Conservative Virginian, 1790–1844.* Madison: The State Historical Society of Wisconsin, 1963.

Hall, Daniel. *Addresses Commemorative of Abraham Lincoln and John P. Hale.* Concord, N.H.: Republican Press Association, 1892.

Hamlin, Charles Eugene. *The Life and Times of Hannibal Hamlin.* Cambridge, Mass.: The Riverside Press, 1899.

Harris, Thomas. *The Life and Services of Commodore William Bainbridge, United States Navy.* Philadelphia: Carey, Lea and Blanchard, 1837.

Hartmann, Cyril Hughes. *The Angry Admiral: The Later Career of Edward Vernon, Admiral of the White.* London: William Heinemann Ltd., 1953.

Hayford, Harrison, ed. *The Somers Mutiny Affair.* Englewood Cliffs, N.J.: Prentice-Hall, Inc., 1959.

Hazen, Jacob A. *Five Years Before the Mast; or, Life in the Forecastle Aboard of a Whaler and Man-of-War.* Chicago: Belford, Clarke & Co., 1887.

Henderson, Daniel. *The Hidden Coasts: A Biography of Admiral Charles Wilkes.* New York: William Sloane Associates, 1953.

Hodgson, Sister M. Michael Catherine, O.P. *Caleb Cushing, Attorney General of the United States.* Washington, D.C.: The Catholic University of America Press, 1955.

Holbrook, Samuel F. *Threescore Years: An Autobiography.* Boston: J. French and Co., 1857.

Hollis, Ira N. *The Frigate Constitution.* Boston: Houghton Mifflin and Co., 1931.

Hoppin, James Mason. *Life of Andrew Hull Foote, Rear Admiral United States Navy.* New York: Harper and Brothers, 1874.

Horsman, Reginald. *The Causes of the War of 1812.* Philadelphia: University of Pennsylvania Press, 1962.

Hoxse, John. *The Yankee Tar.* Northampton, Mass.: John Metcalf, 1840.

Hutchinson, J. R. *The Press Gang Afloat and Ashore.* New York: E. P. Dutton, 1914.

Jackson, David K. *The Contributors and Contributions to the Southern Literary Messenger.* Charlottesville, Va.: Historical Publishing Co., 1936.

Jervey, Theodore D. *Robert Y. Hayne and His Times.* New York: The Macmillan Co., 1909.

Knox, Dudley W. *A History of the United States Navy.* Rev. ed. New York: G. P. Putnam's Sons, 1948.

Krout, John A. *The Origins of Prohibition.* New York: Alfred A. Knopf, 1925.

Lawson, John D., ed. *American State Trials.* Vol. I. St. Louis: F. H. Thomas Law Book Co., 1914.

Lewis, Charles Lee. *David Glasgow Farragut: Admiral in the Making.* Vol. I. Annapolis: U.S. Naval Institute, 1941.

———. *Matthew Fontaine Maury: The Pathfinder of the Seas.* Annapolis, Md.: U.S. Naval Institute, 1927.

———. *The Romantic Decatur.* Philadelphia: University of Pennsylvania Press, 1937.

Lewis, John R. C., and William B. Allen. *Bluejackets with Perry in Japan*, ed. Henry F. Graff. New York: The New York Public Library, 1952.

Lewis, Michael. *England's Sea-Officers: The Story of the Naval Profession.* London: George Allen & Unwin Ltd., 1948.

———. *The History of the British Navy.* Harmondsworth: Penguin Books Ltd., 1957.

———. *The Navy of Britain: A Historical Portrait.* London: George Allen & Unwin Ltd., 1949.

———. *A Social History of the Navy, 1793–1815.* London: George Allen & Unwin Ltd., 1960.

Lloyd, Christopher. *The Nation and the Navy: A History of Naval Life and Policy.* London: The Cresset Press, 1954.

[Lockwood, John A.] *An Essay on Flogging in the Navy.* New York: Pudney and Russell, Printers, 1849.

Lossing, Benson J. *The Story of the United States Navy for Boys.* New York: Harper and Brothers, 1880.

Lovette, Leland D. *Naval Customs, Traditions and Usage.* Annapolis, Md.: U.S. Naval Institute, 1939.

Lowenthal, David. *George Perkins Marsh: Versatile Vermonter.* New York: Columbia University Press, 1958.

Macdonough, Robert. *The Life of Commodore Thomas Macdonough U.S. Navy.* Boston: The Fort Hill Press, 1909.

Maclay, Edgar Stanton. *A Youthful Man-O'-Warsman.* Greenlawn, N.Y.: Navy Blue Co., 1910.

———, ed. *Journal of William Maclay, United States Senator from Pennsylvania, 1789–1791.* New York: D. Appleton and Co., 1890.

McClellan, Edwin. *History of the U.S. Marine Corps.* 1st ed. Washington, D.C.: Historical Section, Headquarters, U.S. Marine Corps, 1925.

McColgan, Daniel T. *Joseph Tuckerman, Pioneer in American Social Work*. Washington, D.C.: The Catholic University of America Press, 1940.

McNally, William. *Evils and Abuses in the Naval and Merchant Service, Exposed; with Proposals for Their Remedy and Redress*. Boston: Cassady and March, 1839.

Maguire, John Francis. *Father Mathew: A Biography*. New York: D. and J. Sadlier and Co., 1864.

Mahan, Alfred T. *From Sail to Steam: Recollections of Naval Life*. New York: Harper and Brothers Publishers, 1907.

———. *Sea Power in Its Relations to the War of 1812*. 2 vols. London: Sampson Low, Marston & Co., Ltd., 1905.

Mainwaring, G. E., and Bonamy Dobrée. *The Floating Republic: An Account of the Mutinies at Spithead and the Nore in 1797*. London: Geoffrey Bles, 1935.

Melville, Herman. *White Jacket, Or, The World in a Man-of-War*. Boston: L. C. Page and Co., 1892.

Meyers, Marvin. *The Jacksonian Persuasion: Politics and Belief*. Stanford: Stanford University Press, 1957.

Murrell, William Meacham. *Cruise of the Frigate Columbia Around the World, Under the Command of Commodore George C. Read, in 1838, 1839, and 1840*. Boston: Benjamin B. Mussey, 1840.

Neeser, Robert W. *Statistical and Chronological History of the United States Navy, 1775–1907*. 2 vols. New York: The Macmillan Co., 1909.

Nelson, Dennis D. *The Integration of the Negro into the United States Navy, 1776–1947*. Washington, D.C.: Government Printing Office, 1948.

Nichols, Roy F. *Franklin Pierce*. 2d ed., revised. Philadelphia: University of Pennsylvania Press, 1958.

———. *Religion and American Democracy*. Baton Rouge: Louisiana State University Press, 1959.

Nordhoff, Charles. *Man-of-War Life: A Boy's Experience in the United States Navy, During a Voyage Around the World, in a Ship of the Line*. New York: Dodd, Mead and Co., 1855.

Nye, Russel B. *George Bancroft, Brahmin Rebel*. New York: Alfred A. Knopf, Inc., 1944.

Packard, Francis R. *History of Medicine in the United States*. 2 vols. New York: Paul B. Hoeber, Inc., 1931.

Parsons, Charles W. *Memoir of Usher Parsons, M.D.* Providence: Hammond, Angell and Co., Printers, 1870.

Paulding, William I. *Literary Life of James K. Paulding*. New York: Charles Scribner and Co., 1867.

Paullin, Charles O. *Commodore John Rodgers: A Biography*. Cleveland: Arthur H. Clark, 1910.

Perkins, Bradford. *Prologue to War: England and the United States, 1805–1812*. Berkeley: University of California Press, 1961.

Pope, Dudley. *The Black Ship*. Philadelphia: J. B. Lippincott Co., 1964.

Porter, David D. *Memoir of Commodore David Porter of the United States Navy.* Albany, N.Y.: J. Munsell, Publisher, 1875.

Pratt, Fletcher. *The Navy: A History.* Garden City, N.Y.: Garden City Publishing Co., Inc., 1941.

———. *Preble's Boys: Commodore Preble and the Birth of American Sea Power.* New York: William Sloane Associates, Publishers, 1950.

Prucha, Francis P., ed. *Army Life on the Western Frontier.* Norman: University of Oklahoma Press, 1958.

———. *Broadax and Bayonet: The Role of the United States Army in the Development of the Northwest, 1815–1860.* Madison: The State Historical Society of Wisconsin, 1953.

Puleston, W. D. *Annapolis: Gangway to the Quarterdeck.* New York: D. Appleton Century Co., Inc., 1942.

Raybeck, Robert J. *Millard Fillmore.* Buffalo: Henry Stewart Inc., 1959.

Richardson, James D. *A Compilation of the Messages and Papers of the Presidents, 1789–1897.* 10 vols. New York: Bureau of National Literature, Inc., 1897.

Risch, Erna. *Quartermaster Support of the Army: A History of the Corps, 1775–1939.* Washington, D.C.: Government Printing Office, 1962.

Robinson, Charles N. *The British Tar in Fact and Fiction; The Poetry, Pathos, and Humor of the Sailor's Life.* New York: Harper and Brothers, 1909.

Rockwell, Charles. *Sketches of Foreign Travel and Life at Sea.* 2 vols. Boston: Tappan and Dennet, 1842.

Rogers, Patrick. *Father Theobald Mathew, Apostle of Temperance.* Dublin: Browne and Nolan Ltd., 1943.

Roosevelt, Theodore. *The Naval War of 1812.* 4th ed. New York: G. P. Putnam's Sons, 1889.

Salter, William. *The Life of James W. Grimes.* New York: D. Appleton and Co., 1876.

Sanborn, Solomon. *An Exposition of Official Tyranny in the United States Navy.* New York: no publisher, 1841.

Schlesinger, Arthur M., Jr. *The Age of Jackson.* Boston: Little, Brown and Co., 1945.

Sellstedt, Lars Gustav. *From Forecastle to Academy.* Buffalo: The Matthews-Northrup Works, 1904.

Sewell, Richard H. *John P. Hale and the Politics of Abolition.* Cambridge, Mass.: Harvard University Press, 1965.

Shapiro, Samuel. *Richard Henry Dana, Jr., 1815–1882.* East Lansing: Michigan State University Press, 1961.

Smelser, Marshall. *The Congress Founds the Navy, 1787–1798.* Notre Dame, Ind.: University of Notre Dame Press, 1959.

Smith, Preserved. *The Enlightenment, 1687–1776.* Vol. II of *A History of Modern Culture.* 2 vols. New York: Collier Books, 1962.

Snedeker, James. *A Brief History of Courts-Martial.* Annapolis, Md.: U.S. Naval Institute, 1954.

Soley, James Russell. *Historical Sketch of the United States Naval Academy.* Washington, D.C.: Government Printing Office, 1876.

Sprout, Harold and Margaret. *The Rise of American Naval Power, 1776–1918.* Princeton, N.J.: Princeton University Press, 1946.

Squibb, Edward R. *The Journal of Edward Robinson Squibb, M.D.* 2 vols. No city: privately printed, 1930.

Stewart, Charles S. *A Visit to the South Seas in the U.S. Ship Vincennes, During the Years 1829 and 1830; With Scenes in Brazil, Peru, Manilla, Cape of Good Hope, and St. Helena.* 2 vols. New York: J. P. Haven, 1831.

Story, William W. *The Life and Letters of Joseph Story.* 2 vols. Boston: C. C. Little and J. Brown, 1851.

Sullivan, William. *Sea Life; Or, What May or May Not Be Done, and What Ought to Be Done by Ship-Owners, Ship-Masters, Mates and Seamen.* Boston: James B. Dow, 1837.

Taylor, Fitch W. *A Voyage Round the World, and Visits to Various Foreign Countries, in the United States Frigate Columbia; Attended by Her Consort the Sloop of War John Adams, and Commanded by Commodore George C. Read.* 2 vols. 3d ed. New Haven, Conn.: H. Mansfield, 1844.

Thompson, Robert Means, and Richard Wainwright, eds. *Confidential Correspondence of Gustavus Vasa Fox, Assistant Secretary of the Navy, 1861–1865.* 2 vols. New York: The Naval History Society, 1918–19.

Thring, Theodore, and C. E. Clifford. *Thring's Criminal Law of the Navy, with an Introductory Chapter on the Early State and Discipline of the Navy, the Rules of Evidence, and an Appendix Comprising the Naval Discipline Act and Practical Forms.* 2d ed. London: Stevens and Sons, 1877.

Torrey, F. P. *Journal of the Cruise of the United States Ship Ohio, Commodore Isaac Hull, Commander, in the Mediterranean, in the Years 1839, '40, '41.* Boston: Samuel N. Dickinson, 1841.

Tuckerman, Henry T. *The Life of John Pendleton Kennedy.* New York: G. P. Putnam and Sons, 1871.

Turnbull, Archibald Douglas. *Commodore David Porter, 1780–1843.* New York: The Century Co., 1929.

Tyler, Alice Felt. *Freedom's Ferment: Phases of American Social History to 1860.* Minneapolis: The University of Minnesota Press, 1944.

Tyler, Lyon G. *The Letters and Times of the Tylers.* 3 vols. Richmond, Va.: Whittel and Shepperson, 1884–96.

Van de Water, Frederic F. *The Captain Called It Mutiny.* New York: Ives Washburn, Inc., 1954.

Webster, George Sidney. *The Seamen's Friend; A Sketch of the American Seamen's Friend Society by Its Secretary, George Sidney Webster, D.D.* New York: The American Seamen's Friend Society, 1932.

West, Richard S., Jr., *Gideon Welles, Lincoln's Navy Department.* Indianapolis, Ind.: The Bobbs-Merrill Co., 1943.

————. *The Second Admiral: A Life of David Dixon Porter, 1813–1891.* New York: Coward-McCann, Inc., 1937.

Westcott, Allan F., ed. *American Sea Power Since 1775.* Rev. ed. Philadelphia: J. B. Lippincott Co., 1952.

White, Leonard D. *The Federalists: A Study in Administrative History, 1789–1801.* New York: The Macmillan Co., 1948.

————. *The Jacksonians: A Study in Administrative History, 1829–1861.* New York: The Macmillan Co., 1954.

————. *The Jeffersonians: A Study in Administrative History, 1801–1829.* New York: The Macmillan Co., 1951.

Williams, Frances Leigh. *Matthew Fontaine Maury, Scientist of the Sea.* New Brunswick, N.J.: Rutgers University Press, 1963.

Willis, Nathaniel P. *Summer Cruise in the Mediterranean, on Board an American Frigate.* Auburn and Rochester, N.Y.: Charles Scribner, 1856.

Wines, Enoch C. *Two Years and a Half in the Navy, Or, Journal of a Cruise in the Mediterranean and Levant, on Board the U.S. Frigate Constellation, in the Years 1829, 1830, and 1831.* 2 vols. Philadelphia: Carey and Lea, 1832.

Wish, Harvey. *Society and Thought in Early America.* New York: Longmans, Green and Co., 1950.

Wold, Ansel, comp. *Biographical Directory of the American Congress, 1774–1927.* Washington, D.C.: Government Printing Office, 1928.

Wood, William Maxwell. *Shoulder to the Wheel of Progress.* Buffalo: Derby, Orton and Mulligan, 1853.

Zimmerman, James F. *Impressment of American Seamen.* New York: Columbia University Press, 1925.

ARTICLES

Afterguard. "Our Navy, Economy, and Good Order," *United States Nautical Magazine,* I (1845), 307–313.

Anderson, Charles R. "A Reply to Herman Melville's *White Jacket* by Rear-Admiral Thomas O. Selfridge, Sr.," *American Literature,* VII (1935), 123–144.

Anonymous. "Notes and Commentaries on a Voyage to China," *Southern Literary Messenger,* XVIII (1852), 192–208.

Anonymous. "Report of the Secretary of the Navy to the President of the United States, December 1, 1829," *The North American Review,* XXX (1830), 360–389.

Aptheker, Herbert. "The Negro in the Union Navy," *The Journal of Negro History,* XXXII (1947), 169–200.

Basaler, R. E. "Splice the Main Brace," *United States Naval Institute Proceedings* [hereafter cited as *U.S.N.I.P.*], LXIII (1937), 1588–92.

Belknap, George E. "The Old Navy," *Naval Actions and History, 1799–1898. Papers of the Military Historical Society of Massachusetts,* XII (1902), 22–69.

Bluff, Harry [Matthew F. Maury]. "Of Reorganizing the Navy," *Southern Literary Messenger*, VII (1841), 3–25.

———. "Our Navy," *Southern Literary Messenger*, VII (1841), 345–379.

———. "Scraps from the Lucky Bag," *Southern Literary Messenger*, VI (1840), 306–320, 786–800.

Bradley, Udolpho T. "Commodore Rodgers and the Bureau System of Naval Administration," *U.S.N.I.P.*, LVII (1931), 307–308.

Brown, Kenneth L. "Mr. Madison's Secretary of the Navy," *U.S.N.I.P.*, LXXIII (1947), 967–975.

C. [ooper], James F. "Hints on Manning the Navy," *Army and Navy Chronicle*, III (1845), 34, 49, 51.

David, Leon. "An Episode in Naval Justice," *Case and Comment*, LVII (1952), 20, 22–25.

Davies, George E. "Robert Smith and the Navy," *Maryland Historical Magazine*, XIV (1919), 305–322.

Dictionary of American Biography. Eds. Allen Johnson, Dumas Malone, Harris E. Starr, and Robert L. Schuyler. 22 vols. New York: Charles Scribner's Sons, 1928–58.

Edel, William W. "The Golden Age of Navy Chaplaincy, 1830–55," *U.S.N.I.P.*, L (1924), 875–885.

Eller, Ernest M. "Truxtun the Builder," *U.S.N.I.P.*, LXIII (1937), 1445–52.

Evans, Frank E. "The Corps a Hundred Years Ago," *Marine Corps Gazette*, I (1916), 43–62.

Griffin, Clifford S. "Religious Benevolence as Social Control, 1815–1860," *The Mississippi Valley Historical Review*, XLIV (1957), 423–444.

Hare, John S. "Military Punishments in the War of 1812," *Journal of the American Military Institute*, IV (1940), 225–239.

Hill, James D. "Charles Wilkes—Turbulent Scholar of the Old Navy," *U.S.N.I.P.*, LVII (1931), 867–887.

Hirsch, Charles B. "Gunboat Personnel on the Western Waters," *Mid-America*, XXXIV (1952), 75–86.

Horan, Leo F. S. "Flogging in the United States Navy: Unfamiliar Facts Regarding Its Origin and Abolition," *U.S.N.I.P.*, LXXVI (1950), 969–975.

Hunt, [?]. "The Navy and the Late Treaty," *Hunt's Merchant's Magazine and Commercial Review*, VIII (1843), 49–56.

Kanof, Abram. "Uriah Phillips Levy: The Story of a Pugnacious Commodore," *Publications of the American Jewish Historical Society*, XXXIX (1949), 1–66.

Langley, H. D. "The Grass Roots Harvest of 1828," *U.S.N.I.P.*, XC (1964), 51–59.

Lathrop, Constance. "Grog: Its Origin and Use in the United States Navy," *U.S.N.I.P.*, LXI (1935), 377–380.

[Lockwood, John A.] "Flogging in the Navy," *United States Magazine and Democratic Review*, XXV (1849), 97–115, 225–242, 318–337, 417–432.

Merrill, James A. "Men, Monotony, and Mouldy Beans – Life on Board Civil War Blockaders," *The American Neptune*, XVI (1956), 49–59.

Mitchell, Donald W. "Abel Upshur: Forgotten Prophet of the Old Navy," *U.S.N.I.P.*, LXXV (1949), 1366–75.

Paullin, Charles O. "Duelling in the Old Navy," *U.S.N.I.P.*, XXXV (1909), 1155–97.

———. "Early Naval Administration Under the Constitution," *U.S.N.I.P.*, XXXII (1906), 1001–30.

———. "A Half Century of Naval Administration in America, 1861–1911," *U.S.N.I.P.*, XXXVIII (1912), 1309–34.

———. "Naval Administration, 1842–1861," *U.S.N.I.P.*, XXXIII (1907), 1435–70.

———. "Naval Administration Under Secretaries of the Navy Smith, Hamilton and Jones, 1801–1814," *U.S.N.I.P.*, XXXII (1906), 1289–1328.

———. "Naval Administration Under the Navy Commissioners, 1815–1842," *U.S.N.I.P.*, XXXIII (1907), 597–641.

———. "Washington City and the Old Navy," *Records of the Columbia Historical Society*, XXXIII (1932), 163–177.

Pleadwell, F. L. "Edward Cutbush, M.D., the Nestor of the Medical Corps of the Navy," *Annals of Medical History*, V (1923), 337–386.

Pratt, Fletcher. "The Basis of Our Naval Tradition," *U.S.N.I.P.*, LXIII (1937), 1107–14.

Prendergast, William B. "The Navy and Civil Liberty," *U.S.N.I.P.*, LXXIV (1948), 1263–67.

Radom, J. Matthew. "The Americanization of the U.S. Navy," *U.S.N.I.P.*, LXIII (1937), 231–234.

Robison, S. S., "Commodore Thomas Truxtun, U.S. Navy," *U.S.N.I.P.*, LVIII (1932), 541–554.

Sawtell, Clement C. "Impressment of American Seamen by the British," *The Essex Institute Historical Collections*, LXXVI (1940), 314–344.

Stearns, Bertha-Monica. "Reform Periodicals and Female Reformers, 1830–1860," *The American Historical Review*, XXXVII (1932), 678–699.

Stevens, William O. "Two Early Proposals for Nautical Education," *U.S.N.I.P.*, XXXIX (1913), 127–133.

Stewart, Charles. "Commodore Stewart's Letter," *United States Nautical Magazine*, II (1845), 172–185.

Strauss, W. Patrick. "Preparing the Wilkes Expedition: A Study in Disorganization," *Pacific Historical Review*, XXVIII (1959), 221–232.

"William Leggett," *United States Magazine and Democratic Review*, VI (1839), 17–28.

UNPUBLISHED MATERIAL

Albion, Robert G. "A Brief History of Civilian Personnel in the U.S. Navy Department." Unpublished manuscript, National Archives Library, 1943.

Bradley, Udolpho Theodore. "The Contentious Commodore: Thomas Ap Catesby Jones of the Old Navy, 1788–1858." Unpublished Ph.D. Dissertation, Department of History, Cornell University, 1933.

Carrigg, John J. "Benjamin Stoddert and the Foundation of the American Navy." Unpublished Ph.D. dissertation, Department of History, Georgetown University, 1953.

Crowe, Sister Catherine. "The National Intelligencer and Humanitarianism, 1841–1850." Unpublished Master's thesis, Department of History, The Catholic University of America, 1954.

Stanton, Sister Clare Francis. "The National Intelligencer and Humanitarianism, 1830–1840." Unpublished Master's thesis, Department of History, The Catholic University of America, 1952.

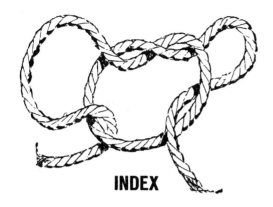

INDEX